TRAVEL, TOURISM AND ECO-TOURISM

TRAVEL, TOURISM AND ECO-TOURISM

Mahesh Chandra Singh

CENTRUM PRESS
NEW DELHI-110002 (INDIA)

CENTRUM PRESS
H.O.: 4360/4, Ansari Road, Daryaganj,
New Delhi-110002 (India)
Tel: 23278000, 23261597, 23255577, 23286875
B.O.: No. 1015, Ist Main Road, BSK IIIrd Stage,
IIIrd Phase, IIIrd Block, Bangalore-560085 (INDIA)
Tel: 080-41723429
Email: centrumpress@gmail.com
Visit us at: www.centrumpress.com

Travel, Tourism and Eco-tourism

First Edition, 2010

ISBN 978-93-80540-78-8

PRINTED IN INDIA

Printed at Balaji Offset, Delhi.

Contents

Preface

Eco-tourism is responsible travel to fragile, pristine, and usually protected areas that strives to be low impact and (often) small scale. It purports to educate the traveller; provide funds for conservation; directly benefit the economic development and political empowerment of local communities; and foster respect for different cultures and for human rights. Eco-tourism is held as important by those who participate in it so that future generations may experience aspects of the environment relatively untouched by human intervention.

Most serious studies of ecotourism including several university programs now use this as the working definition. Eco-tourism appeals to ecologically and socially conscious individuals. Generally speaking, it focuses on volunteering, personal growth and environmental responsibility. It typically involves travel to destinations where flora, fauna, and cultural heritage are the primary attractions. One of the goals of ecotourism is to offer tourists insight into the impact of human beings on the environment, and to foster a greater appreciation of our natural habitats.

Responsible ecotourism includes programs that minimize the negative aspects of conventional tourism on the environment and enhance the cultural integrity of local people. Therefore, in addition to evaluating environmental and cultural factors, an integral part of ecotourism is the promotion of recycling, energy efficiency, water conservation, and creation of economic opportunities for local communities. Thus Ecotourism is part of the general growth in tourism and reflects increased environmental awareness and the desire for more authentic natural and cultural experiences.

The concept of eco-tourism is very complex to define though several attempts have been made by renowned writers to explain it.

The book offers a clear idea and explanation of eco-tourism and practicable site management policy and it can be used by researcher, academics, policy makers, tourism environment and resource management experts.

—Mahesh Chandra Singh

1

Introduction

Eco-tourism

'Eco-tourism' (also known as ecological tourism) is responsible travel to fragile, pristine, and usually protected areas that strives to be low impact and (often) small scale. It purports to educate the traveller; provide funds for conservation; directly benefit the economic development and political empowerment of local communities; and foster respect for different cultures and for human rights. Eco tourism is held as important by those who participate in it so that future generations may experience aspects of the environment relatively untouched by human intervention. Most serious studies of Eco-tourism including several university programs now use this as the working definition.

Eco-tourism appeals to ecologically and socially conscious individuals. Generally speaking, it focuses on volunteering, personal growth and environmental responsibility. It typically involves travel to destinations where flora, fauna, and cultural heritage are the primary attractions. One of the goals of Eco-tourism is to offer tourists insight into the impact of human beings on the environment, and to foster a greater appreciation of our natural habitats.

Responsible Eco-tourism includes programs that minimize the negative aspects of conventional tourism on the environment and enhance the cultural integrity of local people. Therefore, in addition to evaluating environmental and cultural factors, an integral part of Eco-tourism is the promotion of recycling, energy efficiency, water conservation, and creation of economic opportunities for local communities.

Criteria

Eco-tourism is a form of tourism that involves traveling to tranquil and unpolluted natural areas. According to the definition and principles of Eco-tourism established by The International Eco-tourism Society (TIES) in 1990, Eco-tourism is "Responsible travel to natural areas that conserves the environment and improves the well-being of local people." (TIES, 1990). Martha Honey, expands on the TIES definition by describing the seven characteristics of Eco-tourism, which are:

- Involves travel to natural destinations.
- Minimizes impact.
- Builds environmental awareness.
- Provides direct financial benefits for conservation.
- Provides financial benefits and empowerment for local people.
- Respects local culture.
- Supports human rights and democratic movements.

Ideally, Eco-tourism should satisfy several criteria, such as:

- conservation of biological diversity and cultural diversity through ecosystem protection
- promotion of sustainable use of biodiversity, by providing jobs to local populations
- sharing of socioeconomic benefits with local communities and indigenous peoples by having their informed consent and participation in the management of Eco-tourism enterprises
- tourism to unspoiled natural resources, with minimal impact on the environment being a primary concern.
- minimization of tourism's own environmental impact
- affordability and lack of waste in the form of luxury
- local culture, flora and fauna being the main attractions.

For many countries, Eco-tourism is not simply a marginal activity to finance protection of the environment, but is a major industry of the national economy. For example, in Costa Rica, Ecuador, Nepal, Kenya, Madagascar and Antarctica, Eco-tourism represents a significant portion of the gross domestic product and economic activity. The concept of Eco-tourism is widely misunderstood and in practice is often used as a marketing tool to promote tourism that is related to nature. This is an especially frequent malpractice in the realm of Jungle tourism. Critics claim that these greenwashing practices, carried out in the name of Eco-tourism, often consist of placing a hotel in a splendid landscape, to the detriment of the ecosystem. According to them, Eco-tourism must above all sensitize people to the beauty and the fragility of nature. They condemn some operators as greenwashing their operations: using the labels of "green" and "eco-friendly", while behaving in environmentally irresponsible ways.

Although academics disagree about who can be classified as an ecotourist and there is little statistical data, some estimate that more than five million ecotourists-the majority of the ecotourist population-come from the United States, with many others from Western Europe, Canada and Australia.

Currently, there are various moves to create national and international Eco-tourism accreditation programs, although the process is also controversial. National Eco-tourism certification programs have been put in place in countries such as Costa Rica, Australia, Kenya and Sweden.

History

Eco-tourism, responsible tourism, jungle tourism, and sustainable development have become prevalent concepts since the late 1980s, and Eco-tourism has experienced arguably the fastest growth of all sub-sectors in the tourism industry. The popularity represents a change in tourist perceptions, increased environmental awareness, and a desire to explore natural environments. At times, such changes become as much a statement affirming one's social identity, educational sophistication, and disposable income as it has about preserving the Amazon rainforest or the Caribbean reef for posterity.

Criticisms

Definitional Problems and Greenwashing

To approach an understanding of the problem, a clear definition must delineate what is, and is not, Eco-tourism. Ideally, Eco-tourism satisfies several general criteria, including the conservation of biological diversity and cultural diversity through ecosystem protection, promotion of sustainable use of biodiversity, share of social-economic benefits with local communities through informed consent and participation, increase in environmental and cultural knowledge, affordability and reduced waste, and minimization of its own environmental impact. In such ways, it contributes to the long term benefits to both the environment and local communities.

However, in the continuum of tourism activities that stretch from conventional tourism to Eco-tourism proper, there has been a lot of contention to the limit at which biodiversity preservation, local social-economic benefits, and environmental impact can be considered "Eco-tourism". For this reason, environmentalists, special interest groups, and governments define Eco-tourism differently. Environmental organizations have generally insisted that Eco-tourism is nature-based, sustainably managed, conservation supporting, and environmentally educated. The tourist industry and governments, however, focus more on the product aspect, treating Eco-tourism as equivalent to any sort of tourism based in nature. As a further complication, many terms are used under the rubric of Eco-tourism. Nature tourism, low impact tourism, green tourism, bio-tourism, ecologically responsible tourism, and others have been used in literature and marketing, although they are not necessary synonymous with Eco-tourism.

The problems associated with defining Eco-tourism have led to confusion among tourists and academics alike. Definitional problems are also subject of considerable public controversy and concern because of green washing, a trend towards the commercialization of tourism schemes disguised as sustainable, nature based, and environmentally friendly Eco-tourism. According to McLaren, these schemes are environmentally destructive, economically exploitative, and culturally insensitive at its worst. They are also morally disconcerting because they mislead tourists and manipulate their concerns for the environment. Despite objections, green washing continues to grow unabated. The Nature's Sacred Paradise, a theme park in Quintana Roo, Mexico, is responsible for displacing local Mayan communities and illegally keeping endangered species in captivity to attract visitors. The development and success of such large scale, energy intensive, and ecologically unsustainable schemes are a testament to the tremendous profits associated with being labeled as Eco-tourism.

Negative Impact of Tourism

Eco-tourism has become one of the fastest-growing sectors of the tourism industry, growing annually by 10-15% worldwide

(Miller, 2007). One definition of Eco-tourism is "the practice of low-impact, educational, ecologically and culturally sensitive travel that benefits local communities and host countries" (Honey, 1999). Many of the Eco-tourism projects are not meeting these standards. Even if some of the guidelines are being executed, the local communities are still facing other negative impacts. South Africa is one of the countries that are reaping significant economic benefits from Eco-tourism, but negative effects-including forcing people to leave their homes, gross violations of fundamental rights, and environmental hazards-far outweigh the medium-term economic benefits (Miller, 2007). A tremendous amount of money is being spent and human resources continue to be used for Eco-tourism despite unsuccessful outcomes, and even more money is put into public relation campaigns to dilute the effects of criticism. Eco-tourism channels resources away from other projects that could contribute more sustainable and realistic solutions to pressing social and environmental problems. "The money tourism can generate often ties parks and managements to Eco-tourism" (Walpole et al. 2001). But there is a tension in this relationship because Eco-tourism often causes conflict and changes in land-use rights, fails to deliver promises of community-level benefits, damages environments, and has plenty of other social impacts. Indeed many argue repeatedly that Eco-tourism is neither ecologically nor socially beneficial, yet it persists as a strategy for conservation and development (West, 2006). While several studies are being done on ways to improve the Eco-tourism structure, some argue that these examples provide rationale for stopping it altogether.

The Eco-tourism system exercises tremendous financial and political influence. The evidence above shows that a strong case exists for restraining such activities in certain locations. Funding could be used for field studies aimed at finding alternative solutions to tourism and the diverse problems Africa faces in result of urbanization, industrialization, and the over exploitation of agriculture (Kamuaro, 2007). At the local level, Eco-tourism has become a source of conflict over control of land, resources, and tourism profits. In this case, Eco-tourism has harmed the environment and local people, and has led to conflicts over profit distribution. In a perfect world more efforts would be made towards educating tourists of the environmental and social effects of their travels. Very few regulations or laws stand in place as boundaries for the investors in Eco-tourism. These should be implemented to prohibit the promotion of unsustainable Eco-tourism projects and materials which project false images of destinations, demeaning local and indigenous cultures.

Direct Environmental Impacts

Eco-tourism operations occasionally fail to live up to conservation ideals. It is sometimes overlooked that Eco-tourism is a highly consumer-centered activity, and that environmental conservation is a means to further economic growth.

Although Eco-tourism is intended for small groups, even a modest increase in population, however temporary, puts extra pressure on the local environment and necessitates the development of additional infrastructure and amenities. The construction of water treatment plants, sanitation facilities, and lodges come with the exploitation of non-renewable energy sources and the utilization of already limited local resources. The conversion of natural land to such tourist infrastructure is implicated in deforestation and habitat deterioration of butterflies in Mexico and squirrel monkeys in Costa Rica. In other cases, the environment suffers because local communities are unable to meet the infrastructure demands of Eco-tourism. The lack of adequate sanitation facilities in many East African parks results in the disposal of campsite sewage in rivers, contaminating the wildlife, livestock, and people who draw drinking water from it.

Aside from environmental degradation with tourist infrastructure, population pressures from Eco-tourism also leaves behind garbage and pollution associated with the Western lifestyle. Although ecotourists claim to be educationally sophisticated and environmentally concerned, they rarely understand the ecological consequences of their visits and how their day-to-day activities append physical impacts on the environment. As one scientist observes, they "rarely acknowledge how the meals they eat, the toilets they flush, the water they drink, and so on, are all part of broader regional economic and ecological systems they are helping to reconfigure with their very activities." Nor do ecotourists recognize the great consumption of non-renewable energy required to arrive at their destination, which is typically more remote than conventional tourism destinations. For instance, an exotic journey to a place 10,000 kilometers away consumes about 700 litres of fuel per person.

Eco-tourism activities are, in of itself, issues in environmental impact because they disturb fauna and flora. Ecotourists believe that because they are only taking pictures and leaving footprints, they keep Eco-tourism sites pristine, but even harmless sounding activities such as a nature hike can be ecologically destructive. In the Annapurna Circuit in Nepal, ecotourists have worn down the marked trails and created alternate routes, contributing to soil impaction, erosion, and plant damage. Where the Eco-tourism activity involves wildlife viewing, it can scare away animals, disrupt their feeding and nesting sites, or acclimate them to the presence of people. In Kenya, wildlife-observer disruption drives cheetahs off their reserves, increasing the risk of inbreeding and further endangering the species.

Environmental Hazards

Unfortunately, industrialization, urbanization, and unsustainable agriculture practices have all had serious effects on the environment. Eco-tourism is now also playing a role in this depletion. While the term Eco-tourism may sound relatively benign, one of its most serious impacts is its consumption of virgin territories (Kamuaro, 2007). These invasions often include deforestation, disruption of ecological life systems and various forms of pollution, all of which contribute to environmental degradation.

The number of motor vehicles crossing the park increases as tour drivers search for rare species. The number of roads has disrupted the grass cover which has serious effects on plant and animal species. These areas also have a higher rate of disturbances and invasive species because of all the traffic moving off the beaten path into new undiscovered areas (Kamuaro, 2007). Eco-tourism also has an effect on species through the value placed on them. "Certain species have gone from being little known or valued by local people to being highly valued commodities. The commodification of plants may erase their social value and lead to overproduction within protected areas. Local people and their images can also be turned into commodities" (West, 2006). Kamuaro brings up a relatively obvious contradiction, any commercial venture into unspoiled, pristine land with or without the "eco" prefix as a contradiction in terms. To generate revenue you have to have a high number of traffic, tourists, which inevitably means a higher pressure on the environment.

Local People

Most forms of Eco-tourism are owned by foreign investors and corporations that provide few benefits to local communities. An overwhelming majority of profits are put into the pockets of investors instead of reinvestment into the local economy or environmental protection. The limited numbers of local people who are employed in the economy enter at its lowest level, and are unable to live in tourist areas because of meager wages and a two market system.

In some cases, the resentment by local people results in environmental degradation. As a highly publicized case, the Masai nomads in Kenya killed wildlife in national parks to show aversion to unfair compensation terms and displacement from traditional lands. The lack of economic opportunities for local people also constrains them to degrade the environment as a means of sustenance. The presence of affluent ecotourists encourage the development of destructive markets in wildlife souvenirs, such as the sale of coral trinkets on tropical islands and animal products in Asia, contributing to illegal harvesting and poaching from the environment. In Suriname, sea turtle reserves use a large portion of their budget to guard against these destructive activities.

Displacement of People

One of the most powerful examples of communities being moved in order to create a park is the story of the Masai. About 70% of national parks and game reserves in East Africa are on Masai land (Kamuaro, 2007). The first undesirable impact of tourism was that of the extent of land lost from the Masai culture. Local and national governments took advantage of the Masai's ignorance on the situation and robbed them of huge chunks of grazing land, putting to risk their only socioeconomic livelihood. In Kenya the Masai also have not gained any economic benefits. Despite the loss of their land, employment favours better educated workers. Furthermore the investors in this area are not local and have not put profits back into local economy. In some cases game reserves can be created without informing or consulting local people, who come to find out about the situation when an eviction notice is delivered (Kamuaro, 2007). Another source of resentment is the manipulation of the local people by their government. "Eco-tourism works to create simplistic images of local people and their uses and understandings of their surroundings. Through the lens of these simplified images, officials direct policies and projects towards the local people and the local people are blamed if the projects fail" (West, 2006). Clearly tourism as a trade is not empowering the local people who make it rich and satisfying. Instead Eco-tourism exploits and depletes, particularly in African Masai tribes. It has to be reoriented if it is to be useful to local communities and to become sustainable (Kamuaro, 2007).

Threats to Indigenous Cultures

Eco-tourism often claims that it preserves and "enhances" local cultures. However, evidence shows that with the establishment of protected areas local people have illegally lost their homes, and most often with no compensation (Kamuaro, 2007). Pushing people onto marginal lands with harsh climates, poor soils, lack of water, and infested with livestock and disease does little to enhance livelihoods even when a proportion of Eco-tourism profits are directed back into the community. The establishment of parks can create harsh survival realities and deprive the people of their traditional use of land and natural resources. Ethnic groups are increasingly being seen as a "backdrop" to the scenery and wildlife. The local people struggle for cultural survival and freedom of cultural expression while being "observed" by tourists. Local indigenous people also have strong resentment towards the change, "Tourism has been allowed to develop with virtually no controls. Too many lodges have been built, too much firewood is being used and no limits are being placed on tourism vehicles. They regularly drive off-track and harass the wildlife. Their vehicle tracks criss-cross the entire Masai Mara. Inevitably the bush is becoming eroded and degraded" (Kamuaro, 2007).

Mismanagement

While governments are typically entrusted with the administration and enforcement of environmental protection, they often lack the commitment or capability to manage Eco-tourism sites effectively. The regulations for environmental protection may be vaguely defined, costly to implement, hard to enforce, and uncertain in effectiveness. Government regulatory agencies, as political bodies, are susceptible to making decisions that spend budget on politically beneficial but environmentally unproductive projects. Because of prestige and conspicuousness, the construction of an attractive visitor's centre at an Eco-tourism site may take precedence over more pressing environmental concerns like acquiring habitat, protecting endemic species, and removing invasive ones. Finally, influential groups can pressure and sway the interests of the government to their favour. The government and its regulators can become vested in the benefits of the Eco-tourism industry which they are supposed to regulate, causing restrictive environmental regulations and enforcement to become more lenient. Management of Eco-tourism sites by private Eco-tourism companies offers an alternative to the cost of regulation and deficiency of government agencies. It is believed that these companies have a self interest in limited environmental degradation, because tourists will pay more for pristine environments, which translates to higher profit. However, theory indicates that this practice is not economically feasible and will fail to manage the environment.

The model of monopolistic competition states that distinctiveness will entail profits, but profits will promote imitation. A company that protects its Eco-tourism sites is able to charge a premium for the novel experience and pristine environment. But when other companies view the success of this approach, they also enter the market with similar practices, increasing competition and reducing demand. Eventually, the demand will be reduced until the economic profit is zero. A cost-benefit analysis shows that the company bears the cost of environmental protection without receiving the gains. Without economic incentive, the whole premise of self interest through environmental protection is quashed; instead, Eco-tourism companies will minimize environment related expenses and maximize tourism demand.

The tragedy of the commons offers another model for economic unsustainability from environmental protection, in Eco-tourism sites utilized by many companies. Although there is a communal incentive to protect the environment, maximizing the benefits in the long run, a company will conclude that it is in their best interest to utilize the Eco-tourism site beyond its sustainable level. By increasing the number of ecotourists, for instance, a company gains all the economic benefit while paying only a part of the environmental cost. In the same way, a company recognizes that there is no incentive to actively protect the environment; they bear all the costs, while the benefits are shared by all other companies. The result, again, is mismanagement. Taken together, the mobility of foreign investment and lack of economic incentive for environmental protection means that Eco-tourism companies are disposed to establishing themselves in new sites once their existing one is sufficiently degraded.

Improving Sustainability

Regulation and Accreditation

Because the regulation of Eco-tourism is poorly implemented or nonexistent, ecologically destructive greenwashed operations like underwater hotels, helicopter tours, and wildlife theme parks are categorized as Eco-tourism along with canoeing, camping, photography, and wildlife observation. The failure to acknowledge responsible, low impact Eco-tourism puts these companies at a competitive disadvantage.

Many environmentalists have argued for a global standard of accreditation, differentiating Eco-tourism companies based on their level of environmental commitment. A national or international regulatory board would enforce accreditation procedures, with representation from various groups including governments, hotels, tour operators, travel agents, guides, airlines, local authorities, conservation organizations, and non-governmental organizations. The decisions of the board would be sanctioned by governments, so that non-compliant companies would be legally required to disassociate themselves from the use of the Eco-tourism brand.

Crinion suggests a Green Stars System, based on criteria including a management plan, benefit for the local community, small group interaction, education value and staff training. Ecotourists who consider their choices would be confident of a genuine Eco-tourism experience when they see the higher star rating.

In addition, environmental impact assessments could be used as a form of accreditation. Feasibility is evaluated from a scientific basis, and recommendations could be made to optimally plan infrastructure, set tourist capacity, and manage the ecology. This form of accreditation is more sensitive to site specific conditions.

Guidelines and Education

An environmental protection strategy must address the issue of ecotourists removed from the cause-and-effect of their actions on the environment. More initiatives should be carried out to improve their awareness, sensitize them to environmental issues, and care about the places they visit.

Tour guides are an obvious and direct medium to communicate awareness. With the confidence of ecotourists and intimate knowledge of the environment, they can actively discuss conservation issues. A tour guide training program in Costa Rica's Tortuguero National Park has helped mitigate negative environmental impacts by providing information and regulating tourists on the parks' beaches used by nesting endangered sea turtles.

Small Scale, Slow Growth and Local Control

The underdevelopment theory of tourism describes a new form of imperialism by multinational corporations that control Eco-tourism resources. These corporations finance and profit from the development of large scale Eco-tourism that causes excessive environmental degradation, loss of traditional culture and way of life, and exploitation of local labour. In Zimbabwe and Nepal's Annapurna region, where underdevelopment is taking place, more than 90 percent of Eco-tourism revenues are expatriated to the parent countries, and less than 5 percent go into local communities.

The lack of sustainability highlights the need for small scale, slow growth, and locally based Eco-tourism. Local peoples have a vested interest in the well being of their community, and are therefore more accountable to environmental protection than multinational corporations. The lack of control, westernization, adverse impacts to the environment, loss of culture and traditions outweigh the benefits of establishing large scale Eco-tourism.

The increased contributions of communities to locally managed Eco-tourism create viable economic opportunities, including high level management positions, and reduce environmental issues associated with poverty and unemployment. Because the Eco-tourism experience is marketed to a different lifestyle from large scale Eco-tourism, the development of facilities and infrastructure does not need to conform to corporate Western tourism standards, and can be much simpler and less expensive. There is a greater multiplier effect on the economy, because local products, materials, and labour are used. Profits accrue locally and import leakages are reduced. However, even this form of tourism may require foreign investment for promotion or start up. When such investments are required, it is crucial for communities for find a company or non-governmental organization that reflects the philosophy of Eco-tourism; sensitive to their concerns and willing to cooperate at the expense of profit. The basic assumption of the multiplier effect is that the economy starts off with unused resources, for example, that many workers are cyclically unemployed and much of industrial capacity is sitting idle or incompletely utilized. By increasing demand in the economy it is then possible to boost production. If the economy was already at full employment, with only structural, frictional, or other supply-side types of unemployment, any attempt to boost demand would only lead to inflation. For various laissez-faire schools of economics which embrace Say's Law and deny the possibility of Keynesian inefficiency and under-employment of resources, therefore, the multiplier concept is irrelevant or wrong-headed.

As an example, consider the government increasing its expenditure on roads by $one million, without a corresponding increase in taxation. This sum would go to the road builders, who would hire more workers and distribute the money as wages and profits. The households receiving these incomes will save part of the money and spend the rest on consumer goods. These expenditures in turn will generate more jobs, wages, and profits, and so on with the income and spending circulating around the economy.

The multiplier effect arises because of the induced increases in consumer spending which occur due to the increased incomes — and because of the feedback into increasing business revenues, jobs, and income again. This process does not lead to an economic explosion not only because of the supply-side barriers at potential output (full employment) but because at each "round", the increase in consumer spending is less than the increase in consumer incomes. That is, the marginal propensity to consume (mpc) is less than one, so that each round some extra income goes into saving, leaking out of the cumulative process. Each increase in spending is thus smaller than that of the previous round, preventing an explosion. Eco-tourism has to be implemented with care.

Natural Resource Management

Natural resource management can be utilized as a specialized tool for the development of Eco-tourism. There are several places throughout the world where the amount of natural resources are abundant. But, with human encroachment and habitats these resources are depleting. Without knowing the proper utilization of certain resources they are destroyed and floral and faunal species are becoming extinct. Eco-tourism programmes can be introduced for the conservation of these resources. Several plans and proper management programmes can be introduced so that these resources remain untouched. Several organizations, NGO's, scientists are working on this field.

Natural resources of hill areas like Kurseong in West Bengal are plenty in number with various flora and fauna, but tourism for business purpose poised the situation. Researcher from Jadavpur University presently working in this area for the development of Eco-tourism which can be utilized as a tool for natural resource management.

In South-East Asia government and Non-Government Organisations are working together with academics and industry operators to spread the economic benefits of tourism into the kampungs and villages of the region. A recently formed alliance, the South-East Asian Tourism Organisation-SEATO is bringing together these diverse players to allay resource management concerns.

Tour Operators, Travel Agencies & Retailers

Some companies specialise in Eco-tourism, designing their trips to be environmentally, culturally and socially friendly. Companies such as Intrepid Travel, Adventure Life, Frontier, and Marine Conservation Society, Family Nature Summit, Peregrine Adventures, World Expeditions, greentraveller, Explore Worldwide and Exodus offer trips catering for the thoughtful traveller. Some tour operators are keenly aware of the impacts that they may have on specific areas and rotate clients around to different sites for snorkelling, bird watching, and other activities. Others are just beginning to see the advantage of "green" travel destinations.

2

Tourism and Natural Resource Management

Introduction: Recent and Future Trends in Tourism

Tourism can be considered one of the most remarkable socioeconomic phenomena of the twentieth century. From an activity "enjoyed by only a small group of relatively well-off people" during the first half of the last century, it gradually became a mass phenomenon during the post-World War II period, particularly from the 1970s onwards. It now reaches larger and larger numbers of people throughout the world, and is a source of employment for a significant segment of the labour force.

Although domestic tourism currently accounts for approximately 80 per cent of all tourist activity, many countries tend to give priority to international tourism because, while the former basically involves a regional redistribution of national income, the latter has now become the world's largest source of foreign exchange receipts. According to the latest figures compiled by the World Tourism Organization (WTO), foreign exchange earnings from international tourism reached a peak of US$ 476 billion in 2000, which was larger than the export value of petroleum products, motor vehicles, telecommunications equipment or any other single category of product or service.

International tourist arrivals grew at an annual average rate of 4.3 per cent during the 1990s, despite major international political and economic crises, such as the Gulf War and the Asian financial crisis. According to the latest WTO figures, compiled with data received up to August 2001, the turn of the millennium recorded one of the most impressive annual growth rates in international tourism. The September 2001 terrorist attacks in the United States, however, appear to have had a more serious impact on the tourist sector than any other major international crisis in recent decades. The attacks had a particularly severe impact on air transport, business travel and long-haul travel.

Worldwide travel reservations were estimated to have dropped by 15 per cent at the end of October 2001, although not every destination nor every part of the tourism sector was badly affected. For example, while air transport and luxury hotels have suffered from considerable fall in demand, travel within the same country or region, as well as travel by rail and road, appear to have weathered the worst effects of the crisis, or even benefited from it.

Nevertheless, initial forecasts of 3-4 per cent rise in international tourist arrivals for 2001, made before the September 2001 attacks, were subsequently revised downwards to around a 1 per cent increase over the 2000 figures. The latest data, released by WTO in January 2002, show that there was a sharp decline of 1.3 per cent in international arrivals, to a total of less than 690 million, in 2001.7 Given that the northern hemisphere summer holiday season was coming to end by the time the attacks took place, this significant drop confirms that the short-term impacts of the attacks were devastating to international tourism as a whole. The last four months of 2001, in fact, recorded a drop of almost 11 per cent in arrivals worldwide and substantial decreases in all regions of theworld.

It is worth noting, however, that this considerable fall in international arrivals was caused not only by a widespread fear of traveling generated by the attacks – particularly in airplanes and to certain destinations – but also by a downturn in the world economy. The economic downturn that began in the United States during the first half of 2001 had already been affecting the tourism sector before the terrorist attacks were carried out. The attacks merely aggravated the economic slowdown already under way.

According to the most recent United Nations economic forecasts, growth of only 1.5 per cent in gross world product (GWP) is expected in 2002, as compared to 1.3 per cent last year. Such a modest improvement is linked to a number of economic uncertainties, notably the high dependency of the global economy on the recovery of the United States. Higher rates of population growth would thus make 2002 the second consecutive year with no real growth in per capita GWP. This, in turn, is also likely to undermine the short-term prospects for a recovery in international tourism, at least until mid-2002, when the summer holiday season begins in the northern hemisphere, and probably until the end of the year. Although much will depend on the evolution of the world economy during this year, it is also likely that some destinations will experience a prolonged decline in tourism revenues regardless of any world economic improvements.

In the medium and long term, however, international tourism is expected to resume its rapid growth, in view of rising living standards and discretionary incomes, falling real costs of travel, expansion and improvement of various transport modes, increasing amounts of free time and other factors. The World Tourism Organization has recently reiterated its long-term forecasts, made before the September 2001 attacks, of an average annual growth rate in international arrivals of over 4 per cent in the period up to 2020.10 The number of international arrivals is thus expected to reach the striking mark of 1 billion by 2010 and 1.6 billion by 2020.

Main Economic Benefits of Tourism

Tourism, as a sector that comprises an extensive range of economic activities, can be considered the largest industry in the world. International tourism is also one of the fastest growing and most ramified sectors of the global economy, covering a broad range of enterprises, sectors and stakeholders. During the 1990s, when the globalization of tourism reached unprecedented proportions, international tourism receipts had a much higher average annual growth rate (7.3 per cent) than that of gross world product. By 1999, international tourism receipts accounted for more than 8 per cent of the worldwide export value of goods and services, overtaking the export value of other leading world industries such as automotive products, chemicals, and computer and office equipment.

Tourism is also the only major service sector in which developing countries have consistently recorded trade surpluses relative to the rest of the world. Between 1980 and 1996, for instance, their travel account surplus increased from $4.6 billion to $65.9 billion, due primarily to the impressive growth of inbound tourism to countries in Africa, the Caribbean, and the Asia and Pacific regions. The 1990s also experienced a significant growth of international tourism receipts in the 49 poorest developing countries: total tourism receipts in these countries more than doubled from US$ 1 billion in 1992 to over US$ 2.2 billion in 1998.15 Tourism is now the second largest source of foreign exchange earnings in the 49 least developed countries (LDCs) as a whole, after the oil industry, which is concentrated in only three of these countries.

Tourism has become the main source of income for the economies of an increasing number of small island developing States (SIDS) – as well as less developed regions of large countries – with a natural environment appealing to tourists. Foreign exchange earnings can, however, vary significantly among these tourism-driven economies because of 'leakages' arising from imports of equipment for construction and consumer goods required by tourists, repatriation of profits earned by foreign investors and amortization of foreign debt incurred in tourist development.

Besides export earnings, international tourism also generates an increasingly significant share of government (national and local) tax revenues throughout the world. In addition, the development of tourism as a whole is usually accompanied by considerable investments in infrastructure, such as airports, roads, water and sewerage facilities, telecommunications and other public utilities. Such infrastructural improvements not only generate benefits to tourists but can also contribute to improving the living conditions of local populations. This increase in social overhead capital can also help attract other industries to a disadvantaged area and thus be crucial to regional economic development.

The tourism sector is an increasingly important source of employment – including in tourism-related sectors, such as construction and agriculture – primarily for unskilled labour, migrants from poor rural areas, people who prefer to work part-time, and notably women. Because the sector is relatively labour-intensive, investments in tourism tend to generate a larger and more rapid increase in employment than equal investment in other economic activities. Furthermore, given that the sector provides a considerable amount of jobs for women and unskilled workers, tourism can significantly contribute to empowering women and alleviating poverty. At the same time, available data suggests that most workers in the tourism sector, notably in hotels and catering, tend to earn less than workers in socially comparable occupations in both developed and developing countries. In addition, the differential tends to be larger in less developed countries and regions, particularly those with high rates of unemployment amongst unskilled labour. Informal employment relations in small and medium-sized enterprises, which employ about half of the labour force in the hotel and catering sub-sectors worldwide, also contribute to a relatively high proportion of child labour and non-remunerated employment in these sub-sectors in many countries.

The increasing reliance of less diversified economies on tourism also increases their vulnerability to international shocks, such as, natural disasters, regional wars and other unexpected events. The recent crisis generated by fear of international terrorism, for example, caused devastating immediate effects on tourism-dependent economies, including regional economies in large countries. In addition, sudden changes in consumer tastes and sharp economic downturns pose significant risks to such economies, given that demand for mass tourism tends to be relatively income-elastic and can produce drastic negative responses to economic recession in source markets. Nonetheless, it is now generally recognized that tourism can make a vital contribution to employment, export receipts and national income in most countries and regions. Furthermore, tourism is often identified as the most promising driving force for the economic development of less developed countries and regions endowed with areas of natural beauty – including small island developing States – because it offers them a valuable opportunity for economic diversification.

Environmental Impacts of Tourism

While tourism provides considerable economic benefits for many countries, regions and communities, its rapid expansion can also be responsible for adverse environmental (and sociocultural) impacts. Natural resource depletion and environmental degradation associated with tourism activities are sometimes serious problems in tourism-rich regions. The management of natural resources to reverse this trend is thus one of the most difficult challenges for governments at different levels. The fact that most tourists chose to maintain their relatively high patterns of consumption (and waste generation) when they reach their destinations can be a particularly serious problem for developing countries and regions without the appropriate means for protecting their natural resources and local ecosystems from the pressures of mass tourism. The main environmental impacts of tourism are (a) pressure on natural resources, (b) pollution and waste generation and (c) damage to ecosystems. Furthermore, it is now widely recognized that not only uncontrolled tourism expansion is likely to lead to environmental degradation, but also that environmental degradation, in turn, poses a serious threat to tourism.

Pressure on Natural Resources

In addition to pressure on the availability and prices of resources consumed by local residents – such as energy, food and basic raw materials – the main natural resources at risk from tourism development are land, freshwater and marine resources. Without careful land-use planning, for instance, rapid tourism development can intensify competition for land resources with other uses and lead to rising land prices and increased pressure to build on agricultural land. Intensive tourism development can also threaten natural landscapes, notably though deforestation, loss of wetlands and soil erosion. Tourism development in coastal areas – including hotel, airport and road construction – is a matter for increasing concern worldwide as it can lead to sand mining, beach erosion and land degradation.

Freshwater availability for competing agricultural, industrial, household and other uses is rapidly becoming one of the most critical natural resource issues in many countries and regions. Rapid expansion of the tourism industry, which tends to be extremely water-intensive, can exacerbate this problem by placing considerable pressure on scarce water supply in many destinations. Water scarcity can pose a serious limitation to future tourism development in many low-lying coastal areas and small islands that have limited possibility for surface water use and storage, and whose groundwater may be contaminated by saltwater intrusion. Over-consumption by many tourist facilities – notably large hotel resorts and golf courses – can limit current supplies available to farmers and local populations in water-scarce regions and thus lead to serious shortages and price rises. In addition, pollution of available freshwater sources, some of which may be associated with tourism-related activities, can exacerbate local shortages. Rapid expansion of coastal and ocean tourism activities, such as snorkelling, scuba diving and sport fishing, can threaten coral reefs and other marine resources. Disturbance to marine aquatic life can also be caused by the intensive use of thrill craft, such as jet skis, frequent boat tours and boat anchors. Anchor damage is now regarded as one of the most serious threats to coral reefs in the Caribbean Sea, in view of the growing number of both small boats and large cruise ships sailing in the region. Severe damage to coral reefs and other marine resources may, in turn, not only discourage further tourism and threaten the future of local tourist industries, but also damage local fisheries.

Pollution and Waste Generation

Besides the consumption of large amounts of natural and other local resources, the tourism industry also generates considerable waste and pollution. Improper disposal of liquid and solid waste generated by the tourism industry has become a particular problem for many developing countries and regions that lack the capacity to treat these waste materials properly. Disposal of such untreated waste has, in turn, contributed to reducing availability of the above-mentioned resources at the local level. Apart from the contamination of freshwater from pollution by untreated sewage, tourist activities can also lead to land contamination from solid waste and the contamination of marine waters and coastal areas from pollution generated by hotels and marinas, as well as cruise ships. It is estimated that cruise ships in the Caribbean Sea alone produced more than 70,000 tons of liquid and solid waste a year during the mid-1990s. The fast growth of the cruise sector in the region may have exacerbated this problem in recent years. Furthermore, a particular cause of concern for coastal areas and small islands is the illegal disposal of sewage, solid waste and cargo residues by merchant ships, which cause marine and beach pollution.

In addition, relatively high levels of energy consumption in hotels – including energy for airconditioning, heating and cooking– as well as fuel used by tourism-related transportation can also contribute significantly to local air pollution in many host countries and regions. Local air and noise pollution linked to exhaustive tourism development or urban congestion can sometimes even discourage tourists from visiting some destinations.

Damage to Ecosystems

Intensive tourism activity in natural areas can interfere with fragile vegetation and wildlife and cause irreversible damage to ecosystems, particularly if the infrastructure in those areas is not adequately prepared to absorb mass tourism.

Uncontrolled tourism activities can lead to the severe disruption of wildlife habitats and increased pressure on endangered species. As it has been widely documented, it can also disrupt wildlife behaviour, such as, tourist vehicles in Africa's national parks that approach wild cats and thus distract them from hunting and breeding; tour boat operators in the Caribbean Sea that feed sharks to ensure that they remain in tourist areas; and whale-watching boat crews around the world that pursue whales and dolphins and even encourage petting, which tends to alter the animals' feeding and behaviour.

Tourism can also lead to the indiscriminate clearance of native vegetation for the development of new facilities, increased demand for fuelwood and even forest fires. Ecologically fragile areas, such as rain forests, wetlands and mangroves, are also threatened by intensive or irresponsible tourist activity. Moreover, as will be discussed below, it is increasingly recognized that, the rapid expansion of nature tourism (or 'Eco-tourism') may also pose a threat to ecologically fragile areas, including natural world heritage sites, if not properly managed and monitored.

In many countries, coastlines are becoming overbuilt due to tourism development until the damage caused by environmental degradation – and the eventual loss of revenues arising from a collapse in tourism arrivals – becomes irreversible. As mentioned above, intensive tourism development and recreational activities in coastal areas can not only lead to beach destruction and coastal degradation, but can also threaten coral reefs and other marine ecosystems. The delicate ecosystems of most small islands, together with their increasing reliance on tourism as a main tool of socioeconomic development, means that these environmental impacts can be particularly damaging since the success of the sector in these islands often depends on the quality of their natural environment. In addition, pollution of coastal waters – in particular by sewage, solid waste, sediments and untreated chemicals – often leads to the deterioration of coastal ecosystems, notably coral reefs, and thus harms their value for tourism.

The equally fragile ecosystems of mountain regions are also threatened by increasing popular tourist activities such as skiing, snowboarding and trekking. One of the most serious environmental problems in mountainous developing countries without appropriate energy supply is deforestation arising from increasing consumption of fuelwood by the tourism industry. This often results not only in the destruction of local habitats and ecosystems, but also in accelerating processes of erosion and landslides. Other major problems arising from tourist activities in mountain regions include disruption of animal migration by road and tourist facilities, sewage pollution of rivers, excessive water withdrawals from streams to supply resorts and accumulation of solid waste on trails.

Environmental Threats to Tourism

In many mountain regions, small islands, coastal areas and other ecologically fragile places visited by tourists, there is an increasing concern that the negative impacts of tourism on the natural environment can ultimately hurt the tourism industry itself. There is now plenty of evidence of the 'life-cycle' of a tourist destination, that is, "its evolution from discovery, to development, to eventual decline, ... attributed to a site's overuse and the subsequent deterioration of key attractions or facilities." In other words, the negative impacts of intensive tourism activities on the environmental quality of beaches, mountains, rivers, forests and other ecosystems also compromise the viability of the tourism industry in these places.

In addition, tourism in many destinations could be particularly threatened by global environmental problems, notably the potential threat of 'global warming'. There is increasing scientific evidence that human activity has begun to change the average temperature on the Earth's surface. According to the authoritative United Nations Intergovernmental Panel on Climate Change (IPCC), this process of global warming has been caused by several factors associated with the intensification of economic activities, including the emissions of 'greenhouse gases', such as carbon dioxide produced by burning fossil fuels and forests.

Sustainable Tourism: The Way Forward

Countries and regions where the economy is driven by the tourism industry are becoming increasingly concerned with the environmental, as well as the socio-cultural problems associated with unsustainable tourism. As a result, there is now increasing agreement on the need to promote sustainable tourism development to minimize its environmental impacts and to ensure more sustainable management of natural resources. The concept of sustainable tourism, as developed in the United Nations sustainable development process, refers to tourist activities "leading to management of all resources in such a way that economic, social and aesthetic needs can be fulfilled while maintaining cultural integrity, essential ecological processes, biological diversity and life support systems."

These sustainability concerns are, therefore, beginning to be addressed by governments at national, regional and local, as well as international, levels. In addition, given the leading role of the private sector in the tourism industry in most countries, many initiatives have also been taken by this sector. Broadly speaking, the main policy areas regarding sustainable tourism are: (a) the promotion of national strategies for sustainable tourism development, including the decentralizatior. of environmental management to regional and local levels, (b) the use of both regulatory mechanisms and economic instruments, (c) the support for voluntary initiatives by the industry itself, and (d) the promotion of sustainable tourism at the international level.

National and Regional Strategies for Sustainable Tourism Development

Generally speaking, the main priority for national and regional governments is to incorporate tourism planning and development effectively into overall sustainable development strategies. For example, regional development strategies for areas containing water resources that an integrated manner that considers all potential water users. Government policies to promote the domestic tourism industry and to attract foreign direct investment should also ensure that tourism is properly planned and managed so as to minimize adverse environmental impacts and its use of natural resources.

Since the environmental impacts of tourism development are primarily felt at the local and regional levels, national Governments need to promote decentralization of public environment management to the regional and municipal levels. Given that in many countries, local and regional governments already have important responsibilities for tourism development, central Governments should also support capacity building programmes at lower levels in order to enable local and regional authorities to better respond to the challenges of sustainable tourism development in the areas under their jurisdiction. National and local governments also need to develop clear strategies to monitor progress towards sustainable tourism.

Last but far from least, governments at all levels can greatly benefit from working in partnership with all major stakeholders, including local communities, to ensure their active participation in tourism planning, development and management, as well as in the sharing of benefits. Participation of local communities in decision-making and sharing of benefits also helps to generate better awareness of the environmental costs of tourism and thus provides strong incentives to conserve natural resources and protect local environmental assets. Governments, together with the tourism industry and other stakeholders, should also promote or support various efforts to raise public awareness about the impact of tourists cn destinations, to promote respect for local communities and their cultures and to protect the environment. Such public awareness campaigns often succeed in promoting positive behavioural changes not only in tourists, but also in tourism workers and host communities as a whole.

Regulatory Mechanisms and Economic Instruments

Sustainable tourism can also be promoted by a careful mix of government policies comprising both direct regulation and market-based instruments, although financial incentives that encourage environmentally damaging activities, such as energy subsidies, should be reduced or removed. The major challenge for governments is, therefore, to formulate and effectively apply an appropriate mix of regulatory and economic instruments for both sustainable natural resources management and environmental protection.

The most direct tool for promoting sustainable tourism involves the use of regulatory mechanisms, such as, integrated land-use planning and coastal zone management. In many cases, it may be necessary to protect coastlines through rigid building restrictions, such as, existing with externalities is thus to internalize them through taxes so that the full costs of production are reflected in prices.

One well-known example of charging user fees to support environmental conservation is the Bonaire protected marine areas in the Netherlands Antilles. This was one of the first protected marine parks in the Caribbean to become entirely self-financing through the levying of admission fees on scuba divers. The (private) diving industry in Bonaire was initially opposed to the levy because of its potential negative impacts on future demand and revenues, against the background of intense competition offered by many Caribbean diving destinations.

The system, however, has been an unqualified success since it was introduced in January 1992 because many divers (and an increasing number of tourists in general) are willing and able to pay higher prices to support environmental protection. Fees from this scheme also support the active management of the park's coral reef and mangrove ecosystems, as well as educational activities and orientation sessions for divers.

Voluntary Industry Initiatives

As noted above, tourism services in most countries are provided primarily by the private sector, which tends to oppose greater government regulation and taxation of the industry on the grounds that they are ultimately detrimental to efficiency, competitiveness and profits. The predominantly private tourism industry has thus developed several self-regulation and voluntary initiatives to promote greater environmental sustainability. These include waste and pollution reduction schemes, voluntary codes of conduct, industry awards and eco-labels for sustainable tourism. In addition, environmental management schemes to encourage responsible practices have been promoted in various sub-sectors, including hotel and catering, recreation and entertainment, transportation, travel agencies and tour operators.

For example, the World Travel and Tourism Council (WTTC), the main international industry association, has developed an environmental management programme (Green Globe), for both travel and tourism companies and tourism destinations, aimed to raise the level of environmental awareness and to provide a low-cost practical means for improving the environmental performance of the industry. It is also responsible for ECoNETT, an internet-based tool that provides an extensive information resource on all tourism and environmental issues. Another innovative global programme is the International Hotel Environment Initiative (IHEI), led by a council of leading international hotel chains, aimed to promote environmental management in the hotel industry, which is one of the main consumers of resources and sources of waste. Such initiatives are particularly important not only because they can lead to significant reductions of water and energy consumption, as well as liquid and solid waste, but also because they promote positive behavioural changes in both tourists and employees. In addition, they can lead to improved economic efficiency and increased profitability.

At the regional level, it is worth noting the successful implementation of the Blue Flag Programme, which now extends to 18 countries in Europe, in providing an incentive to protect and improve the quality of beaches and coasts. Under this programme, environmental standards at individual beaches in Europe are assessed by measuring compliance with acceptable concentrations of a range of pollutants to ensure clean bathing water. Beaches are also judged by their compliance with guidelines dealing with litter management, the availability of sanitary and beach safety facilities, and environmental education. Beaches that meet these stringent criteria receive Blue Flag awards, which also serve as a marketing tool to attract tourists.

Despite these helpful initiatives of the tourism industry to improve its standards of environmental management and protection, the very proliferation of such voluntary codes of conduct and eco-label awards at global, regional and local levels – which are not, in any case, adopted or recognized by all industry enterprises – can sometimes lead to confusion and difficulty to evaluate and compare them. While national and regional governments should fully support these voluntary initiatives and encourage the dissemination of the best practices in the private tourism industry, there is also a role for independent supervision, monitoring and comparative assessment by relevant government agencies.

In addition, trustworthy codes of conduct, transparent eco-label awards and internationally agreed programmes of action for sustainable tourism are required at the international level. The international community has a particularly crucial role to play in developing a set of internationally recognized accreditation and monitoring systems for assessing the sustainability of tourism services around the world.

International Activities in Support of Sustainable Tourism

Although tourism was not specifically addressed in Agenda 21 – the international programme of action on sustainable development agreed on at the 1992 Earth Summit in Rio de Janeiro (Brazil) – its growing economic importance, significant use of natural resources and environmental impact all contributed to its gradual introduction into the international sustainable development agenda over the past ten years.

One of the first concrete sectoral programmes of action arising from the increasing cooperation between the tourism industry and inter-governmental agencies was 'Agenda 21 for the Travel and Tourism Industry,' an action plan for sustainable tourism development jointly launched by the World Tourism Organization, the above-mentioned WTTC and the Earth Council in 1996. Among its innovative key objectives are the estimation of the economic value for resources, such as wildlife, natural areas and cultural heritage, "whose conservation would otherwise be seen as having no financial value," and the establishment of "essential infrastructure, such as water treatment plants, for residents as well as visitors ... (in order to) stimulate other economic activities." Many tourism-based communities and regions have also formulated their own 'Agenda 21s' at the local and regional levels.

In 1997, the United Nations General Assembly, at its special session to review the five-year implementation of Agenda 21, decided that there was a need to consider the importance of tourism in the context of Agenda 21 and to "develop an action-oriented international programme of work on sustainable tourism." This request was followed up during the seventh annual session of the United Nations Commission for Sustainable Development (CSD), held in New York in 1999, which discussed tourism as an economic sector and held a multi-stakeholder dialogue on the topic.

The Commission adopted an international work programme on sustainable tourism development, which is due to be reviewed during the forthcoming World Summit for Sustainable Development in Johannesburg (South Africa) later this year, as part of the ten-year review of progress achieved since the Earth Summit. The CSD also invited the World Tourism Organization to seek further input from the private sector, non-governmental organizations and other stakeholders in the further development of its proposed global code of ethics that had been drafted in consultation with the industry over the previous two years.

The final 'Global Code of Ethics for Tourism,' introduced by the World Tourism Organization in late 1999, sets a frame of reference for the responsible and sustainable development of international tourism. It includes nine articles outlining the basic rules for governments, tour operators, developers, travel agents, workers, as well as host communities and the tourists themselves. The tenth article deals with implementation and includes a proposed mechanism for conciliation, through the creation of a World Committee on Tourism Ethics made up of representatives of each region of the world and representatives of each group of stakeholders in the tourism sector, governments, the private sector, and labour and non-governmental organizations. The United Nations General Assembly adopted the Global Code of Ethics for Tourism at the end of 2001.

Although progress has been achieved over the past ten years, one of the key remaining challenges for the international community is to devise ways and means to assist developing countries to ensure that their tourism industries become more internationally competitive without damaging their natural resources and environmental assets base. This will require, amongst other things, greater technical and financial assistance, including human resources development, institutional capacity building and the transfer of environmentally sound technologies to many developing countries. The international community could also support the wider use of 'debt-fornature swaps', through which a portion of the foreign debt of developing countries is purchased at a discount by various international partners in exchange for the debtor's country investment of an agreed sum of local currency in environmental protection projects.

Economic Impacts, Economic Values, and Market Segmentation

An important factor in Eco-tourism development is the amount of revenue that remains within local economies (Seidl 1994). For example, economic benefits derived from Eco-tourism can contribute to residents having positive attitudes toward local natural areas (Lindberg and others 1996) and serve as economic incentives for natural resource conservation (Wunder 2000). Alternatively, if local residents bear the costs of tourism without receiving any benefits, they may be unsupportive of not only tourism but also the conservation of natural areas on which tourism is based. Sustainable tourism development must meet the needs of the host population in terms of improved living standards while satisfying the demands of tourism and protecting the natural environment (Seidl 1994). The costs and benefits of protection may not be distributed equally among tourism providers and local residents (Dixon and Sherman 1990).

Measuring the economic impacts of tourism and outdoor recreation has received considerable attention in academic literature. Economic impacts generally are examined within a costbenefit framework with the benefits measured by using expenditure surveys combined with input-output analysis. Travel cost or contingent valuation methods also are commonly used to place dollar values on natural areas or marginal changes in their characteristics. The trend toward greater reliance on user fees in the financial management of public lands also has led to many studies examining fees and pricing policies.

Measuring economic impacts or values derived from tourism necessitates differentiating between the economic benefits derived from the various forms of tourism. One of the problems in determining the economic impact of Eco-tourism, for example, is knowing what is meant by the term (Tisdell 1996). Differentiating between economic benefits derived from Eco-tourism and those derived from general tourism can depend on how each is defined.

When Eco-tourism is defined less restrictively, as simply tourism derived from nature preserves, parks, or refuges, researchers tend to assume that all economic impacts derived from those natural areas are Eco-tourism-derived impacts. Economic impacts are measured by using expenditure surveys of tourists visiting those areas. Tourism expenditures assumed to be generated by a particular natural area may be reported for a well-defined geographic area or combined with input-output analysis to describe secondary impacts. An alternative to surveying tourists is surveying local businesses and residents.

When Eco-tourism is defined more restrictively and confined to particular types of tourism activity or particular types of tourists, researchers attempt to segment tourists into the categories of ecotourist and general tourist. One approach identifies ecotourists as those individuals pursuing recreational activities that are assumed to characterize Eco-tourism. Economic impacts might then be based on the economic value of specific outdoor recreation activities. For example, studies have estimated the economic value of wildlife viewing (Navrud and Mungatana 1994), birdwatching, and whitewater recreation (Johnson and Moore 1993), among other activities.

Another approach confines Eco-tourism to tourists possessing certain attitudes or motives. Attitude or motive-based segmentation combines surveys of tourists with factor and cluster analysis to segment tourists according to their trip motives or socioeconomic characteristics. This method has been used to segment ecotourists from general tourists and ecotour operators from nonecotour operators (Bottrill and Pearce 1995). Segmentation can be used to disaggregate expenditure, travel cost, or contingent valuation survey results into Eco-tourism and general tourism economic impacts. Segmentation also can be used to evaluate how preferences for site management differ among ecotourists and general tourists.

Selecting an appropriate method for segmenting different types of tourism and tourists depends on the location and situation of interest. Focusing on specific natural areas may be appropriate in some cases, whereas focusing on different types of tourists may be appropriate in others. Some tourists may visit one location to escape commercial development, whereas others may expect typical tourist services offered by national franchises. Different tourists may differ in their spending and rates of visitation. Individual trips might take on characteristics of Eco-tourism at some times and characteristics of general tourism at others (Lindberg 1991). Recognition of different types of tourism and tourists, the economic impacts different tourists generate, and the use and nonuse values they hold with respect to their tourism experience can have important implications for how tourism economics research is conducted.

Planning and Development Case Studies

Perhaps the greatest proportion of published Eco-tourism literature presents case studies examining political, social, economic, and environmental issues related to tourism development in specific locations.

Some studies focus more directly on difficulties associated with Eco-tourism planning and development. For example, Eco-tourism development can be adversely impacted by inadequate protection of natural areas on which Eco-tourism is based (Wells 1993). National political and economic priorities can dominate regional or local priorities, thereby leading to national policies that are incompatible with sustainable tourism development (Tosun 1998). In other locations, prodevelopment and proprotection roles might be reversed. Disagreement may exist between national protection interests and the economic development aspirations of local communities (Prunier and others 1993).

Sustainable tourism advocates may not always agree with local residents. What sustainable tourism advocates may see as potential conflicts between tourism development and natural resource protection, local residents may see as desirable economic development. Failure to involve communities in tourism development decisions along with an inability of policymakers to form an integrated regional vision can be obstacles to sustainable development (Ioannides 1995). Progress toward sustainability most likely occurs in communities that recognize the potential costs and benefits of tourism and are willing to take a proactive approach in its planning and management (Godfrey 1998).

Collaboration is a common theme advocated for successful Eco-tourism development. Cooperation and coordination between public and private sectors are important. Several case studies describe integrated roles of natural resources management agencies, tourism service industries, government agencies, and local communities as important factors leading to successful Eco-tourism development. Many studies advocate the need for community involvement and outline community-based tourism development strategies.

Community involvement can be impeded by disagreement over the level or type of tourism development desired (Wyllie 1998). It can be difficult to discern whether tourism development is an appropriate alternative to other types of economic development in different locations (Joppe 1996). A potential problem of basing a local economy on tourism is that tourism injects money into the economy without producing more goods for people to consume. This can result in local price inflation, which is worsened by the presence of tourists who increase demand (Seidl 1994). For many communities, tourism will have a limited growth potential. Economic activity based on tourism and recreation can suffer significant seasonal variability (Keith and others 1996). Eco-tourism is subject to fluctuations owing to ups and downs in the trendiness of given destinations and modes of travel (Seidl 1994). Local residents also may face significant opportunity costs associated with restrictions on local resource use, whereas the benefits of protection may not be readily apparent. Tourism should be viewed as part of an overall economic and environmental plan that includes other industries (Anderson 1994).

Researchers argue that overdeveloped or unsustainable tourism results from the openaccess nature of natural resources on which tourism is based. Overdevelopment can result in damage to natural resources and reduced enjoyment by tourists because of congestion and site degradation. Steele (1995) argues that problems derived from open access can be remedied if control over the resource is assigned to governments, local communities, or private entities who can restrict access. Assigning control to one entity, however, can lead to other problems. For example, governments may feel compelled to maintain open access as a service to the public (Lindberg 1991). Development of seemingly sustainable tourism also can lead to unsustainable tourism development if tourism businesses are unable to resist the temptation to increase visitors (Weaver 1995). Economic incentives often run counter to preservation and favour development (Backman and others 1994). Tourism development also potentially can spark desired or undesired growth in nontourism sectors.

Establishing Criteria for Success

Several studies propose specific principles, criteria, or guidelines by which to judge Eco-tourism development success. Some attempts at sustainable tourism development also have relied on the implementation of charters or codes of ethics designed to guide the activities of tourists and the tourism industry. Dowling (1993) proposes an environmentally based tourism development planning model as one way to implement environmentally compatible sustainable tourism. The usefulness of such prescriptions for Eco-tourism likely are dependent on specific circumstances of specific locations.

Tourism Research and the USDA Forest Service

National forests and other public lands undoubtedly have played a role in attracting tourism in many communities located near them, by providing significant outdoor recreation opportunities in relatively undeveloped settings. Much of this tourism fits within new nature-based tourism, Eco-tourism, and sustainable tourism concepts.

Many of the issues and concerns that motivate interest in new forms of tourism are consistent with the traditional conservation-oriented multiple-use objectives that have characterized national forest management. Although outdoor recreation historically has been an important component of research conducted by the USDA Forest Service, tourism research has not. Although recreation and tourism research address many similar concepts and issues, little integration exists between the two. Increasing recognition of the role of national forests as tourism destinations may imply a need to expand traditional outdoor recreation planning to include inquiry into the economic, social, and ecological impacts of tourism.

Evaluating National Forests as Tourism Resources

An important factor in tourism development is whether natural or cultural resources exist on which to base a tourism industry. New tourism concepts, such as Eco-tourism, may require natural areas or cultures that are relatively unique or pristine. Economic feasibility depends on a site having a marketable product (Seidl 1994). Not all locations are sufficiently unique to draw tourists. If a location is a less popular or highly specialized destination, there can be risks involved in developing a reliance on tourism (Anderson 1991).

Poor accessibility owing to remoteness or inadequate transportation systems can constrain tourism growth. Some communities may be unable to provide or develop necessary complementary tourist services.

Different scales and types of tourism development may be appropriate in different locations. Some communities located near national forests or other public lands likely possess comparative advantages in offering relatively undeveloped natural areas potentially of interest to tourists seeking outdoor recreation opportunities. Whether their comparative advantages in tourism exceed those in other natural resource-based industries is not always clear. Evaluating the existing and potential role national forests can play in attracting local and regional tourism likely would aid national forest managers in natural resource planning.

Forest Management Impacts on Tourism

In addition to the natural resource endowments provided by national forests, how those endowments are managed will significantly impact the numbers and types of tourists that will be attracted. Traditional multiple-use objectives of national forests may be incompatible with certain types of tourism. For example, it is plausible that certain types of tourists may be unwilling to accept any signs of intensive forest management for commercial timber production. Locations that can enhance or maintain their relative environmental quality will improve their comparative advantage over other destinations. Also, certain recreational activities may be incompatible with others, thereby resulting in conflicts between different tourists seeking different forms of recreation. Hikers may be at odds with off-road vehicle users, hunters may be at odds with birdwatchers, and motorized boaters may be at odds with nonmotorized boaters. Accommodating every type of tourist may be infeasible in every location. Tourism planning may require aligning forest management with the preferences of tourists in specific locations. User surveys could assist in identifying specific outdoor amenities and forest management activities that attract or repell different types of tourists and aid in developing appropriate forest management prescriptions in specific locations.

Evaluating Economic, Social, and Ecological Tradeoffs

Recent literature on tourism tends to differentiate between mass tourism, which is viewed as environmentally and culturally destructive, and alternative forms of tourism developed on a smaller scale so as to minimize adverse impacts to local environments and cultures. These alternative forms of tourism, it is argued, provide local residents greater employment opportunities, maintain a greater share of economic benefits within the local area, and result in less negative impacts (Hampton 1998). In contrast, mass tourism is associated with large-scale, high-density accommodations, contrived attractions, seasonal markets, and limited benefits to the local economy with minimal concern for carrying capacity and a lack of local involvement (Weaver 1995). One advantage of tourism development on a larger scale, however, is the ability for local government agencies to control accommodation standards and recoup tax revenues through licensing, which is more difficult with more fragmented and small-scale tourism development (Carey and others 1997). Different types and scales of tourism development imply economic, social, and ecological tradeoffs.

Virtually any kind of tourism activity will result in some impact to natural resources somewhere (Cater 1993, Hunter 1997). Despite strong ethical and environmental motives, ecotourists still are seeking primarily pleasure and entertainment (McKercher 1993a). As Prunier and others suggest, a person who wishes to be a "green" holidaymaker should remain at home. Wildlife biologists are concerned that even Eco-tourism can adversely affect wildlife (Jacobson and Lopez 1994). Moscardo and others (1996) suggest that rather than embracing a simplified dichotomy between "good" and "bad" tourism, a more useful analytical framework may be to examine the dimensions underlying the different manifestations of tourism. A successful tourism industry in one area may not fit in another.

In their discussion of recreation carrying capacity, Stankey and McCool (1984) suggest that the question of "how much is too much?" may focus on the wrong issue. Rather, the focus should be on identifying what kinds of resource and social conditions are appropriate and acceptable in different settings. In considering if tourism development is appropriate in a given location, the comparative advantages of different types and scales of tourism development need to be evaluated. Social, economic, and ecological constraints need to be identified. Successful tourism development will depend less on how tourism is labeled than on the natural endowments in given locations and the existing infrastructure, local expertise, and community support necessary to complement those endowments. Studies could address what types and scales of tourism development are appropriate in certain locations from economic, social, and ecological perspectives.

National Forest Fees and Local Economic Impacts

In recent years, there has been increasing interest in charging user fees for access to public lands. Revenue can be made both by entrance fees charged to tourists and by use permits charged to businesses offering tourist services such as guided tours on public lands. Fees can help public agencies recoup the costs of natural resource management and reduce congestion at certain sites by creating economic disincentives to visit. Entrance fees to parks and natural areas frequently are set below amounts visitors are willing to pay and below amounts required to finance park budgets (Laarman and Gregersen 1996). Low fees often persist because of a lack of information regarding site demand, and potential impacts of charging higher fees often are unknown (Lindberg and Johnson 1994). Pricing potentially can lead to greater efficiency, fairness, and environmentally sustainable nature-based tourism (Laarman and Gregersen 1996). For national forests, this may imply setting user fees that are sufficient to capture positive unpriced benefits derived from forest resources.

For local communities, however, a significant socioeconomic factor in tourism development is the proportion of tourism income that can be captured by the local economy. Such income is generated through employment in tourism-related services such as food and lodging, gasoline, local tour guiding, and sale of souvenir and outdoor recreation equipment. Charging access fees to public lands potentially reduces visitation and can result in adverse economic impacts to local communities where access to public lands is a primary attraction. User surveys incorporating contingent valuation, travel cost, or other methods could be used to provide information about the impact of fees on rates of visitation. Such studies could be combined with economic impact assessments within local communities to describe different fee levels in terms of potential local economic impacts. The fiscal benefits of access fees on public lands could be evaluated within a broader context to include the tourism industry in which public lands are a part.

Defining the Role of the Forest Service in Tourism

National forests likely will have an increasingly significant impact on tourism in communities located near them. As the U.S. population continues to grow and become more urban, so do ever-increasing demands for outdoor recreation opportunities. Such increased demands will place growing pressure on National Forests and other public lands to provide the types of nontimber amenities desired by many recreationists. These changes will lead to increasingly difficult decisions about national forest management as managers try to balance traditional multiple-use objectives. The role the USDA Forest Service intends to play in tourism development in local communities is not clearly defined. Should the agency be more actively involved in local tourism development planning? Are there types of tourism the agency should encourage or discourage? How would the role of the agency differ depending on local economic, social, and ecological conditions, and in relation to economic diversification, community resiliency, and economic dependence on public lands? These likely will be some of the questions confronting researchers and policymakers in the future.

Key Strategies of Eco-tourism Development

To ensure that tourism at a protected area is sustainable, it is necessary to implement a strong and effective management program that involves all stakeholders in dynamic, creative ways.

Zoning for Visitor Use

The appropriate zoning of an Eco-tourism site is fundamental to all other management strategies. Zoning is the division of a site into a number of different sectors, or zones, for the purpose of distributing different types of use or non-use (i.e., protection) in the most appropriate places. The number and types of zones depend upon:

a) the management objectives and priorities of the site;
b) the quality and variety of the natural and cultural resources and the degree of alteration they have suffered; and
c) the types of use that have been planned (many types of use conflict with one another an d thus must be separated geographically). Each zone is managed to maintain or achieve a particular natural setting within which Eco-tourism and other activities take place, and thus, each zone has its own set of rules and regulations for activities carried out within its boundaries.

Typically, a site or a protected area within it, has one or two zones dedicated primarily for public use (such as Eco-tourism) and two or three other zones where public use is of secondary consideration.

Visitor Site Planning and Design

At most Eco-tourism sites, visitor use is concentrated in only a few locations, or "visitor sites," both to facilitate its management and to limit its impact upon the natural environment. Because of the concentration of people and infrastructure, it is important that these visitor sites be well planned.

The main goals in good visitor site planning are:

- efficient use of the space by locating infrastructure in places where it will be most easily, safely and effectively used by the visitors, employees (e.g., guides, cooks) and site managers;

- minimal impact of visitor use and infrastructure development upon the surrounding environment; and
- planning infrastructure in accordance with the determined capacity of the natural area to receive a defined number of visitors (e.g., building a fixed number of cabins for the maximum allowable number of guests).

Site planning requires the preparation of an actual plan and topographic map on which all existing and planned Eco-tourism infrastructure is placed, be it an ecolodge, a trail, a campsite or a latrine. All infrastructure should be located to establish the geographical relationship with the significant natural and cultural features before any construction begins. Site planning also means that "best practices" for Eco-tourism activities and infrastructure must be followed.

A good site plan requires the professional services of a topographer and a landscape architect that are experienced in Eco-tourism development, or similarly experienced specialists.

Sustainable Infrastructure Design

Eco-tourism implementation requires infrastructure different from that of a conventional tourism setting, particularly if visitor lodging or food service is involved. In natural areas, Eco-tourism infrastructure must blend in with the surroundings, use predominantly renewable energy sources and manage sewage and food waste without damaging the surrounding environment. In the last 20 years or so, significant advances have been made that allow infrastructure planners and designers to minimize these impacts.

Several organizations have developed effective "best practice" guidelines for Eco-tourism architectural design and development.

Revenue-Generating Mechanisms

As we all know, money makes the world go 'round. The major goals of Eco-tourism are to generate income for conservation and to benefit local communities and other stakeholders that are also participating in the Eco-tourism program in or near a protected area. The degree to which a visitor site produces income depends in large part upon its importance as a tourism destination and, secondarily, upon its management and marketing capabilities.

In order to generate revenue, the following questions must be answered:

- Which mechanisms are needed to generate revenues?
- How should revenues be managed?
- How should income be spent?

It is important to recognize that income generation should never become an end in itself. The ultimate goal is site conservation. If adding another Eco-tourism activity to increase funding for a site is going to interfere with effective long-term site conservation, then it should probably not be carried out.

There are many ways to generate income in an Eco-tourism site, some of which may not apply to all situations.

Visitor Impact Monitoring and Management

Every time a visitor sets foot in an Eco-tourism site, he/she causes a negative impact. This is an unavoidable fact. The job of Eco-tourism managers is to minimize those impacts and ensure that, via Eco-tourism management strategies, the positive impacts outweigh the negative ones. Monitoring and managing visitor impacts are fundamental Eco-tourism management strategies; unfortunately, they are also ones most frequently left unattended. If the effects of Eco-tourism activities on the site's natural environment and on the surrounding communities are unclear or unknown, then there can be no certainty of success.

Careful monitoring of impacts, both positive and negative, needs to be a primary activity of a site's overall management plan. This costs money and requires trained personnel and the assistance of interested stakeholders.

Naturalist Guides – The Heart of Eco-tourism

Most Eco-tourism takes place in remote natural areas where it is typically not feasible for visitors to fully experience the attractions without the accompaniment of trained, knowledgeable guides. Even in more easily accessible areas, the success of Eco-tourism depends in large part on the abilities of naturalist guides to interpret the environment in ways that inspire and educate visitors. Guides can also help to monitor the impact of tourists when accompanying them.

It is crucial for protected area managers to establish a guide licensing system because naturalist guides can:

- significantly enrich the visitor experience through education and consequently
  a) create new supporters of the site's conservation goals and
  b) generate additional demand for tourism in the area;
- ensure that the negative impacts of visitation are minimized and that positive impacts are maximized;
- generate income for themselves and for others in local communities;
- strengthen links between conservation and community development goals;
- increase the safety of visitors; and
- be additional eyes and ears for protected area administrations and proxies for protected area management.

Because the role of naturalist guides is so very important to an Eco-tourism program, a site's administrators need to effectively manage guides' involvement with the site to ensure that their activities conform to Eco-tourism standards. There are two basic mechanisms to accomplish this:

i) provide mandatory training of all naturalist guides who work within a site; and

ii) license all naturalist guides who work in the site, thus maintaining control over their activity.

Through implementation of each of these Eco-tourism management strategies, a protected area will be well positioned to harness the potential of Eco-tourism as a force for conservation and sustainable community development.

Eco-tourism in Mountain Areas

Mountains are one of the world's most important tourist destinations. Their soaring peaks and beautiful landscapes are becoming increasingly attractive as a place of escape in a stressful, urbanized world. But tourism presents both opportunities and dangers for mountain regions. Tourism revenues have become a primary source of income for many mountain communities. Yet, the influx of visitors into mountain regions poses a threat to these unique and often pristine environments. Mountain people are the stewards of mountain ecosystems, so any decision to develop tourism must be made with their involvement and agreement. Most of all, tourism must be sustainable, planned to ensure that the beauty of mountains can be enjoyed by present and future generations.

The Call of the Wild

More than 50 million people visit mountains each year. They are drawn to these areas by the physical beauty of alpine environments, the many forms of recreation available in mountainous terrain and the opportunities for experiencing cultural heritage in the communities found there. The clean, cool air and awe-inspiring scenery of mountain areas, combined with the unique customs, arts, crafts and culinary traditions of the communities that live there, make trips to the mountains attractive holiday options.

Sport-based tourism in particular has boomed in mountain regions over the past 30 years. It has expanded from the traditional areas of North America and the European Alps to largely untouched mountain regions, including parts of Central Asia, the Himalaya, Karakorum, Caucasus, Andes and even Antarctica.

Typical mountain activities include hiking, skiing, snowboarding, climbing and birdwatching. However, extreme sports, such as bungee jumping, hydrospeeding, rafting, paragliding and canyoning are becoming increasingly popular, especially with affluent urban thrill-seekers. Another growth area for alpine tourism focuses on mountains as a source of well-being and health. An ever-increasing number of mountain tours offer opportunities for contemplation and meditation.

The tourism boom has undoubtedly brought benefits to many of the world's mountain regions. Thanks to tourism revenues, mountain people, many of whom are economically disadvantaged, can aspire to greatly improved living standards. Mountain tourism has given young men and women the option of building a future in their home community, instead of becoming part of the rural exodus to cities. The influx of visitors has also created a market for products made by local crafts workers, as well as for produce from the land.

Yet although tourism – and mountain tourism in particular – is one of the fastest growing economic sectors in the world, it is also one of the least regulated. Short-term profits need to be balanced against long-term losses if the industry is to become a lasting source of benefit for mountain people.

A Double-edged Sword

Experience has already shown that mountain tourism can have a range of damaging effects. It can degrade and stress fragile mountain ecosystems, destroying the qualities that make these environments so alluring. Mountains are among the world's most important repositories of biodiversity, yet construction, pollution and noise all threaten this precious asset. In many of the developing world's most beautiful mountain regions, litter and waste have emerged as key problems, as well as trees being felled to supply timber and fuelwood. The mysticism of sacred mountain sites is often diminished by the numbers of people who come from all over the world to make pilgrimages. Tourism means more transportation networks and links, which can blight the mountain environment, disrupt traditional ways of life and threaten the existence of local languages. If mountains become the world's playgrounds, there is a risk that mountain people will lose their own cultural identity.

Counting the Cost of Fun in the Snow

Winter sports are booming, with resorts now operating all over the world. The snow sport business has spawned a large and complex commercial network that includes hotels, shops, restaurants, cable cars and ski schools. For many isolated mountain communities, it has meant a new lease on life. But in some cases, it has also come at a high price. Building ski runs often involves destroying swathes of forest, planting pylons for chairlifts and cable cars and building roads and tunnels. In the Alps, emissions from the millions of vehicles that bring visitors to the slopes threaten the health of trees and worsen the effects of global warming. Paths and ski runs harm sensitive mountain ecosystems and disturb plant and animal life. And constructions that look acceptable under a mantle of snow can become a scar on the landscape once the winter fun is over.

How not to Kill the Golden Goose

Tourism can provide benefits for mountain people and visitors alike if sensitively planned and managed. Often, the development of tourism in mountain areas is concentrated in the hands of outside interests, with little of the profits going to local communities. This is especially true of developing countries and emerging economies, where venture capital is in short supply.

Mountain tourism needs to be developed according to specific local conditions and cultures, an approach that will help communities gain a niche in an increasingly competitive market. Policy-makers could favour activities that build on local knowledge and traditions to ensure that tourists respect the natural and cultural diversity of the places they visit and encourage mountain people to view their home as a source of pride.

Because it is notoriously volatile, and often seasonal, the tourism industry needs to be developed as part of an overall economic development strategy, with diversification to ensure local economies do not become reliant solely on tourism revenue. Governments can help mountain communities by investing profits in programmes to ensure sustainable livelihoods for local people. Non-governnmental organizations and the private sector can also help get the tourism equation right by offering education and training in responsible tourism practices.

Eco-tourism in Mountains

One promising answer to the challenge of developing mountains wisely for recreation is Eco-tourism. As well as being the International Year of Mountains, 2002 was also the International Year of Eco-tourism, and there is a strong and important link between the two. Eco-tourism can help reduce poverty and hunger, a key issue in mountain areas where a high proportion of the world's poor and food-insecure live. It also has considerable potential for strengthening communities and for protecting mountain ecosystems.

Defined by the International Eco-tourism Society as "responsible travel to natural areas which conserves the environment and improves the welfare of local people," Eco-tourism currently accounts for between 2 and 4 percent of global tourism. This form of holidaymaking makes a point of putting something back into the area and culture being visited, in terms of revenue and financial support for conservation projects, but often also in-kind. Some tourism operators plant trees to combat desertification, collect garbage from trekking regions and ensure tourists use biodegradable wrapping on food and drink. During many eco-holidays, tourists help out with projects that protect endangered species and habitats. Handled properly, Eco-tourism can be a valuable tool in advancing tourism, especially for poor mountain communities in the developing world, without destroying natural resources and the environment.

Cultural and Eco-tourism in the Mountainous Regions of Central Asia and in the Himalayas

Tourism is coming to the previously isolated mountainous regions of Central and South Asia. The challenge is to ensure that it is well-managed and that its benefits are shared by all.

The spectacular mountainous regions of Central Asia, the Hindu and the Himalayas, closed for many years to visitors from abroad, now attract growing numbers of foreign tourists attracted by the unique cultures and natural beauty of these hitherto isolated areas.

However, while growing tourist numbers are bringing economic opportunities and employment to local populations, helping to promote these little-known regions of the world, they have also brought challenges with them: How to ensure that local communities fully benefit from the development of tourism and that growth in tourism helps to preserve and sustain the natural and cultural riches of these regions, rather than putting them in danger?

This project, the Development of Cultural and Eco-tourism in the Mountainous Regions of Central Asia and the Himalayas, generously sponsored by the Norwegian Government as well as by UNESCO Regular Programme funds, aims to establish links and promote cooperation between local communities, national and international NGOs, and tour agencies in order to involve local populations fully in the employment opportunities and income-generating activities that tourism can bring.

An interdisciplinary project, drawing on the expertise of international NGOs and tourism professionals in the seven participating countries, the project is making a practical and positive contribution to alleviating poverty by helping local communities to draw the maximum benefit from their region's tourism potential, while protecting the environmental and cultural heritage of the region concerned.

Mountain areas concerned by the project include Ladakh in India, Masouleh in Iran, the Northern Tien Shen Mountains in Kazakhstan, the mountainous region around Lake Issy Kul in

Kyrgyzstan, a Biosphere Reserve of the UNESCO Man and the Biosphere Programme (MAB), Humla in Nepal, Chitral and the Kalash Valleys in Pakistan and the Pamir Mountains in Tajikistan. Local project partners include the Mountain Institute and Snow Leopard Conservancy in Ladakh (India), the Aga Khan Rural Support Programme in Chitral (Pakistan) and the Kazakh Mountaineering Foundation and the Novinomad Eco-tourism Development Company in Kazakhstan and Kyrgyzstan, respectively.

In Tajikistan, UNESCO is working with ACTED, L'Agence d'aide a la cooperation technique et au development, in the Pamir Mountains, and in Nepal with the Nepal Trust in Humla, one of the poorest and most isolated regions of the country. Project activities include training local tour guides, producing high-quality craft items and promoting home-stays and bed-and-breakfast type accommodation, while fully involving local communities in these income-generating activities. Recommendations on best practices, Web resources and a database on community profiles, including maps, research data and regional attractions and resources, are all included in the project.

The aim is to promote these unspoilt regions of the world for foreign tourists and researchers, while helping local communities to benefit fully from the economic opportunities that their environments can bring.

Hill & Mountain Cosystems

Importance of Hill &Mountain Areas

* Home to most indigenous populations
* Provider of essential resources
* Major source of water supply
* Centres of culture and indigenous knowledge systems
* Repositories of unique forms of biodiversity & ecosystems.

Hill & Mountain Tourism

* Nature and adventure tourism (trekking, rock climbing, mountaineering, rafting)
* Winter sports (alpine skiing, cross-country skiing)
* Summer holidays in warmer countries (accommodations in holiday cottages, less activity-oriented)

* Pilgrimages (traditional tourism, particularly in the Himalayan).

Impacts of Tourism on Hills & Mountains

* Basic infrastructure – electricity, water, waste disposal, transport and transportation related, development and securing of infrastructure, utilities
* ccommodation infrastructure for lodges/resorts/ restaurants/cafes/bars
* Additional services – e.g., shops and other commercial establishments
* Recreational activities – main and complementary activities
* Recreation infrastructure – paths/trails, sports facilities, golf courses, cable cars etc.
* Directly and indirectly induced developments – regional migration, urbanisation, changing values etc.

Environmental Impacts

* Establishment of protected or conserved areas to meet tourist demand
* Defining new uses of marginal or unproductive lands
* Programmes to protect the attractiveness of locations
* Assist refurbishment and reuse of heritage buildings & abandoned properties
* Pollution
* Visual impact
* Degradation / alteration of ecosystems
* Construction activities & infrastructure development
* Depletion of and Access to Natural Resources –land, water.

Eco-tourism ...Sustainable Enough?

Tourism & Environmental Issues

* Exploitative trends of mainstream tourism
* Contribution as a million dollar industry
* Towards conservation of the destination.

Reasons for Growth

* Environmental awareness
* Aroused interest among middle class
* Promotion of nature through print and electronic media.

Tourism & Environment

The stress is on niche tourism products;

- Wildlife Tourism
- Nature-based Tourism
- Eco-tourism
- Sustainable Tourism.

Tracing History of Eco-tourism

- 1st coined by tour operator in Costa Rica – 70s
- Defined by IUCN –1996
- Became popular with industry
- Lucrative option
- Cover up for bad practices
- Boost after IYE 2002.

Fall Out

- Tourism in ecologically sensitive regions is being qualified as Eco-tourism
- Opening up more and newer areas
- New forms added – rural, adventure etc.
- Entry of new players – Forest Dept.
- Tourism industry claims on a few eco-friendly practices.

Critical Areas Being Targeted

Andaman Islands, North East, Numerous PA's, Other ecologically rich & sensitive areas.

Components

- Contribute to conservation of biodiversity
- Benefit indigenous / local communities
- Minimum consumption of resources
- Address site specific issues
- Stress upon local participation, ownership and business opportunities
- Cater to small groups by small-scale businesses
- Include an interpretation / awareness experience
- Involve responsible behaviour on the part of tourists and tourism industry.

Case Study: Andamans

- Low volume high end tourism
- High-end tourism infrastructure
- Private sector investment
- Reduction of no development zone from 200m / 500m to 50m from HTL
- 40 islands to be opened by Forest
- Dept. for Eco-tourism
- 7 studies & master plans-MoT-WTOUNDP master plan (1996-97) selected by tourism vision.

MoT-WTO-UNDP Master Plan (96-97)

- Linking with other SE Asian destinations ! resulted in twinning Port Blair & Phuket
- Targets to be achieved: growth, marketing & high quality international tourism
- Relaxation of development norms & regulations (draconian CRZ!)
- No environmental sustainability, livelihood generation for local community.

Impacts

Impacts of Eco-tourism on Indian Coast;

- Habitat fragmentation from infrastructure
- Denial of access to coastal communities
- Competition over natural resources
- Ecosystem degradation:
- Leveling of sand dunes
- Destruction of mangroves
- Disturbance to wildlife – e.g. turtle nesting sites
- Destruction of coral reefs.

Community Based Tourism Projects

- Management Plan for Community based conservation and Eco-tourism in the Nanda Devi Biosphere Reserve
- Initiation and complete management of tourism activity in the area by the Village Council
- Abiding with regional, national and international guidelines on sustainable tourism

- Declaration on Nanda Devi Biodiversity Conversation and Eco-tourism, 2001 onwards.

Khonoma, Nagaland

- Tourism is seen as a vehicle for bringing development
- Needs of community are prioritized over tourism needs
- Impacts of tourism are identified beforehand and adequate systems and mechanisms put in place to minimize impacts
- Eco-tourism, as a set of values, would mean-
    * no disturbance to natural areas or areas under traditional land use like agriculture;
    * low infrastructure that blends with the local setting & architecture;
    * an enriching and learning experience for tourists, which becomes the unique selling proposition and hence brings benefits to the local community.

Planned and well managed tourism with regular monitoring strengthened by research;

- Need for alternative technologies
- Training of local people for implementation
- Value addition to intrinsic properties of the village
- Planning for better utilisation of energy within the village
- Bringing in community managed Eco-tourism to Khonoma
- The Khonoma Village Council to drive the process.

3

Eco-tourism to Contribute to Wildlife Conservation

Wildlife Tourism

Definition

Wildlife tourism can be broadly defined as trips to destinations with the main purpose of visit being to observe the local fauna.

This therefore implies that wildlife tourism includes other niche markets such as bird watching and the exploration of marine life (such as whale watching).

As bird watching has grown to be a significant niche market in its own right, the definition of wildlife tourism has been restricted to trips to destinations with the main purpose of visit being to observe local fauna, excluding birdlife.

Estimate of Global Market Size

The global market size of wildlife tourism is estimated as being 12 million trips each year. Africa accounts for around one half of all these trips, with South Africa, Kenya, Tanzania and Botswana being the top destinations.

Some destinations rely heavily on wildlife tourism, but could survive without it (wildlife tourism contributes roughly $500 million to the Kenyan economy, or 14% of GDP). On the other hand, places such as the Galapagos islands rely almost exclusively on wildlife tourists (wildlife tourism contributes £60 million to the local economy).

Other destinations are enjoying increased influxes of visitors due to strong interest in certain mammals. For example there has been considerable growth in whale watching at Kaikoura in New Zealand and Puerto Piraminde in Argentinean Patagonia.

Potential for Growth

Interest in wildlife is growing considerably, in particular as its exposure in the international media increases. As with bird watching, the National Geographic channel and other renowned television channels have generated increased interest amongst consumers.

There is still considerable potential for growth within this market, and it is expected to expand by between 8% and 10% per annum over the next decade. The age group that will most influence this growth will be the increasingly wealthy, healthy, and active 55+ age group.

Brief Profile of Consumers

Wildlife tourists are some of the most diverse of any niche market. They range from the experienced specialists who like to seek "virgin" places that remain relatively undiscovered, to the inexperienced tourist travelling on a package to one of Africa's well-known game reserves.

Across this spectrum, consumers vary considerably in age, gender, and socioeconomic grouping. Package tourists vary from budget travellers through to those staying in small exclusive lodges or tented camps.

However, specialists tend to be independent travellers, who are likely to stay in basic accommodation, and are generally very flexible with their travel arrangements.

Whilst the luxury-end of the package market tends to be the most demanding in terms of infrastructure and services, they also generate the greatest income. These consumers tend to be in the third-age group (50-65 years), often including the early retired.

Main Source Markets

The main source markets for wildlife tourism are:

- United States
- Europe (UK, Germany and Netherlands being the top 3 markets)
- Canada
- Australia.

Main Competing Destinations

Africa is the market leader and accounts for around one half of all wildlife tourism trips worldwide. The traditional wildlife destinations of South Africa, Kenya, Botswana and Tanzania receive the greatest volume of visitors. However, there are a number of emerging wildlife destinations which demonstrate the desire of consumers to seek out new destinations, in particular these are:

- Antarctica (whales, penguins and seals)
- Bolivia (New World's largest concentration of large animals such as the Giant River Otter and Jaguar)
- Finland (particularly Hiidenportti National Park for bears, wolves and lynx).

It's 2010, the Year of the Tiger, BUT, time is running out to conserve the wild tigers of Asia. 100 years ago, 100,00 tigers lived in habitats across Asia. Now, only about 3,000 of these magnificent animals survive. They have lost 40% of their remaining habitat in the past 10 years alone. Ecosystems, endangered species, biodiversity and loss of habitats are inextricably linked with the livelihoods of the poor. 'There will be no room left for tigers and other wildlife in Asia without a more responsible and sustainable program for economic growth and infrastructure development' The tiger may be only one species, but the tiger's plight highlights the biodiversity crisis in Asia'. said Robert

Zoellick, President, The World Bank Group

Keith and Steve introduced the delegates to contemporary case studies on Eco-tourism and wildlife conservation they are respectfully engaged in Namibia and Indonesia. While Eco-tourism is not a panacea for tiger conservation, it was generally agreed by delegates that properly planned and well managed, it should be one of the more beneficial tools to be applied.

Keith's presentation was a case study of efforts undertaken in Namibia to provide incentives for local communities to live with wildlife, including predators.

The relevance of a Namibian case study is that the types of incentives in use may prove applicable for Tiger Range States.

The three core messages of this presentation include:

- Devolution of Rights over Wildlife and Tourism to Communities

- The parallel successes of Tourism Joint-Ventures (JV's) and Wildlife Recovery
- Impact at the Destination-Level.

'The devolution of rights over wildlife and tourism to local communities has created the "greatest African wildlife recovery story ever told" – and predators are an integral part of the story.' Keith Sproule

Steve Noakes cited the experiences of Ecolodges Indonesia and the challenges facing the wild tiger habitat within Way Kambas National Park which have been identified by the local National parks staff, including:

- Protection flora-fauna & ecosystem of the Park-illegal poaching, illegal logging,
- Forest fire, encroachment, livestock invasion, etc.
- Law enforcement-effectiveness of coordination with local Government law agencies
- Human – elephant conflict mitigation: improvement strategy and facilities
- Area rehabilitation and reforestation of ex-forest fire, ex-settlement (deadly wells), ex-encroachment, etc.
- Building biodiversity research and database-information system, to develop more effective conservation strategy
- Effectiveness of management organization & human resources through education & training
- Community development and participation/involvement through improve education & awareness programs.

The 'bottom-line' of his presentation was 'Tourism not a panacea for wildlife conservation, poverty reduction & related MDG targets. But it can play an important part. It needs workable partnerships – government, private sector, community, conservation and development sectors.

Community Based Eco-tourism

Place – Power – Prognosis: Community-based Conservation, Partnerships and Eco-tourism Enterprise in Namibia

Private Eco-tourism enterprises, partnered with communal conservancies, are purported to be central to the success of Namibia's conservancies in achieving biodiversity conservation and poverty alleviation (World Resources Institute et al. 2005; NACSO 2006). Eco-tourism, premised on stunning wildlife and scenery, has attracted an international, 'up market' clientele to Namibia and generated revenues, employment and additional benefits for participating conservancy communities.

Community-based conservation is based on the idea that if conservation and development can be simultaneously achieved, the interests of both are served (Berkes 2004). Community conservation stresses the role of local residents in decision-making for natural resources (Adams and Hulme 2001). Communitybased conservation has been practiced in many forms, but in the broadest sense includes conservation by, for, and with the local community. The co-existence of people and nature, as distinct from protectionism and the segregation of people and nature, is its central characteristic (Western and Wright 1994). Recent commons scholarship stresses that local levels of collective action are necessarily linked to higher levels of social and political organization in a globalized world. Indeed, Namibia's conservancies have many and increasing cross-scale and cross-level linkages, including important linkages with international tourism enterprises.

Centrally and internationally conceived approaches in community-based conservation emerged in the 1980s in Southern Africa to buttress national parks as wildlife reserves, and better conserve wildlife as an economic development alternative to agriculture in semi-arid regions (Adams and Hulme 2001). These have been termed community-based natural resource management or CBNRM (Fabricius et al. 2004). CBNRM has featured the devolution of certain bundles of wildlife use rights to local communities, premised on making wildlife pay, with benefits exceeding the costs of living with wildlife such as crop and property damage. The central theory is that benefits from wildlife for local and indigenous peoples will promote conservation.

The revenue and resource sharing devolution to communities under CBNRM was led by Zimbabwe and Namibia in Southern Africa and was a direct outgrowth of wildlife management on the private land estates in both countries preceding independence. In the 1970s, Zimbabwean legislation was passed that conferred strong proprietor rights over wildlife to private, white landowners. This same type of legislation was passed in Namibia in the 1970s under the South African administration, prior to independence. There was strong political demand after independence in both Zimbabwe and Namibia to transfer the economic success of wildlife management on private lands to communal lands and relieve a racist divide in rights to use wildlife, where indigenous use of wildlife had been criminalized under colonial rule.

Design principles for long-enduring common property institutions at local levels have been recognized at varying levels of detail (Ostrom 1990; Agrawal 2002). These are norms and rules determining who is excluded from a particular resource use or area, and how participants deal with subtractability in ways that sustain collective agreement and mutually shared benefits. Namibia's wildlife is a common property resource for which excludability, or the control of access is difficult, given the mobile nature of wildlife, and where collective use involves subtractability, where each user is capable of subtracting from the welfare of others.

Under Namibia's CBNRM program, communal area residents form a common property institution called a conservancy and enjoy rights in wildlife and related tourism development devolved under national legislation. Conservancies are approved by and registered with the Ministry of Environment and Tourism. Registration requires a defined conservancy boundary, voluntary registered membership, a representative conservancy management committee, a constitution and a commitment to producing a benefits distribution plan.

Namibia's CBNRM program drew lessons from regional experience (Jones 2006 interview; Owen-Smith 2006 interview) especially Zimbabwe's Communal Areas Program for Indigenous Resources, Campfire.

There was a deliberate effort to avoid pre-determined administrative boundaries such as Campfire's use of rural district ward boundaries and ADMADE's use of nationally defined Game Management Area boundaries. Rather, Namibia's conservancies self-organized and negotiated their own boundaries, to help reinforce devolution of wildlife use rights and benefits to community level. Formal registration of conservancy members, and legal gazetting reinforced external recognition (Ostrom 1990), again a significant departure from both CAMPFIRE and ADMADE. As well, the wildlife revenues and other benefits developed under conservancies were intended to accrue solely to the conservancies and were not to be shared with central or regional government, as they were under CAMPFIRE and ADMADE.

Institutional Linkages and Partnerships – An Evolution

The roots of Namibia's CBNRM program date back to 1982. The Namibian Wildlife Trust was concerned about severely depleted wildlife in northern Namibia. This conservation NGO deployed a conservationist to collaborate with four local headmen, who shared concern about the dramatic loss of wildlife in the region. The headmen appointed community game guards who were knowledgeable hunters and trackers from local communities. The aim was to stop poaching (Jacobsohn 2006 interview). The game guards monitored wildlife, reporting wildlife incidents and suspicious activities to the headmen, who in turn informed the government wildlife enforcement agency. The community game guards, in contrast to other CBNRM approaches emerging in Southern Africa were not enforcement personnel employed in salaried positions by the state.

By the late 1980s, wildlife populations had noticeably recovered and the community game guard program was considered a major contributing factor. This coalition of local conservation effort, featuring leadership and collaboration in a basic NGO and community partnership, spurred wider application. Increased demand for the program led to formation of a new Namibian NGO, Integrated Rural Development and Nature Conservation (IRDNC), to facilitate and support the development of CBNRM in the wider Kunene and Caprivi regions. IRDNC remains the leading NGO dedicated to CBNRM in Namibia.

The next stage in the evolution of Namibian CBNRM followed independence in 1990. The new black majority government extended rights in wildlife to communal area residents that previously had been granted only to white farmers on private lands by the colonial South African administration. IRDNC's leadership, based upon their knowledge and experience gained in the community game guard program, were engaged by the government to help design and conduct community surveys. This led to policy and legislation for a national CBNRM program under the *Nature Conservation Amendment Act, 1996*.

USAID provided donor assistance through the World Wildlife Fund (WWF US). USAID and WWF (US) have remained the main donors to CBNRM, although other international donors have come in. During this same period the Namibian Association of CBNRM Support Organizations (NACSO) was formed as a national umbrella organization for other NGOs supporting institutional development, natural resources management, business enterprises and livelihoods at the local conservancy level (Louis 2006 interview). Thus, we see a further evolution of cross-scale linkages and partnership formation that started locally in a remote part of northern Namibia, moved to national level, and in turn attracted and mediated international donor support. The national conservation NGOs, led by the IRDNC, filled various CBNRM facilitation and support roles, including technical support for annual game counts, wildlife monitoring and reporting, capacity-building in project planning and budgeting, and funding for salaries, vehicles, field offices and equipment at the local conservancy level. In a number of instances, NGOs have served as boundary or bridging organizations (Cash and Moser 2000; Cash et al. 2006; Berkes in press) linking international donor support to the local conservancy level.

The support and facilitation of local conservancies by national NGOs has centred on locally elected conservancy management committees and the community game guards, who remain the central feature of conservancy conservation efforts. Community game guards are now full-time staff monitoring wildlife on behalf of the conservancy management committees, with technical support from NGOs (Stuart-Hill et al. 2005). The accumulated evidence indicates that wildlife conservation has been achieved under CBNRM. Subject to ranges of natural variability, especially due to drought, overall wildlife numbers have recovered and increased since the 1980s. The national NGOs are headquartered in Windhoek and some have regional field stations or a regional mandate. NGO operations feature professional and technical staff cadres such as biologists, GIS technicians, social scientists and project managers, equipped with all-wheel drive vehicles, modern offices and sophisticated tools, including the latest in computing and remote sensing. Funding for this CBNRM network and establishment comes from the international donor community through multi-lateral and/or bilateral programmes.

Communal conservancy formation has increased exponentially over a relatively short period. There were only four conservancies in the late 1990s and over 50 by 2007 (Weaver 2007 interview). The first conservancies now regularly participate in regional forums to share experiences and develop planning and management skills with the support of NGOs. Thus, we see an emergence of both multiple crossscale and cross-level interactions (Cash et al. 2006). Social learning, knowledge sharing and trust have been emergent properties between certain conservancy and NGO partners, reflecting the greater duration of their interactions and experiences working together (Armitage et al. 2009; Berkes in press).

It is noteworthy that the evolution of CBNRM in Namibia has taken almost three decades. A growing network of national and regionally-based NGOs facilitating and supporting CBNRM has helped mediate and channel international donor support and purportedly offset competition among NGOs for donor funds. This network has also appropriated significant CBNRM funding from international donors to sustain itself. Partnerships between conservancies and Eco-tourism enterprises have played an increasing role in the last decade and I now focus attention on this particular aspect

Torra Conservancy and Eco-tourism Enterprise Partnership

The Torra Conservancy has received international recognition as a successful case of community-based conservation. Torra is premised on conserving and commercially exploiting the wildlife endemic to the spectacular and remote arid wild lands of the Kunene region. Wildlife move seasonally through the wider region that Torra shares with other conservancies, Skelton Coast Park and Etosha National Park. The Torra Conservancy was one of the first communal conservancies gazetted in June 1998, with 450 registered members drawn from Damara and Riemvasmaker, Herero and Owambo pastoral villages in the conservancy area (NACSO 2006). It achieved operational self-sufficiency in 2002 following support from international donors and national NGOs. Revenues from wildlife conservation cover the annual operating costs of the conservancy: staff salaries and other annual program operational expenses. The main revenue-generating enterprise is Damaraland Camp, an up-market, exclusive Eco-tourism resort (daily rates range from US$560–$670/person) owned and operated by Wilderness Safaris, a South African tour company.

Eco-tourism is environmentally responsible travel to relatively undisturbed areas in order to enjoy and appreciate natural and cultural features, while promoting conservation, low negative visitor impact, and beneficial socioeconomic involvement by local populations (Ceballos-Lascurain 1996). Damaraland Camp has fulfilled this concept, receiving international awards in recognition. The camp occupies an exclusive, wilderness site with dramatic scenery. It is accessible only by light aircraft or all-wheel drive vehicle. The main lodge and tented accommodations are luxuriously appointed, using natural materials that blend unobtrusively into the setting. Solar power and other 'green' practices for wastewater and solid waste management are featured. The camp offers local natural and cultural history tours delivered by local village members hired and trained from the conservancy membership.

Wilderness Safaris pays an annual land rent and monthly bed levies to Torra and employs over 20 conservancy members full-time. Training and employment for conservancy members has also been achieved in some 40 additional jobs in the wider Wilderness Safari lodge network. Damaraland Camp's annual income contribution to the conservancy has grown steadily from ~N$50,000 in 1997 to over N$300,000 in 2005 (Wilderness Safaris 2005). The conservancy has earned well in excess of N$2,000,000 from the camp since its inception ($1 US equalled about $7.5 N in this period). Damaraland Camp has been the single largest contributor to conservancy revenues and the single largest employer (Wilderness Safaris 2005). Indeed, up-scale Eco-tourism lodges generated over N$7.6 million for all of Namibia's conservancies in 2005, amounting to nearly 56% of overall conservancy income (NACSO 2006).

A key feature of the partnership between Wilderness Safaris and Torra Conservancy is the land tenure arrangement for the Damaraland Camp. Wilderness Safaris was first introduced to the community by IRDNC. IRDNC acted as a broker and facilitated 'role playing' with a local community committee to prepare them for negotiations with Wilderness Safaris.

Wilderness Safaris negotiated a lease for the Damaraland Camp (Salole 2003) on communal lands that form part of the Torra Conservancy.

Wilderness Safaris assumed 100% financing and risk for Damaraland Camp under an initial 10 year joint venture agreement with the Torra Conservancy which has been extended. An end goal was 100% ownership of Damaraland Camp by the conservancy.

This has not progressed and there is little prospect for this in the foreseeable future. Reportedly, the significant capital re-investments required to maintain an exclusive and remote operation like the Damaraland Camp have exceeded the conservancy's fiscal capacity to attain outright ownership or even a strong equity position in the development.

The Torra Conservancy case illustrates a substantive partnership between the local community level and an international tourism enterprise. The conservancy has made an exclusive and attractive site available for the Eco-tourism development. Local conservancy members have been trained and hired to run the operation, bringing their local knowledge and culture into the Eco-tourism product and activities. The international partner has invested its capital to develop the property and applied its expertise, global reach and resources to promote and attract international tourist patronage, generating significant local wages and revenues for those privileged with jobs and the conservancy management committee. These features draw on the respective strengths of the partners (Berkes 2007). However, partnership arrangements have also perversely served to limit empowerment and benefits at the local community level. Further discussion follows to elaborate on these observations.

Benefits of Sustainable Eco-tourism

Increasing awareness of the problems of mass tourism is leading many holidaymakers to seek more responsible and sustainable forms of tourism.

One of the most common forms of sustainable tourism is Eco-tourism, the term most commonly used to describe any form of holiday or recreation in natural surroundings. The Eco-tourism Society also adds the concept of social responsibility in its definition of Eco-tourism as:

> *"Purposeful travel to natural areas to understand the culture and natural history of the environment, taking care not to alter the integrity of the ecosystem, while producing economic opportunities that make the conservation of natural resources beneficial to local people."*

Thus, Eco-tourism is a form of tourism to relatively undisturbed natural areas for the main purposes of admiring them and learning more about their habitats. Eco-tourism also seeks to reduce its impacts on the area visited. It also contributes to the conservation of natural areas and the sustainable development of adjacent areas and communities, generating further awareness among resident and nearby populations and visitors.

Although a relatively new part of the tourism industry, Eco-tourism has spread rapidly throughout the world. The most popular Eco-tourism destinations are spread relatively evenly throughout the world and include sites in Central and South America, Canada and the USA, Antarctica and Australia.

Another important Eco-tourism destination is Africa. For example, Kenya employs 55,000 people in its wildlife tourism industry alone. The Kenya Wildlife Service recorded $24 million of revenues from wildlife tourism in 1990. For 1995, it was $54 million with 25% of earnings paid to communities in areas adjacent to parks and reserves.

A recent study of Amboseli National Park in Kenya determined that each lion there was worth $27,000 and each elephant herd as much as $610,000 in tourist revenue per year.

Case Studies of Rainforest Eco-tourism

One of the major attractions in Eco-tourism is the rainforest. The benefits and problems of Eco-tourism can be analysed through case studies of rainforest Eco-tourism in Rwanda and Brazil.

Do Rainforests Benefit From Eco-tourism?

Income from tourism must reach the people who will ultimately decide the forest's future if Eco-tourism is going to be influential in saving rainforests. Unfortunately, too often the money generated does not benefit these people.

All to often it goes to the North, where the tourists originated, giving little economic protection to the forests. Profits leak back to the North through tour companies, plane tickets, foreign-owned accommodation and use of non-local supplies. As a result, the World Bank estimates that only 45% of worldwide revenues from tourism remains in the host country.

The percentage is often lower in the South. A study of the Annapurna region of Nepal, a popular Eco-tourism destination, found that only 10 cents of every dollar spent stayed in the local economy-and that much of that small amount ended up in the large cities or in the hands of the wealthy elite.

Tourist dollars should help to improve management of conservation areas on which the tourism is based. However, the money from tourism often does not end up with the agencies that manage these areas. In Costa Rica, for example, the park service does not earn enough money from its entrance fees to manage and protect its numerous parks. Only 25% of its budget comes from fees. The other three quarters must come from donations.

Tourists often resent paying large sums of money on entrance fees. Although these fees are only a small portion of the money spent on a trip they can be the most important dollars spent in protecting the resource because they go directly toward protecting the site.

Can Eco-tourism Harm the Rainforest?

Despite many scientific advances, we know very little about rainforest ecology. Thus, it is difficult to know how many people can visit a rainforest in a day without disrupting the forest ecology. There is some evidence that just the presence of travellers walking on trails through the forest changes the behaviour of animals in the forest.

A major impact on the forest are the pressures caused by accommodating the physical needs and comforts of tourists; impacts of providing wood for fuel, accommodation and access routes, together with the problems caused by tourists' rubbish, put a large stress on the environment. For example, litter has been strewn along the trails of popular Himalayan tourist routes, and the alpine forest decimated by trekkers looking for fuel to heat their food and bath water.

Only a limited number of people can visit an area before that area is adversely affected. However, deciding that number is often very difficult.

Case Study: Manuel Antonio National Park, Costa Rica

In Costa Rica, Manuel Antonio National Park is a victim of its own popularity. It is a popular tourist spot for both international and Costa Rican tourists who come to see its beautiful beaches and natural scenery. It is also the home of one of the last surviving populations of spider monkeys in the country.

The popularity of the park has led developers to build many hotels in the area. This excessive building in the area combined with high visitation in the park has threatened the monkey population as well as other wildlife.

While half of the park has been closed to tourists, it is necessary to severely restrict visitors to the rest of the park, and even to enlarge it, if a viable ecosystem is to be maintained. However, there is opposition to any further restriction to local land use and access to the park by the local tourist industry.

Costa Rica is one of the few countries that has a national policy to promote Eco-tourism as a non-consumptive use of their rich rainforests. Costa Rica has the difficult task of trying to foster its tourist industry while limiting the number of visitors to sensitive environments. However, the enormous success of the industry has overwhelmed the forest and prompted a call for a comprehensive study into methods to manage and limit tourist impact on the forest.

Does Eco-tourism Affect The People of the Rainforest?

The pressures of Eco-tourism go beyond the natural world. Eco-tourism can also disrupt local people and their social structures. Indeed, it is difficult to bring the benefits of tourism to traditional people without disrupting their way of life.

Ecotourists bring their modern material comforts, such as preserved foods, cameras, razors and so on, with them. These can often be unimagined luxuries for local people who cannot pay for them without major changes in their lifestyles.

The local use of the forest for firewood, meat and agriculture can sometimes conflict with tourists' wishes to keep the land pristine. To protect the tourist industry, regulations are sometimes made that prevent locals from using these forest resources. With their livelihood eroded and often without the skills to work in the tourism industry, local people can be left with no alternative income. There have been many cases where the original inhabitants of an area are pushed out so outsiders can move in to try to profit from tourism.

Careful planning is needed to attract enough tourists to make money and still maintain the unspoiled forest and indigenous communities within them. Opening an area to tourists without such planning can quickly destroy the forests upon which the tourism is based. Alta Floresta is one example of a tourist project that has been planned with care.

Case Study: Alta Floresta, Brazil

Alta Floresta, a town in the Brazilian highlands, is the home of an innovative research centre and Eco-tourism centre. The research centre was set up to study sustainable ways of using the forest and to help people in the area benefit from the changes that come from Eco-tourism.

The project emphasises community involvement through schools, hospitals and training programs. Local people are trained in sustainable farming practices and the harvesting of non-timber forest products. Instead of being forced out of the economy, they are trained to work in the tourist centre and lodge, thus becoming an integral part of the whole project. The tourist centre also educates travellers on the biology of the rainforest and causes of its destruction.

Eco-tourism Development and Management

Tourism is the world's largest industry. It accounts for more than 10% of total employment, 11% of global GDP, and total tourist trips are predicted to increase to 1.6 billion by 2020. As such, it has a major and increasing impact on both people and nature.

Effects can be negative as well as positive. Inappropriate tourism development and practice can degrade habitats and landscapes, deplete natural resources, and generate waste and pollution. In contrast, responsible tourism can help to generate awareness of and support for conservation and local culture, and create economic opportunities for countries and communities. WWF is taking action to reduce negative impacts, and to encourage responsible tourism that enhances not only the quality of life, but also natural and cultural resources in destinations.

The Purpose of these Guidelines

These guidelines identify some general principles, and highlight some practical considerations for community-based Eco-tourism. They seek to provide a reference point for field project staff, and to encourage a consistent approach. However, prevailing conditions and levels of knowledge about Eco-tourism vary considerably between countries and projects, and this will dictate how the guidelines are interpreted and used at a local level.

The guidelines are not intended to be a detailed 'how to' manual, but rather stand as a collection of issues and topics to be considered and addressed. In some countries, such as Brazil, WWF has been involved in the development of specific policies and good practice manuals for Eco-tourism which relate to local circumstances and go into more detail.

Although the guidelines are primarily intended for use within WWF, they may also be of value to partner organisations and other agencies, and demonstrate to a wider audience, WWF's interest and approach in this field. They are based on experience obtained from WWF projects, and from published literature and case studies. A list of helpful reference sources is also included. Throughout the text, information on individual WWF Eco-tourism projects is provided in boxes. Though these are only referenced where their content is relevant to a specific point, the information contained in them complements the guidelines as a whole.

In total, twelve guidelines are presented. These have been grouped into four sections that relate to different stages of community-based Eco-tourism initiatives. These are:

A. Considering whether Eco-tourism is an appropriate option;
B. Planning Eco-tourism with communities and other stakeholders;
C. Developing viable community-based Eco-tourism projects;
D. Strengthening benefits to the community and the environment.

Although this is a broadly sequential ordering, all the issues raised by the guidelines should be considered together to obtain a comprehensive picture.

What is Community-based Eco-tourism?

Eco-tourism is a frequently debated term. Sometimes it is used simply to identify a form of tourism where the motivation of visitors, and the sales pitch to them, centres on the observation of nature. Increasingly, this general sector of the market is called 'nature tourism'. True 'Eco-tourism', however, requires a proactive approach that seeks to mitigate the negative and enhance the positive impacts of nature tourism. The International Eco-tourism Society defines Eco-tourism as responsible travel to natural areas that conserves the environment and sustains the well-being of local people.

This definition not only implies that there should be a recognition of, and positive support for, the conservation of natural resources, both by suppliers and consumers, but also that there is a necessary social dimension to Eco-tourism. The term 'community-based Eco-tourism' takes this social dimension a stage further. This is a form of Eco-tourism where the local community has substantial control over, and involvement in, its development and management, and a major proportion of the benefits remain within the community.

How the community is defined will depend on the social and institutional structures in the area concerned, but the definition implies some kind of collective responsibility and approval by representative bodies. In many places, particularly those inhabited by indigenous peoples, there are collective rights over lands and resources. Community-based Eco-tourism should therefore foster sustainable use and collective responsibility. However, it must also embrace individual initiatives within the community.

Some further general characteristics of Eco-tourism have been identified by UNEP and the World Tourism Organisation as:

- involving appreciation not only of nature, but also of indigenous cultures prevailing in natural areas, as part of the visitor experience;
- containing education and interpretation as part of the tourist offer;
- generally, but not exclusively, organised for small groups by small, specialised and locally owned businesses (while recognising that foreign operators also market and operate Eco-tourism);
- minimising negative impacts on the natural and socio-cultural environment;
- supporting the protection of natural areas by generating economic benefits for the managers of natural areas;
- providing alternative income and employment for local communities; and
- increasing local and visitor awareness of conservation.

While definitions can be useful, what is more important is the appropriateness and quality of action, not what it is called.

The processes involved in Eco-tourism include all aspects of planning, developing, marketing and managing resources and facilities for this form of tourism. Visitor provision includes access to natural areas and cultural heritage, guiding and interpretative services, accommodation, catering, sales of produce and handicrafts, and transport.

Appropriate recreational and special interest activities, such as trail walking, photography and participatory conservation programmes, may also be part of Eco-tourism. In some locations, hunting and fishing may be included as appropriate activities, provided that they are carefully researched and controlled within a management plan that supports conservation. This kind of sustainable use relies on local knowledge, provides significant local income, and encourages communities to place a high value on wildlife, resulting in net conservation benefits.

Checking the Preconditions for Eco-tourism

It is important to avoid spending time pursuing Eco-tourism and raising expectations in circumstances which are highly likely to lead to failure. An initial feasibility assessment should be made before instigating a communitybased strategy.

Some preconditions relate to the situation at a national level, others to conditions in the local area. The main aspects to check are as follows.

Reasonable conditions for undertaking tourism business are:

- an economic and political framework which does not prevent effective trading and security of investment;
- national legislation which does not obstruct tourism income being earned by and retained within local communities;
- a sufficient level of ownership rights within the local;
- high levels of safety and security for visitors (both in terms of image of the country/region and in reality);
- relatively low health risks and access to basic medical services and a clean water supply; and
- practicable means of physical access and telecommunication to the area.

Basic preconditions for community-based Eco-tourism:

- landscapes or flora/fauna which have inherent attractiveness or degree of interest to appeal either to specialists or more general visitors;
- ecosystems that are at least able to absorb a managed level of visitation without damage;

- a local community that is aware of the potential opportunities, risks and changes involved, and is interested in receiving visitors;
- existing or potential structures for effective community decision-making;
- no obvious threats to indigenous culture and traditions; and
- an initial market assessment suggesting a potential demand and an effective means of accessing it, and that the area is not over supplied with Eco-tourism offers.

Some preconditions may be more relevant than others, depending on the local circumstances, and these may change over time. For example, in Namibia cross-border conflict in Caprivi has seriously affected market demand in that region but action is being taken to enable promising Eco-tourism initiatives there to resume when the situation stabilises.

If the preconditions are met, this does not necessarily mean that Eco-tourism will be successful, only that it is worth proceeding to the next stage of consultation and assessment.

Checking these preconditions will require informed judgement. The concept of preconditions and fast pre-feasibility checks is increasingly applied among donor agencies in the tourism field. A useful guide to this process, giving far more detail than can be attempted here, has been produced by GTZ (1999).

Adopting an Integrated Approach

The small scale of most community-based Eco-tourism initiatives means that their impact, both on nature conservation and on income and employment for the community as a whole, is limited. They can be more influential and successful if they are integrated within other sustainable development initiatives at a regional and local level.

Eco-tourism can be integrated with other sectors of the rural economy, creating mutually supportive linkages and reducing financial leakage away from the area. It can also be coordinated with agriculture, in terms of the use of time and resources and in providing markets for local produce.

In principle, multiple sector activity within local communities should be encouraged. Eco-tourism markets are small, seasonal and sensitive to external influences such as political changes or economic instability in the host or generating country. On the other hand, Eco-tourism can shield against threats to other sectors.

As well as horizontal integration within the community, the success of local Eco-tourism initiatives may depend on vertical integration with national level initiatives to support and promote responsible tourism. In addition to making linkages with what may already exist, efforts should be made to influence national policies in favour of Eco-tourism, including coordination between tourism and environmental ministries and policies. National level support is needed in terms of linking conservation and tourism activities and responsibilities, appropriate legislation and assistance towards small enterprises and community initiatives, and national and international promotion. In Brazil, for example.

At an early stage in work on Eco-tourism it is important to be aware of the work of other national and international agencies in this field and to seek mutually beneficial coordination.

Finding the Best Way to Involve the Community

Involving the community is a critically important and complex subject for successful community-based Eco-tourism. Opportunities and solutions will vary considerably in different areas and between communities. An important principle is to seek to work with existing social and community structures, though these can create challenges as well as opportunities. It can also help to identify potential leaders and people with drive. The main objective should be to achieve broad and equitable benefits throughout the community. Issues of gender may also be important and Eco-tourism can provide good opportunities for women.

Community-based Eco-tourism requires an understanding, and where possible a strengthening, of the legal rights and responsibilities of the community over land, resources and development. This should apply in particular to the tenure of community-held lands and to rights over tourism, conservation and other uses on these lands, enabling the community to influence activity and earn income from tourism. It should also apply to participation in land use planning and development control over private property.

It is important to remember that Eco-tourism is a business. As well as community-led initiatives, private enterprise and investment should be encouraged where appropriate, within a structure which enables the community to benefit, and have decision-making power over the level and nature of tourism in its area.

There are various ways in which the community can relate to private enterprise. The degree of community involvement and benefit can develop over time. For example, there are some Eco-tourism initiatives in the Amazon where lodges, that have been built with private investment, offer a concession to the community, an agreement to hand the business over to them after a specified period, and provision for an employment and training programme for local people. Options for community involvement with enterprise include the following.

1 Private tourism businesses employing local people. Although a useful form of employment, it is very important to guard against poor wages and conditions and to ensure that training is offered to local people, including in management.

2 Local individuals selling produce and handicraft to visitors directly or through tourism businesses. This has often proved to be a good way of spreading benefits within a community.

3 Private tourism businesses (internally or externally owned) being granted a concession to operate by the community, in return for a fee and a share of revenue. There are many examples where this has worked well.

4 Individuals, with links to the broader community, running their own small tourism businesses. Success can vary and lack of skill and tourism knowledge has often proved a weakness.

5 Communally owned and run enterprises. Sometimes these suffer from lack of organisation and incentive, but this can be overcome with time.

Action can be taken to strengthen relationships between the community and private partners. This includes:

- advice and training for communities on their rights and negotiating practies;
- ensuring transparent, simple and consistently applied deals give sufficient incentive to private enterprises, recognise commercial realities, and minimise administrative burdens and uncertainty; and

- establishing committees involving local people, private operators and possibly government agencies and NGOs, to ensure understanding and smooth operation of agreements, and to help local communication.

The method of distribution of income earned by communities to individual members needs careful attention. This can sometimes be covered in legislation relating to communal rights. There are examples where communally-earned income from Eco-tourism has been directly divided between households or placed in community development funds or separate trusts for use on community projects such as health or education programmes.

Working Together on an Agreed Strategy

All community-based Eco-tourism initiatives should be centred on a clear strategy agreed and understood by the local community and all other stakeholders with an interest in tourism and conservation.

The strategy should enable a comprehensive picture to be formed of needs and opportunities in an area, so that a range of complementary actions can be taken. One of the main benefits from working on a strategy is to provide the community with the tools and knowledge necessary for decision making.

The strategy should be community-led and community-focused. However, it is essential that people with experience and knowledge of tourism and conservation are involved in its preparation.

People involved should include representatives of the local community, knowledgeable tourism operators, local entrepreneurs, relevant NGOs, conservation agencies including protected area managers, and local authorities. Links should be made as appropriate to the regional and national government level.

Inputs to the strategy should include:

- careful consultation within the community covering attitudes and awareness of tourism, possible opportunities and pitfalls, existing experience, concerns and level of interest;
- a comprehensive market assessment; and
- an assessment of the natural and cultural heritage, including opportunities presented for Eco-tourism and sensitivities and constraints.

It is also helpful to set out a clear statement of strengths, weaknesses, opportunities and threats.

The output of the strategy process should be an agreed vision for Eco-tourism over a specified period, together with an identification of aims, objectives and strategic priorities, an action plan, and a way of monitoring results. The action plan should identify practical initiatives, including a timescale and an indication of responsibility and resources required. It is very important, in order to avoid frustration, not to be too ambitious in terms of targets and timing.

The actions identified may include specific development or marketing projects. In some locations at least as much, or more, attention may need to be paid to action to manage tourism, including policies on development control and the handling of existing visitors. In many places, the relationship between the local community and a protected area may be an important element of the strategy, including agreed action on the level of any park admission fees and their subsequent use for conservation or within the community, which is an important issue for Eco-tourism.

Ensuring Environmental and Cultural Integrity

A fundamental characteristic of community-based Eco-tourism is that the quality of the natural resources and cultural heritage of an area should not be damaged and, if possible, should be enhanced by tourism. Adverse impact on the natural environment should be minimised and the culture of indigenous communities should not be compromised. Eco-tourism should encourage people to value their own cultural heritage. However, culture is not static and communities may wish to see change.

A practical approach is to identify the limits of acceptable change that could be brought by tourism and then to consider what level of tourism activity would generate this change.

It is very important that communities decide on the level of tourism they wish to see. Consultation during the process of drawing up an Eco-tourism strategy should reveal the kinds of changes that might be viewed positively or negatively by local people. They can then be helped to consider what this might mean in terms of the numbers and types of visitor to look for, when they should come and their length of stay. For example, in one community in the Amazon it was felt that more than eight visitors per month would be disruptive. Two important principles are:

- products developed should be based on the community's traditional knowledge, values and skills; and
- the community should decide which aspects of their cultural traditions they wish to share with visitors.

A similar approach can be adopted with respect to determining limits of acceptable change and of acceptable use as far as the natural environment is concerned. Here scientific knowledge may be required to enable a judgement to be made, taking account of the conditions of different sites at various times of the year. Often it is found that the quantity of visitors at any one time is a more critical factor than the overall level of visitation. Useful tools in the management of visitors include the following.

1 Agreements with tour operators over the number and size of groups to bring.

2 Codes of conducts for visitors.

3 Application of systematic environmental, social and cultural impact assessment on all proposed development. This should also be concerned with details of what is offered to visitors, such as the choice of products sold to them (for example avoiding artefacts with a sacred significance) or the use of inappropriate sources of fuel.

4 Zoning both within and outside protected areas. This should cover both the siting of facilities and the degree of access allowed. In some locations, village communities have identified specific zones for Eco-tourism, both with respect to facility provision and wildlife conservation measures. A common approach is to locate tourist lodges some distance away from community villages.

The planning process should ensure that monitoring measures are in place so that it is possible to tell when limits of acceptable change have been reached. Furthermore, strategies for making the necessary adjustments to overcome any problems identified will need to be established.

There are many examples in the Mediterranean where environmental degradation has occurred but also places where sound planning control and community involvement have prevented over-exploitation.

Ensuring Market Realism and Effective Promotion

The main reason why many community-based Eco-tourism projects have failed is that they have not attracted a sufficient number of visitors. Often, assumptions made about the marketability of a particular location or experience have been unrealistic and not based on research. As a result, promotional activity has been misdirected. A problem has been the lack of tourism knowledge not only among local communities themselves but also among advisors and supporting agencies.

A thorough market assessment should be undertaken for the destination as a whole and for the individual Eco-tourism project. This should consider the following.

1 The patterns, profiles and interests of existing visitors to the area, based on visitor surveys. In principle, it is far easier to get more out of existing visitors than to attract new ones.

2 The location of the area with respect to established tourist circuits in the country. Proximity to these and opportunities for deflection make a considerable difference.

3 The level, nature and performance of existing Eco-tourism products which are competitors but also potential collaborators.

4 The activities of inbound tour operators and ground handling agents in the country and coverage by international tour operators.

5 Existing information and promotional mechanisms in the area.

The unique or particular qualities that an area might offer in comparison to other existing products should be identified. From knowledge of the market, an initial profile of target visitors should be drawn up. Attention needs to be paid to the different opportunities and requirements of experienced ecotourists, more general mid-market visitors who enjoy seeing nature and local culture, backpackers, and educational markets. In some areas, the domestic visitor market may offer more potential than international travellers.

The level and nature of marketing should also take into account the environmental and cultural integrity of the area and implications for visitor numbers. A marketing plan should be prepared for all projects, which relates market research to a promotional programme. A vital ingredient for many projects is to form a close working relationship with one or more specialist tour operators.

These should be selected carefully to ensure they are well established and are delivering reliable business. Contact, directly or through handling agents, should be made in the early stages, before the development of the offer has occurred, so that the operator can advise on what can be sold and adjustments, if necessary, can be made. Setting up a fully saleable programme can take time. An initial step may be to test market the programme with one or two groups. This also has the advantage of acquainting the community with the experience of handling guests.

It is not sufficient for community-based Eco-tourism projects to rely simply on tour operators to supply visitors. For example, although pre-arranged groups may be easier to handle, backpackers or independent travellers may often be better suited to the product in question, but tend not to purchase inclusive packages through operators in their home country. The marketing plan, therefore, will also need to address issues such as local information delivery, internet promotion, media and guidebook coverage, linkages with other projects, and promotion though national tourism campaigns.

Putting Forward Quality Products

A second common reason for failure concerns the quality of execution of the project, both in terms of what is offered and proper business planning. Quality is about delivering an experience that meets or exceeds visitor expectations. These, in turn, will vary according to the type of visitor coming, which reinforces the need for effective market research.

Although luxury and sophistication may not be sought, an important section of the Eco-tourism market, often handled by tour operators, is looking for a rich wildlife experience, comfortable and reliable accommodation and efficient business handling. It can sometimes be difficult for communities to deliver this. On the other hand, the special sense of discovery, welcome and privilege which a community visit can provide is something valued by many visitors. There are three key requirements.

1 Attention to detail, ensuring that what is offered, at whatever level, is well delivered.

2 Quality and accuracy of promotion and information, giving reassurance but also ensuring that expectations match reality. All visitors in this market are increasingly looking for a high level of information provision.

3 Authenticity and ambience. Ecotourists respond to genuine and traditional values and experiences and they do not want this to be manufactured for them.

Some issues relate to specific components of the offer.

1 The quality of the wildlife and landscapes, in terms of relative uniqueness, attractiveness and abundance. If this is high, a project has a greater chance of success. Without it, the quality of the associated facilities and derived experiences becomes more important.

2 The mix of natural and cultural experiences. Many visitors are looking for a combination.

3 Accommodation: cleanliness is of primary importance, but issues such as ablution and toilet arrangements, general functionality, privacy and overall design and ambience can be significant. Different requirements in terms of investment and sophistication exist between lodges and camping grounds.

4 Guiding and interpretation: a fine balance between local colour and story telling, and scientific knowledge and accuracy is often sought. This may require involvement of different people, including an opportunity for local people to be trained as guides and interpreters.

5 Local produce and handicrafts: although visitors may look for authenticity, it is very important to avoid the depletion of cultural artefacts and other resources. Quality products can be made and sold which reflect an area's traditions and creativity without devaluing them.

6 General experience of village life, including folklore: this can prove an experience highly valued by visitors. It can provide an incentive to keep local culture and pass on local knowledge.

7 Participation: some visitors value the opportunity to participate in activities.

Conservation participation programmes are a specific sub-sector of Eco-tourism and can be community-based.

Managing Impacts

Attention to detail in a number of aspects of both the development and operation of Eco-tourism projects can significantly improve their delivery.

The design of all new buildings should be carefully considered. Traditional styles and locally available materials should be used. In some communities, useful income has been earned through, for example, the supply of thatching. Often it can be better to use existing buildings rather than engaging in new development, and this should be considered first.

Action should be taken, both at the development stage and in operating facilities, to reduce consumption of water and energy, reduce waste and avoid pollution.

Low energy technologies appropriate to the location should be applied where possible. Recycling should be encouraged and all forms of waste disposal should be carefully managed, with a principle of taking as much waste away from the site as possible. Use of environmentally friendly transport should be positively favoured, both in the planning of programmes and in the information supplied.

In order to minimise economic leakage, every effort should be made to use local produce and services, and to favour the employment of local people. This may require action to identify local, sustainable sources. Producers can be assisted through the formation of local groups and networks, and help with contacts, marketing and pricing.

Local communities should be encouraged and helped to take account of these issues themselves without any effect on their living standards, through information, training and demonstration. Feedback to them from visitors will help. Influencing the actions taken by visitors and tour operators is very important. Some elements of good practice can be included as firm requirements in contracts with the private sector.

A number of national and international tourism certification schemes provide formal recognition of good practice in managing impacts on the environment and local communities. In selecting a scheme, the criteria it uses should be carefully considered. In particular, certification should be based on action taken rather than simply expressed intention.

Providing Technical Support

Communities will require ongoing access to advice and support in the development, management and marketing of responsible, good quality Eco-tourism products.

Many of the issues raised in these guidelines point to the importance of capacity building and training programmes with local communities. It is important to get the level of delivery and content right. This should be carefully discussed with the communities themselves. In general, it has been found that short, technical courses have had little impact. Longer courses, including learning by doing and on the job training, have proved necessary.

Important topics to consider include:

- product development issues;
- handling visitors, customer care and hospitality skills;
- marketing and communication;
- environmental management;
- working and negotiating with commercial operators;
- management skills, legal issues and financial control;
- guide training, including content and delivery; and
- basic language training.

A useful way of generating ideas, giving confidence and putting across knowledge is through contacting, visiting or meeting other projects which are already experienced in community-based Eco-tourism. There are various examples where this has been particularly successful.

Most projects require some form of financial support. However, the nature of the financial assistance must avoid inhibiting incentive and causing problems within and between communities. Soft loans and long-term credit, well targeted to local needs, may be most appropriate. The use of local committees to approve financial offers has proved successful in some areas. It is important to demonstrate to governments and donor agencies the success of small community-based projects, including appropriate credit schemes, in order to encourage more financial assistance programmes.

The importance of effective marketing has been covered under Guideline 7. As well as technical marketing advice, projects can be assisted through access to national research data, help with visitor surveys, and linkages to marketing outlets such as national tourist board promotions and websites. The establishment of registers of community-based Eco-tourism projects, if possible backed by efficient reservation systems, should be encouraged.

A very valuable way of providing technical support is through establishing networks between projects. Some countries have associations of communitybased tourism initiatives. These not only raise awareness and provide marketing support but can also promote common quality standards, deliver training and financial assistance and generally represent the sector in the commercial and political arena.

Obtaining the Support of Visitors and Tour Operators

Eco-tourism experiences should raise awareness of conservation and community issues among visitors and tour operators and include mechanisms for enlisting their support.

Significant additional benefits can be achieved through improving communication with visitors themselves and with the tour operators who bring them.

These benefits include greater awareness of environmental and social issues, modifying behaviour when visiting, and generating direct support for local communities and conservation causes.

In almost all cases, the experience of a community-based tourism programme will have an impact on how people think in future about the area and habitats they have visited. However, this can be made more or less meaningful depending on the information they receive before, during and after the visit, and how it is delivered. Careful attention should be paid to the messages put out by tour operators to their clients and to the quality of guiding and interpretation on site. Mechanisms for follow-up contact should be explored. Visitors should be encouraged to 'multiply' their experience by writing and talking about it.

A number of codes of conduct for visitors have been produced. Some are generic, others are area or site specific. These tend to cover questions such as prior reading and understanding, selection of operators and destinations, respect for local cultures, minimising environmental impact, purchasing decisions, activities to avoid, and conservation issues to support. Similarly, codes for tour operators cover issues such as particular environmental and cultural issues in the destination concerned, selection of sites, relationship with indigenous communities, messages to put across to staff and clients, and more specific instructions and regulations. These codes can be adapted for all Eco-tourism destinations. Raising finance or other forms of support from visitors (such as participation in research) has become quite a common practice in Eco-tourism destinations. This is often through a levy applied by tour operators or through inviting donations. Although some operators resist this, the effect on tour prices can be relatively small. Visitors appear to applaud the opportunity to make a contribution, creating a marketing advantage for the operator. Money may be put into a local development fund. Visitors may be invited to discuss beneficiary schemes and to get to know them. These can be conservation initiatives or social programmes within the community.

Monitoring Performance and Ensuring Continuity

Eco-tourism Projects should be Designed and Managed for Long-term Viability and Success

A recurring problem with many community-based Eco-tourism projects that have been established as part of externally funded and assisted initiatives, has been a tendency not to continue satisfactorily after the life of the aid programme.

It is very important that:

- a reasonable time span is allotted to the project so that withdrawal of assistance does not occur too early;
- an 'exit strategy' is worked out at an early stage;
- all bodies providing assistance take care to impart know-how to local individuals and organisations throughout the course of the project;
- a strategy of long-term local ownership is maintained; and
- use is made of national or local authority and private sector support that may be ongoing.

Projects will be considerably strengthened by regular monitoring and feedback to assess success and identify weaknesses that may need to be adjusted. Simple indicators should be agreed and made known to the community. These should cover economic performance, local community reaction and wellbeing, visitor satisfaction and environmental changes. Monitoring should be kept simple and feedback should be obtained from visitors, tour operators and local people. Training of local participants in monitoring processes may be required. Certification and award schemes can play a role in maintaining as well as establishing good practice. To ensure maximising benefits from Eco-tourism and minimising negative impacts on natural environments and surrounding communities, all stakeholders must commit themselves to following some principles and guidelines in their operations, in a concerted effort. WTO has identified the following principles and guidelines for Eco-tourism development and management, which need to be adapted to suit the special conditions of each country, region and local destination:

1. Eco-tourism must contribute to the conservation and improvement of natural areas and to the sustainable development of adjacent areas and communities.
2. Eco-tourism requires specific policies, strategies and programmes for each particular destination; it cannot be sustainability developed by simply copying what has been done elsewhere, let alone be left to grow in a disorderly and anarchic manner.
3. Eco-tourism needs practical and effective systems of coordination between all the players involved, including governments, private enterprises and the local community.
4. The planning of Eco-tourism must include strict criteria for territorial zoning, including in surrounding seas, designating reserves, low-and medium-impact areas. These criteria should be strictly enforced and respected by all parties.
5. The physical planning and design of eco-tourist facilities –especially hotels and other means of accommodation, restaurants, information centres in national parks and the like-should be carried out in a manner to avoid or minimise any negative impact they may have upon the natural and cultural environment. Building materials, architectural styles, furniture and decor should ideally be local, while low pollution energy sources should be used.
6. Similarly, the means of transport and communications to access Eco-tourism areas should be low contaminating. Sports involving noisy or highly polluting means of transport should definitely be prohibited in these areas.

7. The practice of Eco-tourism in national parks and protected areas should strictly comply with the management rules governing such areas.
8. Reciprocally, these management plans should take into account the fact that they will be used by tourists, and make suitable provisions for a sustainable use and visitation.
9. The carrying capacity of island systems in relation to tourism is all-important, and integrated long-term strategies and plans must take into account these carrying capacities.
10. Appropriate legal and institutional mechanisms should be established to facilitate and make effective the orderly participation of the local island community in the entire Eco-tourism process, including policy definition, planning, management and monitoring. Awareness raising and capacity building are essential ingredients for this.
11. In line with this, institutional, financial, fiscal or other mechanisms should also be established to ensure that a significant proportion of the income generated from Eco-tourism remains with the local community or serves conservation purposes.
12. It is however important to ensure that Eco-tourism is a good, economically sustainable business and that profits are generated from it. If there are no prospects for profit, then private entrepreneurs will not invest and there will be no benefits to distribute for local communities or conservation purposes.
13. All those concerned with the Eco-tourism business must be aware of the costs of mitigating any possible negative impacts, and such costs must be incorporated in the pre-investment cost-benefit analyses of any Eco-tourism project.
14. Compliance with general tourism regulations and codes should be stricter in the case of Eco-tourism in small islands, combining supervision and monitoring, with awareness raising campaigns among business people and tourists, training of service suppliers, and eventually sanctions against those who do not comply. Self-regulation and voluntary initiatives related to the environmental and

socio-cultural sustainability of Eco-tourism should be encouraged but duly checked.

15. Consideration should be given to the prospects of establishing the obligation of certification systems for Eco-tourism facilities and operations, to guarantee that their quality is consistent with the principles of sustainability. Accreditation of existing local certification systems should also be considered, as a means to give them higher credibility in the eyes of consumers and foreign tour operators.
16. Education and training are prerequisites for sustainable Eco-tourism development and management. Company managers and employees, as well as the local population need training on general and specific aspects of Eco-tourism, tailored to the needs of each. In particular, Eco-tourism needs highly qualified guides, who should ideally be natives from the island.
17. Ecotourists need detailed and specialised information, both before and during the trip. The provision of complete information is precisely one of the elements that differentiate the Eco-tourism experience from traditional tourism, and it can take various forms, such as brochures, guide-books, leaflets, maps, interpretation centres, ecomuseums, signposted nature trails, and, of course the guides themselves.
18. Promotional material for Eco-tourism should contain substantial information on the experience to which potential tourists are invited, including details on flora, fauna, geology and in general on the ecosystem to be visited. It should also include truthful information about the accommodation and catering services, as well as recommendations on what may and may not be done at the destination. All this information before the purchase will help the potential clients to discriminate between genuine Eco-tourism operators and others that only seek to take advantage of a fashion.
19. Both the marketing channels and the promotional means for Eco-tourism products should be consistent with the type of tourism the consumer is being offered and with the typology of ecotourists.

4

Sustainable Development-based Eco-tourism

It is almost impossible, with a title for a paper such as this, to avoid getting into a discussion on definitions, and debate about the merits and shortcomings of Eco-tourism as a tool for or component of sustainable development. There are many critics of Eco-tourism, who see it as a form of environmental opportunism that allows continued exploitation of natural environments by mass tourism. Mass tourism cloaked in a green name. Eco-tourism is certainly a buzz word, and is becoming as ambiguous as the word 'natural' on the supermarket shelf. Here is another definition of Eco-tourism:

> *"A form of tourism inspired primarily by the natural history of an area, including its indigenous cultures. The ecotourist visits relatively undeveloped areas in the spirit of appreciation, participation and sensitivity. The ecotourist practices a non-consumptive use of wildlife and natural resources and contributes to the visited area through labour or financial means aimed at directly benefiting the conservation of the site and the economic well-being of the local residents. The visit should strengthen the ecotourist's appreciation and dedication to conservation issues in general, and to the specific needs of the locale. Eco-tourism also implies a managed approach by the host country or region which commits itself to establishing and maintaining the sites with the participation of local residents, marketing them appropriately, enforcing regulations, and using the proceeds of the enterprise to fund the area's land management as well as community development." Ziffer, K., 1989: 6.*

This is a tough definition of Eco-tourism but we believe it is appropriate and necessary in order to highlight the special nature of genuine Eco-tourism-what Eco-tourism should strive to be. Further, it is important to emphasise that Eco-tourism does not equal nature tourism, rather it is a distinct niche/segment of the more general nature tourism sector.

The Nature-based Tourism-Eco-tourism Spectrum

One of the reasons for continued debate on the merits of Eco-tourism to achieve sustainable development is that there is no blueprint for successful Eco-tourism development in all of its facets. Rather, there are examples of different projects in which particular components are innovative or well-implemented. Sites and potential projects need to be considered on a case by case basis, as many local factors-environmental, human, political, economic, social, cultural etc will work for the benefit of, or to the detriment of, an Eco-tourism project.

In some cases it will be very hard to 'develop' Eco-tourism. For example, in Cuc Phuong National Park mass tourism is already well established and the Park has developed facilities, hardened sites, opened up areas, to cater for these tourists. It will be very hard for Eco-tourism to be developed, unless the Park is able to restrict the number and movement of visitors, unless it can create specific Eco-tourism zones to direct ecotourists away from the present built up areas. But this may place even more environmental pressure on the Park.

Despite the lack of a blueprint, the last few years have seen a number of Codes of Sustainable Practice, Codes of Responsible Behaviour, Guidelines for Eco-tourism and Sustainability etc developed for tourists, tour operators, national park managers, policy makers alike. These have been developed by environmental NGOs; NGOs dedicated to raising awareness of the negative impacts of tourism and striving to make the tourism industry more responsible and sustainable; national parks and nature reserves; and, within the tourism industry itself, international or regional tourism organisations; tour operators; outdoor equipment suppliers....

Carrying Capacity and Limiting Numbers

Eco-tourism markets are expanding faster than any other tourism market segment. Eco-tourism is inherently limited in the extent to which it can be developed and promoted, given that it cannot support large numbers without setting in train a process of succession and change which destroys the reason for its existence.

A big difficulty for Vietnam and other countries wishing to embrace Eco-tourism is the idea that in order to achieve a sustainable Eco-tourism industry planners/managers/policy makers must impose limits. How difficult is it to impose restrictions on the number of visitors to an area...when there is the lure of expansion, as people queue up at the gate? And in a country with a huge domestic population...the concept of limiting numbers appears almost ludicrous and is certainly controversial. It is natural that there will be concerns about equity and elitism, especially if fees or charges are used as a means to limit numbers.

The Principles for Sustainable Tourism (Tourism Concern/ WWF)

1. *Using resources sustainably:* the conservation and sustainable use of resources-natural, social and cultural-is crucial and makes long-term business sense;
2. *Reducing over-consumption and waste:* reduction of over-consumption and waste avoids the costs of restoring long-term environmental damage and contributes to the quality of tourism;
3. *Maintaining Diversity:* maintaining and promoting natural, social and cultural diversity is essential for long-term sustainable tourism, and creates a resilient base for the industry;
4. *Integrating Tourism into Planning:* tourism development which is integrated into a national and local strategic planning framework and which undertakes environmental impacts assessments, increases the long-term viability of tourism;
5. *Supporting Local Economies:* tourism that supports a wide range of local economic activities and which takes environmental costs and values into account, both protects those economies and avoids environmental damage;
6. *Involving local communities:* the full involvement of local communities in the tourism sector not only benefits them and the environment in general but also improves the quality of the tourism experience;

7. *Consulting Stakeholders and the Public:* consultation between the tourism industry and local communities, organisations and institutions is essential if they are to work alongside each other and resolve potential conflicts of interest;
8. *Training Staff:* staff training which integrates sustainable tourism into work practices, along with recruitment of local personnel at all levels, improves the quality of the tourism product;
9. *Marketing Tourism Responsibly:* marketing that provides tourists with full and responsible information increases respect for the natural, social and cultural environments of destination areas and enhances customer satisfaction;
10. *Undertaking Research:* on-going research and monitoring by the industry using effective data collection and analysis is essential to help solve problems and to bring benefits to destinations, the industry and consumers.

How to decide when enough is enough, when restrictions need to be imposed? The management tools of 'limits of acceptable change' and carrying capacity are very important management tools to assist in achieving sustainability NOT ONLY for Eco-tourism or nature tourism, but for the tourism industry as a whole. However their application is far from easy and unfortunately there exists a lack of understanding and awareness of the concept as applied to tourism.

Carrying capacity has four branches: physical, biological, psychological, social. All are related to the number of visitors/ tourists to a site or area:

- Physical is the actual number of visitors a site can hold;
- Biological is the point at which environmental degradation occurs to the extent that it is irreversible or unacceptable;
- Psychological is the point at which the tourists feels the quality of their experience is damaged by the number of other tourists and/or their behaviours, and
- Social is the level at which the local inhabitants of the site (possibly the tourist attraction themselves) feel disrupted, intruded upon etc.

As carrying capacities include qualitative as well as quantitative aspects, there is consequently no 'correct' or empirical figure for an area. Nevertheless it is vital that an attempt is made to arrive at some estimations of the carrying capacity of each site, using the best methods and knowledge available. This research will assist in management decisions. Putting such work in the 'too hard' basket is counter to the principles underlying sustainable development.

The target audience/market needs to be carefully considered in establishing carrying capacity. Eco-tourism does not cater for all and any type of tourist, just as a beach-side resort holiday does not appeal to all.

There is a cultural component relating to carrying capacity that may be obvious but is important to highlight: An Australian will have a different concept of psychological and social carrying capacity and even physical and biological carrying capacity from their Vietnamese or Asian colleague. At the most basic, the perception of and tolerance towards crowding will be very different.

The Target Market(s) and Managing for the Target Market(s)

The above leads to some questions:

- WHO, WHAT TYPE of tourist does Vietnam want to cater for?
- high, middle or low income;
- short stay visitors, long stay visitors, high spenders, low spenders;
- those seeking relaxing beach resort holidays away from it all;
- those seeking physical challenge and close encounters with locals in remote areas, e.g.: trekkers;
- those interested purely in cultural and artistic features of Vietnam who also like to travel and stay in comfort;
- those who travel in tours on the major routes, or those who travel independently;
- those who want to travel to natural, undisturbed areas and learn about the environment;
- those who stay in small hotels and guest houses, those who prefer large;
- visitors from the region ie: ASEAN, China, Japan, Korea, or Europeans or Australasians;
- domestic tourists...

- Can Vietnam target and successfully cater to all these categories?
- Does Vietnam, in developing Eco-tourism, want to provide 'add on attractions' for tourists already coming to Vietnam or does it want to try to attract a new market?
- What are the implications for achieving genuine Eco-tourism when the domestic tourist often acts as though the environment is a resource to be 'exploited and developed'-exemplified in the consumption of wildlife for food and medicine?
- Is the Vietnam domestic tourist compatible with the international visitor to natural areas or the international ecotourist?
- Is there a difference between Asian tourists and Western tourists?

If Vietnam wishes to bring the international ecotourist to visit its protected areas, then this decision will have considerable implications for how it handles the domestic tourist and manages those areas.

It is important to match the numbers and types of ecotourists/ nature tourists with the characteristics of the destination. This requires the monitoring of nature/ecotourists. Understanding customer groups, their motivations and characteristics, is essential for promotion, marketing, planning for improvement of facilities and services including information needs, controlling impacts via restrictions on numbers or zoning of protected areas for different types of use and different types of visitors.

The Recreational Opportunity Spectrum (ROS) developed by Clark and Stankey is a useful management tool to assist here. The ROS is an integrating framework for resource management, its underlying rationale being the assumption that providing a diverse range of recreational opportunities will best assure quality recreational experiences as it will provide for the many tastes and preferences that motivate people to participate in recreation.

Division of the resource into zones with certain biological, social and managerial characteristics helps establish objectives and guidelines for their management, regulations and limits on activities, and enables assessment of optimum and maximum carrying capacity conditions and the level of change tolerated

(Koeman 1989). Inadequate data collection on the market can lead to decision makers developing an area in such a way that they lose their market.

Numerous studies of visitors to national parks around the world have shown that nature tourists are generally more accepting of conditions different from home than are other types of tourists, that they do not demand international glamour, but are satisfied with or want to use local goods and materials and eat local foods....and that they are more demanding in seeking information about their destination.

Nature/ecotourists are also generally willing to spend more, to make an active contribute to conservation causes or community development by their visit or during their visit. Part of the attraction to the ecotourist or dedicated nature tourist is the ability to experience an undeveloped area which is in stark contrast to the urban existence of many travellers from the industrialised world. They are looking for something new and meaningful.

Thus Eco-tourism can be promoted without excessive capital requirements and infrastructure developments. Though this may mean there is no need to build a concrete hotel inside a park with air-conditioning and TV, it does not mean that nothing needs to be done to cater for ecotourists. It is very important that a quality experience be offered.

Quality includes considerations such as the amount and type of information and interpretation, the environmental and cultural sensitivity and skills of guides and park managers, the level of professionalism, dedication and hospitality exhibited by all involved, the degree of local community involvement, the direction of fees paid by the ecotourists to conservation and local community development projects...

There is an inherent risk, however, in assuming that everyone calling themselves an ecotourist is environmentally sensitive and aware. Amongst those included in the definition of ecotourist are those persons who visit a natural place for a few days, unlikely to ever return...they may not care of the long-term repercussions of their activities, especially if they have paid a considerable amount for their travel. The phenomenon of affluent tourists jet-setting the world to visit famous natural sites has been coined the "this year the Galapagos, next year Antarctica" syndrome.

Environmental Education and Awareness

There are initiatives underway in Vietnam to improve environmental education in schools in Vietnam, however it is still obvious that lack of environmental education and information for students (from preschool level up), the general public, tourists and local communities alike is a major problem in developing sustainable Eco-tourism. Environmental education and information dissemination is of prime importance to the realisation of genuine, sustainable Eco-tourism or nature tourism in Vietnam. We need to educate the tourists, both present and potential, both domestic and international.

- Where are all the interpretative and environmental information centres in national parks and nature reserves in Vietnam?
- Investing in such centres is investing in the future, investing for sustainability. Should they be given greater priority than the purchase of vehicles, or even the building of large new park headquarters?
- Is it not essential that every new park HQ have an interpretive/environmental information centre included?

Allocating the space is not all however; the centres need to have extensive materials developed, staff trained in management, hospitality skills, language, culture of local communities, environmental education and sustainable tourism.

There is the very real danger that any Eco-tourism initiative/ project in Vietnam will be overtaken, overrun, swamped by mass tourism to natural areas, or general nature-based tourism (that has none, or only some of the principles of Eco-tourism). A problem not only of lack of environmental awareness but also simply because of sheer numbers!

"The National Parks in North America are being "loved to death" by almost 400 million visitors in 1991 "trampling over the fragile habitat, ruining the flora with the pollution from their cars, scaring the animals, destroying the wilderness..." In Kenya, the central circuit of Amboseli National Park has been reduced to semi-desert by visitors' vehicles, while in the Maasai Mara, which receives 200,000 visitors a year, the construction of a large number of lodges outside the controlled area threatens to overload the system."

Supply-oriented Management

It is important to note that Eco-tourism CAN be, but is NOT automatically, a form of sustainable tourism. To achieve sustainable Eco-tourism involves balancing economic, environmental and social goals within an ethical framework of values and principles. Eco-tourism faces considerable challenges, not least is the challenge to keep foremost a supply-oriented management perspective. A supply-oriented management perspective has as its primary considerations the nature and resilience of the resource, cultural or local community preferences, and interpretive and conservation programmes. Essentially a supply-oriented management perspective puts the resource-national park, protected area, local culture and community-before the demands of tourists. Growth can only go so far, and not nearly as far as with other forms of tourism given the dominance of ecosystem and ecological considerations.

Who is Responsible for Eco-tourism?

Eco-tourism/nature tourism cannot be solely developed by the Ministry or government agency of tourism or by the national park department as tourism crosses over many sectors. There is a need for strong interagency cooperation and linkages. This could be achieved through a Sustainable (Eco) Tourism Taskforce. The Task-force could be responsible for working towards the development of a national Eco-tourism or nature tourism strategy for Vietnam, which could have as goals the establishment of a Sustainable (Eco) Tourism Association and Sustainable (Eco) Tourism Commission. Further, Eco-tourism needs cooperative, collaborative arrangements between Govt. at all levels, parks, NGOs, local communities, tour operators. In developing a national Eco-tourism strategy, these stakeholders need to be fully included in the process.

National Eco/Nature Tourism Strategy for Vietnam

If Vietnam wants to promote nature tourism; tourism to both protected areas and NON protected natural areas, then it needs to develop a national Eco-tourism or nature tourism strategy. We recommend that a Think tank on the Development of a National Eco-tourism Strategy be convened as a first step. The objectives of the Think-tank could be to gather together key decision makers and implementers from the tourism, planning, environmental, educational, socioeconomic sectors in Vietnam to:

1. discuss the need for a National Eco-tourism Strategy (NES) or Nature Tourism Strategy (NNTS) for Vietnam;
2. clarify where or to what extent tourism and Eco-tourism can occur in protected and non-protected natural areas in Vietnam, by clarifying what use rules apply to the different categories of protected areas ie: nature reserves, national parks, marine/coastal zones etc;
3. learn about Eco-tourism, alternative tourism and sustainable tourism principles and management tools, actions/strategies...;
4. learn about the development and composition of National Eco-tourism Strategies from other countries, their implementation and component activities or programmes;
5. consider options for a national definition of Eco-tourism;
6. suggest key elements of a NES or National Nature Tourism Strategy (NNTS);
7. draft a methodology and timetable for the development of a draft Strategy;
8. call for recommendations/nominations for working groups or agencies to be responsible for actively developing key elements of the Strategy according to the agreed timetable;
9. call for recommendations/nominations for the body responsible for carrying forward the initiative ie: 'tying it all together', and
10. consider the areas in which Vietnam/the above bodies require capacity strengthening/training/technical advice to assist in the development and implementation of the NES/NNTS.

Tour Operators

Tour operators are an extremely important component of successful Eco-tourism. The way they function, their choice of destination, the way they package and sell trips, the type of support services they provide, and their cost structure, are all important factors to understand how to make changes in the way nature tourism impacts host countries.

It is important that the role of private small business in the tourism industry be recognised and encouraged. Private operators (or guest houses or guide services etc) are often smaller than government owned operations. They have the potential to be more efficient, flexible and innovative...in a carefully controlled and regulated Eco-tourism market. Small is supposed to be beautiful in Eco-tourism.

It is also essential that cases of Eco-Exploitation: using 'green' or 'eco' to falsely sell a tourism product that is far from ecologically responsible or sustainable, are exposed, whether the culprits are state or private operators.

A quote: "You don't become an ecotourist operator by just having nature as your destination...what do you do with waste? What do you do with hazardous chemicals? How do you transport? Do you buy locally?...Are you encouraging wildlife? What are you doing with your sewage?

It is these kind of nitty gritty things that will make the difference between Eco-tourism being a force for the environment or simply being another threat."

A good step, if Vietnam wants to promote sustainable tourism, would be to develop, adopt and disseminate National Codes of Conduct or Practice for Sustainable Tourism and Eco-tourism. A formal system of accreditation-such as a 'green stars' system could be considered and worked on for Eco-tourism operators. Non compliance to such a 'green stars' system by those proclaiming to be Eco-tourism operators would mean they are required to disassociate from (not use) the term Eco-tourism.

Ideally, these activities should be undertaken in co-operation and consultation with all tourism stakeholders, not decided by government alone, in order to ensure acceptance of the measures. How to get such a consultation process going? How about looking at allowing the establishment of a non-government body to bring together all operators in Vietnam-a Vietnam Sustainable (Eco) Tourism Association? Could the Chamber of Commerce and Industry's proposed *Business Council for Sustainable Development* play a valuable role?

This Association could work together with the Sustainable (Eco) Tourism Task-force to establish an independent Sustainable (Eco) Tourism Commission to be responsible for assessment, certification and policing of the industry. The Commission could have broad representation from the various stakeholder segments e.g.: government; protected area managers; hotels; tour operators; travel agents; guides; foreign tour operators; airlines; transport firms; local authorities; conservation organisations; NGOs. The Eco-tourism Society has produced *Guidelines for Nature Tour Operators*, which our Project is going to translate into Vietnamese, hopefully for distribution nation wide. In the future, such guidelines could be adopted by managers of protected areas as rigorous standards as part of a supply-oriented management regime. Though this may undermine freedom to practice for all and any tour operator, and incur considerable additional costs, operators, whether state or private, would have to comply.

The challenge is for host countries, regions and national parks to enlist the support of operators, for the purposes of conservation, education of tourists, appropriate behaviour etc., not simply rely on imposing restrictions from above. Cooperative partnerships need to be formed.

Tour Operators Segmentation

Practices need to be established that prevent the doers-those operators who are proactive and eager to cooperate on constructive conservation and community development projects, who are active in conserving and improving the areas they visit-from being placed at a competitive disadvantage in the industry.

Pro-active "Doers" in the Tourism Industry: Sharing Responsibilities

Boo (1990) notes that small companies visiting national parks seem to be contributing more to conservation than large ones. She provides an example of a responsible operator, 'Journeys' in the US, which donates a portion of the land costs of their trips to a non-profit conservation organisation and offers 'active conservation tours' such as a cleanup of the Machu Pichu trail.

Multatuli Travel in the Netherlands establishes relationships with local NGOs in Indonesia, Philippines and elsewhere and brings tourists to visit and contribute to their development projects.

Tour participants of such tours are likely to make contributions of their own. There are many more examples...

Such operators should not be placed at a disadvantage in the competitive tourism industry for being so environmentally aware, responsible and proactive, rather they should be acknowledged and in doing so the level playing field would be raised for the entire industry, so that others will also become active doers.

Local, Community Participation

- What is the main reason for developing Eco-tourism?
- Is it purely economic ie: is it to be used for generating foreign currency for national or provincial general revenue?
- Is it for developmental purposes ie: to provide local, rural communities with the opportunity to raise their standard of living and quality of life, increase their participation in natural resource management and conservation?
- Is it for conservation, ie: to provide national parks with the opportunity to strengthen conservation capabilities through increased income, and community participation in Eco-tourism?

Tourism to protected/natural areas can benefit rural, remote regions when other industries are centred on cities and towns, ports and transportation routes. There is a growing gap between the rural and urban areas in Vietnam, the former are missing out on many of the benefits and advancements of a more open economy...Eco-tourism can assist in spreading the benefits of development, stimulating economic activity and growth and provide an opportunity for diversification of the economy (Boo, E. 1990).

Eco-tourism can be a tool for conservation and rural development, but this will only materialise:

> *"if a concerted effort is made to incorporate local populations into the tourism industry. Involvement with local people and consequent rural development will not happen automatically. In some cases [including Vietnam] tourism to protected areas is not benefiting the surrounding population. Nature [eco] tourism will not contribute to rural development unless rural people are brought into the planning and development of the industry".*

The Galapagos Islands of Ecuador, a UNESCO natural heritage site, have suffered considerable social conflicts (in addition to severe environmental problems) due to tourism.

"Competition between the wealthier tourism sector and others is producing direct cultural conflict, aggravated by the fact that most of the tourism labour force is brought in from mainland Ecuador. Newcomers now outnumber those who grew up with and learned to value the special, fragile nature of the islands". Careful consideration should also be made to the distribution of benefits of Eco-tourism amongst local populations-does the project benefit the local poor, often ethnic minority population, or is it controlled by local elites and hence reinforce long-standing inequalities between the majority and minority groups?.

In elephant conservation projects on wildlife reserves in Zambia, local people, including former poachers, have been provided stable jobs and incomes as guards and tourist and hunting safari guides through training initiatives. This has raised the quality of safari tours.

What is the extent of participation? Eco-tourism projects are often directed by expatriates who are not necessarily familiar with local conditions and needs. Training local people to manage their own projects can avoid misunderstanding and possible hostility. Training should thus not only be for low paid and low status jobs, but for higher level management jobs.

Local resentment to being cut-off from the benefits of tourism can be explosive. An oft-cited case is the Maasai in Kenya. Widespread resentment exists amongst the Maasai nomadic pastoralists over the inadequate compensation paid to them for their displacement from traditional grazing lands with the establishment of national parks. The Maasai have resorted to killing wildlife in the parks in protest. Experience shows that with local people fully integrated into tourism projects, and receiving the benefits, infringements such as tree felling (Nepal) and poaching of wildlife (Zimbabwe) reduce markedly.

It is important to be aware of the abuse of the term "participation". Participatory approaches have been used in some cases to increase acceptability of tourism projects and as a means to detect potential conflicts and mitigate 'local threats' early on, rather than being truly committed to fostering democratic decision-making and empowerment of local people. Participation means different things in different societies and political structures. The level of participation will influence the sustainability and success of Eco-tourism in Vietnam.

"Quite clearly, employment is no substitute for sustainable access to resources. The 'hire the natives' approach to compensation also tends to create a small salaried class of locals at the same time that exclusionary policies are negatively impacting the economic situation of the remainder of the community and for relations between the park and the local community".

In 1997 an interactive conference-*Eco-tourism at a Crossroads: Charting the Way Forward*-was held by the Kenya Wildlife Service, The Eco-tourism Society of Kenya and The Eco-tourism Society (US). The conference's primary purpose was to use Kenya as a case study for other nations to examine, as Kenya's tourism industry is almost at a crisis point and requires urgent action. Participants-300 in all-were from government (38%), private sector (35%), NGOs (185) and local communities (9%). One of the recommendations that came out of the conference was the need for a Community Eco-tourism Association to represent communities seeking to create Eco-tourism projects; assist them with any land use and tourism revenue distribution problems, as well as with questions of business, legal, and market plans for Eco-tourism (Elper-Wood, M. 1998).

Economic Values, Revenues and Management Systems

The magnitude of benefits countries receive from nature tourism/Eco-tourism depends in large part on the scale of the tourism, the size of the country, and the complexity of the country's economy. The same can be said at the regional and local level.

Too much reliance on tourism renders an area susceptible to seasonal, economic fluctuations and changes in tourist tastes. It is best for tourism to be one of several activities, and to fit in with traditional activities e.g.: to compliment agriculture rather than competing with it or causing its decline.

Care also needs to be taken to not place excessive emphasis on the economic (tourism) value of parks as this can lead to decision makers believing that parks exist primarily for economic profit. If tourism then fails to meet economic expectations, other more damaging economic activities could be taken up.

"What will happen when forests, wildlife and other natural assets are increasingly valued in monetary terms? For instance, the visitor-attraction worth of each lion at Kenya's Amboseli Park has been estimated at US$27,000 per year and each elephant herd at US$610,000. To stress the profit-making potential of Eco-tourism, will the next step be to calculate the visitor attraction worth of a Maasai, a Karen or an Igorot?" In Vietnam, as in other countries, a hindrance to developing sustainable Eco-tourism is the problem of 'general revenue'. That is, park tourism revenue becomes general revenue for the central government, and/or provincial government, and there is considerable uncertainly about how much will be returned to the park as its budget allocation each year.

This system can hinder conservation and also Eco-tourism:

- it makes the protected areas highly susceptible to government budget cuts during economic downturns;
- it does little to encourage local park personnel to develop and participate in Eco-tourism or improve training in tourism;
- it does little to encourage the park to provide or improve educational information for tourists;
- it does little to promote conservation and strengthen commitment to and pride in the park (Boo, E. 1990).

Development of Eco-tourism requires improved internal and financial management incentives. It requires a dedicated portion of park revenue to be controlled by park management to provide an incentive for efficient administration (with some still going to central government so that national support for the parks will be maintained) (Ziffer, K. 1989).

With such a system in place ecotourists will be satisfied as they generally like to know, or even demand to know, how the money they pay is spent on conservation and development projects. If they know it is not simply going to general revenue they are more likely to make voluntary contributions. It cannot be assumed that protected areas will be able to generate sufficient tourist revenues to be self sufficient. In many cases tourism should not be considered as a path towards self-sufficiency but as a means to defray the costs of operations. Eco-tourism will not be appropriate for all protected areas in Vietnam, nor for all parts of a particular protected area (Ziffer, K. 1989).

Nepal and the Annapurna Area: the Environmental Impact of Uncontrolled Tourism to Natural Areas

Tourism is one of the main sources of foreign exchange income for Nepal. Each year, over 36,000 trekkers and 36,000 porters visit the Annapurna region which supports 40,000 local inhabitants.

About 60 per cent of these trekkers come during four months of the year. They are concentrated in few places, resulting in devastating impacts on both local cultural and natural environments.

Forest is cleared each year to construct hotels, lodges and furniture and to provide fuel for cooking, hot showers and campfires. 400,000 hectares of forest are cleared each year. This is a deforestation rate of three per cent per year. One hectare of cleared forests loses 30-75 tons of soil annually. This has led to devastating landslides and floods.

86 per cent of Nepal's energy comes from forests. In the Annapurna virtually everybody depends on fuelwood for cooking as there are no alternative sources of energy. The total daily wood consumption by and on behalf of each trekker equals the amount used by a Nepalese family of five for a week.

Tree lines have been raised and entire ridges previously cloaked in rhododendron (one of the attractions of the area and Nepal's national flower) denuded. Few trees are left within the Annapurna Sanctuary itself.

Virtually all food and housekeeping items have to be imported from Kathmandu and elsewhere, inflating local economies and introducing non-nutritious diets.

Inadequate sanitation facilities and indiscriminate practices by tourists and trekking groups have left virtual 'minefields' of human excreta and toilet paper. Toilets, if they exist at all, are often dangerously close to water sources. Non-biodegradable litter such as plastics, tins and bottles, used primarily by tourists, are disposed of in nearby streams or strewn in piles at the edge of the settlements.

Tourism, as a messenger of outside values and behaviours, has also affected local cultures. Village youths are easy prey to the seductiveness of Western consumer culture as tourists are laden with expensive trappings: hi-tech hiking gear, flashy clothes, cameras and electronic goods.

The Project, Implemented by the King

ACAP strives to ensure that the beneficiaries from trekking tourism and conservation activities will be the local people, at the same time making them the guardians of their resources. The approach is that of a grassroots philosophy that strongly discourages a handout philosophy. As a result traditional subsistence activities are woven into a framework of sound resource management, supplemented by small scale conservation and alternative energy projects to minimise the impact of tourists and upgrade the local standard of living."

In our recent visit to Ba Be National Park, we were upset to hear that the Park does not charge an entrance fee, rather this is collected by the local district authorities, with none of the revenue being given to the Park. It has also been said that both the Park and the district authorities are charging entrance fees for international visitors. Is this not bad publicity?

There appear to be tensions between the Park and district and provincial authorities. These tensions seem to be related to some extent to disagreement over the development of tourism in the Park and lack of clarity on the responsibilities for tourism in the Park.

The Park seems almost 'anti-tourism', or rather scared of it. This is not surprising if the Park feels powerless to exert any control over the development and growth of tourism, particularly if it is mass tourism.

The Park has the potential for small, controlled, low impact trekking Eco-tourism that includes overnight stays in villages within the park. The villages can hence benefit from tourism to the park by charging overnight and meal fees, as well as through the sale of agricultural produce (fruits, home cultivated NTFPs such as mushrooms and orchids and honey) and crafts. Residents from the villages can also be trained in language and guiding skills and employed by the park to lead the trekking tours. The present system of issuing permits for overnight stays needs radical change if local villages are to be allowed to benefit from Eco-tourism.

However, despite the potential, if the government's aim is to increase mass tourism (albeit nature-based tourism) to the area, and the Park has no control over tourism within its boundaries, any Eco-tourism initiative started could be overrun, in a short period of time.

For example, local authorities have begun to promote the Tay new rice festival as a means to bring in more tourists. Last year approximately 10,000 persons visited over a two day period. Naturally the lake is the major feature of the park, and over 100 diesel powered boats appeared to serve the crowds of tourists. The Park is very concerned with the use of diesel engines by locals, which are causing both water and noise pollution. Is this use compatible with an Eco-tourism experience and conservation of the park? Lack of co-operation and unclear management responsibilities will be detrimental in the long run to conservation of the area and the development of Eco-tourism.

Small and Local is Beautiful?

Eco-tourism is concerned with small scale, locally owned, built, managed facilities. Eco-tourism has three important benefits for developing countries:

1. facilities and infrastructure are simpler and less expensive than those demanded by conventional mass tourism;
2. being locally owned and operated Eco-tourism projects are not caught up in the need to conform to corporate Western multinational tourism concerns, and therefore can have a much higher input of local products, materials and labour. This means greater multiplier effects in the local economy, and also reduces import leakages and the remittances from expatriate labour which result from large-scale, foreign owned operations;
3. profits accrue locally instead of flowing back to the parent country.

BUT investing in Eco-tourism in developing countries is lucrative. In the face of foreign investors, try to think small and local. If foreign money is required, find the right partner, whether a company or an NGO, who has a more philanthropic bent, who understands the philosophy of Eco-tourism and has experience in Eco-tourism.

Vietnam is currently concerned with attracting foreign investment in tourism, in drawing up master plans for areas with large scale tourism and recreation projects to the sum of millions of USD dollars. Such scales and priorities are not appropriate for Eco-tourism.

The benefits of Eco-tourism to Vietnam can be lost due to:

- the international organisation of Eco-tourism (tours agents and other middlemen in host countries take their percentages);
- foreign investment in Eco-tourism (revenue is returned to the investor's country);
- inflationary pressures at a local level due to foreign involvement (demand for produce, materials, imported goods etc);

- loss of sovereignty with foreign 'take-over', and
- lack of participation of locals (in employment, training, management and operation etc). Locals may also be excluded from the natural attraction, their 'backyard', by price or other means.

A World Resources Institute report noted that Zimbabwe retains only an estimated 10% of nature tourism expenditures, while the Annapurna region in Nepal retains less than 10% (Ziffer, K. 1989). In Belize, 65% of the Belize Tourism Industry Association.

It is somewhat disturbing to hear that tourism developments (involving foreign investment) of Dan Kia resort near Da Lat, the Victoria Hotel in Sa Pa, the Dong Mo Cultural Village in Ha Tay are Eco-tourism developments.

Conclusion and Recommendations

There is no example of tourist use that is completely without impact. Eco-tourism does leave a mark on protected areas. It is a compromise that allows tourism but set limits, controls, strict management systems, monitoring feedback mechanisms etc. It is a compromise between the primary role of protected areas-protection and preservation of the environment-and providing local communities with development opportunities that can at the same time enhance conservation goals, if carried out properly.

Eco-tourism can effect and influence mainstream mass tourism, and indeed it can help make the rest of the tourism industry adopt more sustainable principles and act more responsibly and sustainably. This phenomenon is observable around the world.

However, I would argue that now Vietnam needs to be concerned with trying to make the entire tourism industry sustainable, not focus on Eco-tourism to achieve sustainable tourism development. In relying on, and waiting for Eco-tourism to reform the rest of the industry irreparable damage may be done and reforms, if they occur at all, will come slowly and may come too late. Eco-tourism and sustainable tourism principles need to be adopted together in a two-pronged approach.

Key Factors Required for Successful Eco-tourism

- Aim for strategic, holistic and detailed planning;
- Careful and integrated management:

a. forging strong inter ministerial co-operation between the ministries of planning and investment, science technology and environment, tourism, education and training, agriculture and rural development, and

b. being committed to management that facilitates and ensures input from all stakeholders: tour operators, protected area managers, government, NGOs, local communities etc;

- Establish a national Sustainable (Eco) Tourism Task force to develop a National Eco-tourism or Nature Tourism Strategy;
- Create an environment conducive to the establishment of a private sector Eco-tourism Association, independent Eco-tourism Commission and Community Eco-tourism Association;
- Intervene in the market e.g.: fees to protected areas, limits on numbers, regulations and Codes of Conduct for the industry (developed with the industry);
- Consider each natural area individually (eco and env impacts of tourism, what the area has to offer, local community needs and interaction with the environment, local infrastructure etc);
- Focus on the local and regional level-it is easier for nature tourism/Eco-tourism to be developed successfully at these levels;
- Start small and go slow;
- Believe that small is beautiful and quality is paramount;
- Invest in awareness raising, education and training for tourists, tour operators, local guides, protected area managers, local communities, local authorities;
- Aim to maximise local benefits for conservation and economic development;
- Aim to maximise local participation and involvement at all levels;
- Aim to maximise use of local products, materials;
- Aim to focus on recycling, waste management, alternative technologies and fuels. Manuals have been produced that provide practical information on such topics, we have a few and will be getting more;

- Constantly monitor and evaluate and develop a feedback mechanism for modifying growth and minimising impacts and setting limits.

The Impact of the Shadow State on Eco-tourism Policy

The shadow links that are ultimately responsible for decision making in Belize indicate evidence of a process that is more formalised than simply a matter of *ad hoc* or unco-ordinated corruption. Rather the links between the public and private sector, local elites and external capital constitute a shadow state, and this is nowhere more apparent than in the inability of the formal state apparatus to enforce environmental legislation in the Eco-tourism industry.

Unlike Sierra Leone, Belize—once dependent on primary commodities—is a major tourist destination for North America and Europe. Tourism is a relatively recent development that really began with the expansion of tourist facilities in the 1980s, but it is now Belize's single largest foreign exchange earner, and the Belize Tourist Board (BTB) estimated that in 1994 tourism earned the country Bz$150 million (US$75 million). According to BTB statistics, the three major tourist markets for Belize are the USA, Canada and Europe, and the number of visitors from the USA increased by 55% during the period 1991 to 1995.

However, the purpose of this article is to examine the similarities and differences between the Belizean and Sierra Leonean cases. This article will investigate the possible existence of a shadow state in Belize through an analysis of the Eco-tourism industry, its relationship with external capital, local elites and licit and illicit investment and trading networks. The existence of shadow links between the private sector, the public sector and criminal elements means that enforcement of environmental legislation is problematic in Belize. Since the country is promoted as an Eco-tourism destination, enforcement of regulations to ensure that tourism developments do not damage the environment is important. Belize has an extensive framework of environmental legislation, including the Environmental Protection Act, and it has established a Department of the Environment whose stated aim is to prevent and control pollution.

A common complaint among locally based tour guides and the conservation community was that, while legislation was in place, it was rarely enforced. Godsman Ellis, President of the Belize Eco-tourism Association, stated that policing was not carried out in the face of the country's low financial resources, limited manpower, inadequate technological and administrative resources, and its open borders, and that very few cases of environmental violations had been brought before the courts, despite the legislation that had been put in place. One interviewee, who was involved in marine conservation in Belize, stated that, although environmental impact assessments were legally required for all new tourism developments, the government office responsible for monitoring such assessments was completely overwhelmed by requests for assessments because it was so poorly staffed. In addition, when conservation authorities have tried to press for prosecutions for breaches of environmental legislation, they have faced opposition from powerful sets of interest groups. One example of this was an Ambergris Caye, when there was debate between the resident 'gringo' community, the local community and conservation officers over the fate of resort owners whose catamaran ran aground in the Hol Chan Marine Reserve, causing extensive damage to the coral reef. The incident occurred against a background of highly publicised environmental breaches by 'live-aboard' dive ships owned by external investors. The most high profile incidents involved the *Fantome* and the *Rembrandt Van Rijn* in the marine protected areas, Glovers Reef and Half Moon Caye (respectively). The companies that owned the vessels were offered options to compensate for the damage they had caused or risk having their licences revoked, but the local press reported that there was a perception that the owners were not sufficiently punished because of their high profile connections in Belize. The catamaran incident also occurred against a history of local resentment against foreign land and property owners who had settled on Ambergris Caye. A Department of Environment Report detailed that several foreign-owned resorts or hotels were not abiding by the legal requirements for construction and management of piers. This was especially contentious because several residents had complained that, while the regulations state all piers must be open to the public, any Belizean who went to the pier would immediately be removed by the owners or managers of the establishment.

In the case of the catamaran in San Pedro, those involved in the conservation community, such as Mito Paz, the Director of

Green Reef, were highly critical of the catamaran incident and felt that the owners should be taken to court. Those who opposed high levels of foreign ownership speculated that the catamaran ran aground because of the carelessness and general disrespect for the environment they associated with newcomers to the island. In contrast, external investors in the tourism industry in San Pedro were concerned that the incident was being used by local opponents to criticise the gringo community as a whole. One member of the gringo community, who had assisted in pulling the catamaran off the reef, vigorously argued that it was an accident that could have happened to any boat. In fact, the owners of the boat took the step of writing a public apology in the local *San Pedro Sun* in an attempt to quell rumours about negligence. In it they stated that the engine had failed and the winds had died, and so the boat ran on to the reef before the anchor could be dropped.

Despite the arguments between different interest groups in the tourist areas of Belize, it was clear that ultimately there was a perception among both sets of interest groups that a shadow decision-making process was underway and that this would determine the outcome regardless of the legislation. This indicated a perception that breaches of environmental legislation and wider problems with criminality among foreign and local elites were either overlooked, tolerated or actively supported and encouraged by key members of state agencies, because parts of the state apparatus had been co-opted by these powerful networks of elites. It is also important to provide the political context in which the shadow state operates. Within Belize it is essential to acknowledge the deep divide between supporters of the People's United Party (PUP) and those of the United Democratic Party (UDP). This division permeates local politics, can be exploited by foreign elites in the tourism industry and plays a central role in determining the coverage of certain issues in the Belizean press. In terms of the tourism industry it is important because key. gures in either party are able to offer significant levels of patronage to their supporters. The stakes became higher in 1997 because it was an election year when the opposition PUP were feted to win (and they achieved a landslide victory). Political opponents and economic competitors in Belize have pointed to the role of the current and former Ministers of Tourism and the Environment as major players in the tourism industry. The former Minister of Tourism and the Environment, Glenn Godfrey (PUP), has been able to utilise contacts in his own constituency, which covers the two prime tourist areas of Caye Caulker and Ambergris Caye. In particular, the construction of a new airstrip and condominiums on Caye Caulker have been credited to Godfrey. Indeed, one interviewee suggested that conservation organisations in Belize were. rm supporters of the PUP; political opponents of this party were keen to point out that conservation NGOs might have 'turned a blind eye' to his activities because they were PUP supporters.

The shadow state has also affected organisations that engage in lobbying on conservation issues, especially when they have fallen foul of the deep political divide between the PUP and UDP. The Lamanai Room Declaration of 1997, which detailed major environmental abuses in Belize and was signed by numerous local conservation agencies, including the Audubon Society and Coastal Zone Management Project, was criticised for political bias by those who supported the then UDP government. Victoria Collins, Editor of the *San Pedro Sun,* suggested that the Lamanai Room Declaration was perceived by UDP supporters as designed to strengthen the position of the PUP amid public speculation that an election was to be called.

The then Minister of Tourism and the Environment, Henry Young, accused the parties at Lamanai of trying to topple the UDP government. Over the course of the UDP government term, Young became a developer in Placencia, where large areas of ecologically important mangroves were cut to make way for tourism developments. Political opponents of such developments speculated that local business elites and external investors were able to seek protection from prosecution for environmental breaches because of their links with politically prominent. gures in Belize and with the ruling UDP. It is clear that, in accordance with Reno's model of the shadow state, local elites utilise informal networks to reward their clients. The Eco-tourism industry provides one example of the manner in which those elites can bestow political and economic favouritism upon their international and local supporters.

In promoting tourism as a development strategy, elites often aim to entice foreign investors and large international tour operators into the country to underwrite their own investments and patron-client networks. The involvement of foreign interests in the Belizean tourism industry has assisted the creation of a shadow state. The convergence of legal and illegal business interests with government interests is apparent in the development of coastal tourism. The dominance of foreign capital in the tourism industry is made possible by the compliance of and collaboration with local companies and the political and economic elite. This is especially the case in Belize, where there is a legal stipulation that international tour operators and investors/must have a Belizean partner. In Belize a few key families own or are major. gures in the operation of a number of tourism-and transport-related businesses, and as a result tourists brought in by overseas operators can be funnelled through a series of businesses all owned by one family or elite group which is ultimately reliant on international tour operators. Historically, on Ambergris Caye three key families, Blake, Alamilla and Parham, who were also related through marriage, have been economically dominant. They held sway over the development of the island through gun running to the Santa Cruz Maya in Mexico during the middle of the 19th century, and later thanks to ownership of coconut and timber plantations, and other land. Furthermore, Gach Guerrero, Secretary of the conservation organisation, Green Reef, is also owner of Amigo Travel and manager of Island Air, a member of the Board of the Ambergris Caye Historical Society, an officer of the Belize Tourism Industry Association, and the 1997 and 1998 chairman of the International Sea and Air Festival. Similarly, the Vega family on Caye Caulker own the tour operator Belize Odyssey and the Vega Inn, are involved in environmental and tourism consultancy and a. shing business, and members of the family sit on the BTIA, the Protected Areas National Council and the Coastal Zone Management Programme. However, it is not unusual in a country with a relatively small population to. nd that certain individuals and families have a major role in the public and private sectors.

An examination of the ways that land for tourism development is sold and resold in the coastal zone reveals the extent to which external capital is involved in the expansion of Eco-tourism in Belize. For example, large parcels of land on Ambergris Caye are owned by a US-based company, Sunset Coves Ltd. The role of Sunset Coves on Ambergris Caye was the subject of some debate in the local press, specially the *San Pedro Sun*. Sunset Coves began as a San Pablo Town Board project, and the land was paid for by local islanders who were promised they would be full partners in its development. The scheme had support and assistance from the local MP (and former Minister of Tourism and the Environment) Glenn Godfrey. However, Sunset Coves went into receivership in 1996 because of an unpaid debt of Bz$300 000 ($150 000), and as a result it was sold to Raymond Yusi of Western Caribbean Properties, based in California. This pattern of sale of land to external investors is common in the tourist dominated islands of Belize. The *State of the Coastal Zone Report* (1995) indicated that leased national lands were often sold to external investors or subdivided in joint ventures and then sold on to the highest bidders, who were primarily non-residents. An examination of the tax and valuation rolls for Ambergris Caye revealed that there was a small number of US citizens, including Albert Dugan, Corrie McDermott, Gerry McDermott and Ian Ritchie, who owned or controlled the sales of large swathes of land on the island. Ian Ritchie was formerly the owner of Southwinds Property, which facilitated the purchase of properties in Belize by external investors; he is also owner of a major resort (Captain Sharkey's) on Ambergris Caye and is beginning land speculation in Roatan in Honduras. A Department of Environment Compliance Monitoring Site report for San Pedro states that: Several foreigners who live or own hotels/resorts along the beach prohibit people from using or passing through the beach reserve ... totally disregarding the 66 feet reserve as required by the National Lands Act ... these people do not even own the beach and yet they lay claim to ownership by not allowing anyone to use the beach.

In their election manifesto for 1998– 2003, *Set Belize Free,* the PUP claimed that tourism had decline thanks to corrupt practices that allowed 'unscrupulous foreigners to side step Belizeans' and that the BTB had been 'plagued by mismanagement and corruption'.

Caye Chapel (owned by a former mining millionaire from Kentucky) has proved to be a controversial tourism development that highlights the links between foreign investors, support from local political and economic elites and local perceptions of corrupt business practices. The island was completely re-landscaped and artificially expanded to provide an exclusive tourist resort. The development of the island included building a beach and a golf course, and dredging for sand to build the beach and to allow larger boats to dock at the island. In the process, the dredging stirred up the sea bed, disturbed lobster, sheries and destroyed Caye Caulker shing grounds. The island has been perceived in Belize as an example of an environment being totally remastered in the pursuit of tourism development. The alliances which form the shadow state in Belize ensured that the island could be overhauled to conform to the image of Cayes presented to potential visitors. There was a great deal of local speculation about the way in which the owner of the island appeared to be able to dredge around it and build a beach without proper permission. Those who opposed the development of Caye Chapel speculated that the owner was allowed to undertake such activities because he was protected by the highest political authorities in the country in return for free trips to the island, and that the owner had been careful to pay the relevant officials in order to avoid environmental regulations. For example, one interviewee stated that Caye Chapel was a glaring example of what happened to the environment in Belize when a corrupt politician and a foreign millionaire cooperated, and that it was all about money and there was no-one willing to stop it. Caye Chapel will have its own airstrip and casino to allow gamblers to direct from Miami to the island. Critics of such tourist developments have complained that while the USA and UK berate Belize for failing to tackle money laundering, drug trafficking and a possibly corrupt offshore sector, it is the citizens of these countries that are most likely to avail themselves of the facilities on offer in Belize.

Another example of the links between local elites and external property investors was the highly controversial plan to build a dolphin park called Cangrejo Caye. Aspects of the process to create the park indicate that common forms of public consultation were circumvented in order to push through a major tourist development despite local opposition. Cangrejo Caye was to be developed by a Mexican company, Dolphin International, and it offered tourists an opportunity to swim with 'semi-captive dolphins', along the lines of the highly successful and lucrative dolphin park in Xcaret in Mexico. The residents of Ambergris Caye were first informed of the plans for the park when an advert appeared in *Destination Belize 1997* that encouraged tourists to visit it before it was even built. As a result Dolphin International embarked on a public relations campaign, and local business people who were the promoters of Dolphin International ensured that donations to local charities received favourable coverage in the local press, including when the company sponsored the San Pedro football team and it was renamed the Dolphins in honour of its new backers.

In addition, Dolphin International, which also used the name Cangrejo Caye Educational Experience Ltd., invited a number of Belizean 'movers and shakers' to a free weekend at its dolphin resort at Xcaret in Mexico. Cangrejo Caye was part of a redevelopment programme for Ambergris Caye that included shrimp farming by Nova Shrimp Ltd., the construction of an airstrip and a new pier, all of which was to be developed under the auspices of the North Ambergris Caye Development Corporation (NACDC).

The dolphin park was opposed by some local tour guides who viewed it as unwelcome competition and as contrary to the spirit of Eco-tourism in Belize. Tour operators Daniel and Elodia Nunez openly opposed the park because they disagreed with the idea of keeping wild animals in a captive environment to satiate tourist desires. They stated that they believed that the dolphins at Xcaret were slowly dying, partly because dolphins like to swim freely over large distances in order to feed and so keeping them in pens would be cruel and detrimental to the environment, since the dolphins would eat out such a small area.

According to Daniel and Elodia Nunez, in 1998 the park was forced by local opposition to accept demands for a full environmental impact assessment before construction was begun. This strong pro-conservation lobby was identified by Victoria Collins, Editor of the *San Pedro Sun*, as a major factor in preventing the construction of Cangrejo Caye. Opponents of the development there were keen to speculate that the owners had failed to pay off the right officials in the opposition People's United Party (PUP), which was tipped to win the next election. Indeed, after the PUP had won the general election of 1998, the Urban Planning Officer for Ambergris Caye, Al Westby, remarked that the investors from Dolphin International had been invited back once more to Belize to discuss the future development of Cangrejo Caye further. The case of the dolphin park can also be viewed as an indicator of the extent of the shadow links between state agencies and the private sector.

National Tourism Policy

In order to develop tourism in India in a systematic manner, position it as a major engine of economic growth and to harness its direct and multiplier effects for employment and poverty eradication in an environmentally sustainable manner, the National

Tourism Policy was formulated in the year 2002. Broadly, the "Policy" attempts to:-

- Position tourism as a major engine of economic growth;
- Harness the direct and multiplier effects of tourism for employment generation, economic development and providing impetus to rural tourism;
- Focus on domestic tourism as a major driver of tourism growth.
- Position India as a global brand to take advantage of the burgeoning global travel trade and the vast untapped potential of India as a destination;
- Acknowledges the critical role of private sector with government working as a pro-active facilitator and catalyst;
- Create and develop integrated tourism circuits based on India's unique civilization, heritage, and culture in partnership with States, private sector and other agencies; and
- Ensure that the tourist to India gets physically invigorated, mentally rejuvenated, culturally enriched, spiritually elevated and "feel India from within".

Scheme for Product/Infrastructure and Destination Development

The focus under this scheme is on improving the existing products and developing new tourism products to world class standards. For infrastructure and product development, the Ministry of Tourism has been providing Central Financial Assistance to the State Governments during the 9th Five Year Plan which resulted in strengthening of the infrastructure and product development in the country. The scheme has been restructured during the 10th Five Year Plan to meet the present day infrastructure requirements. The past experience had been that a large number of small projects had been funded under the Scheme, spreading the resources very thinly, which at times had not created the desired impact. The focus in the Tenth Plan has been to fund large projects of infrastructure or product development in an integrated manner.

Under the revised scheme, the destinations are carefully selected based on the tourism potential. Master planning of these destinations is undertaken so as to develop them in an integrated holistic manner. The master plan is suppose to tie up all backward and forward linkages, including environmental considerations. Realizing the importance of destination development, the total outlay for this sector has been increased substantially. Important tourist destinations in each State, in consultation with the State Governments, are taken up for development. This include activities ranging from preparation of master plans to implementation of the master plans. The destinations are selected in consultation with the State/UT Governments.

Scheme for Integrated Development of Tourist Circuits

Under this Central Financial Assistance scheme the Ministry of Tourism Government of India has been extending assistance to States for development of tourism infrastructure. Experience has shown that in the past funds under the CFA have been used to fund a large number of small isolated projects, spread throughout the length and breadth of the country resulting in the resources being spread very thinly. Therefore, in order to provide quick and substantial impact, during the 10th Five Year Plan, this new scheme of Integrated Development of Tourist Circuits have been taken up. The objective of the scheme is to identify tourist circuits in the country on an annual basis, and develop them to international standards. The aim is to provide all infrastructure facilities required by the tourists within these circuits. The Ministry of Tourism aim at convergence of resources and expertise through coordinated action with States/UTs and private sector.

Scheme of Assistance for Large Revenue Generating Projects

It is recognized that the development of tourism infrastructure projects requires very large investment that may not be possible out of the budgetary resources of the Government of India alone. In order to remove these shortcomings and to bring in private sector, corporate and institutional resources as well as techno-managerial efficiencies, it is proposed to promote large revenue generating projects for development of tourism infrastructure in public private partnerships and in partnerships with other Government / Semi-Government agencies.

Large revenue generating project, which can be admissible for assistance under this scheme, should be a project, which is also a tourist attraction, or used by tourists and generates revenue through a levy of fee or user charges on the visitors. Projects like Tourist trains, Cruise vessels, Cruise Terminals, Convention

Centres, Golf Courses etc. would qualify for assistance. However, this is only an illustrative list.

Hotel & Restaurant component will not be eligible for assistance under the scheme either on a stand-alone basis or as an integral part of some other project. Besides hotel & restaurants, procurement of vehicles and sports facilities like stadiums will also not be eligible for assistance under the scheme.

Scheme for Support to Public Private Partnerships in Infrastructure (Viability Gap Funding)

Development of infrastructure require large investments that cannot be undertaken out of public financing alone. Thus, in order to attract private capital as well as techno-managerial efficiencies associated with it, the government is committed to promoting Public-Private Partnerships (PPPs) in infrastructure development. This scheme has been put into effect for providing financial support to bridge the viability gap of infrastructure projects undertaken through Public Private Partnerships.

Scheme for Market Development Assistance (MDA)

The Marketing Development Assistance Scheme (MDA), administered by the Ministry of Tourism, Government of India, provides financial support to approved tourism service providers (i.e. hoteliers, travel agents, tour operators, tourist transport operators etc., whose turnover include foreign exchange earnings also) for undertaking the following tourism promotional activities abroad:

- Sales-cum-study tour
- Participation in fairs/exhibitions
- Publicity through printed material.

Recent Initiatives

During 11th Five Year Plan (2007-2012) Ministry of Tourism propose to continue supporting creation of world class infrastructure in the country so that existing tourism products can be further improved and expanded to meet new market requirements and enhance the competitiveness of India as a tourist destination. In consultation with the State Governments and UTs the Ministry of Tourism have identified several tourist circuits and destinations for integrated development. During the current financial year the Ministry has sanctioned so far Rs.323.00 crore for various projects throughout the country. This is an all time record and will facilitate timely execution of projects during the working season.

Some of the important infrastructure projects which have been sanctioned in the current financial year are:

Beach and Sea Tourism

- MOT has sanctioned a project of Rs.5.00 crore for development and beautification of Beach Promenade in Puducherry.
- Another project for development of walkway along the bank of river Arasalar and Vanjiiar in Karaikal, Puducherry (Rs.4.78 crore)
- The project of Development of Marina bach in Tamilnadu has been sanctioned (Rs.4.92 crore).

Eco Tourism

- A project of Eco tourism for development of Horsely Hill in Chittoor Distt. of Andhra Pradesh has been sanctioned.
- The project of development of Satkosi in Orissa (Rs. 4.25 crore) has been sanctioned in which Interpretation Centre, Landscaping, Elephant camps, Trekking park, Watch Towers and parking facilities, etc. are proposed to be developed.
- MOT has sanctioned a project for development of Eco tourism in Morni-Pinjore Hills and Sultanpur National Park in Haryana for which Rs. 2.63 crore have been sanctioned.
- The project of Integrated Development of Tribal Circuit with special focus on Eco tourism in Spiti in Himachal Pradesh has been approved for Rs. 6.98 crore.
- Development of Wayanad in Kerala for an amount of Rs.2.01 crore.
- Development of Tourist Circuit (Western Assam Circuit) Dhubari-Mahamaya-Barpeta-Hajo has been sanctioned for an amount of Rs.4.97 crore.
- Development of Mechuka Destination (Rs.4.41 crore in Arunachal Pradesh).
- Development of Tourist Destination at Khensa at a cost of Rs.4.58 crore in Nagaland.

- Circuit-Udhyamandalam-Madumalai-Anaimalai, Tamil Nadu Rs.4.39 crore.

Projects for NE Region

- The INA Memorial Complex at Moirang in Manipur is being renovated and tourist facilities are being developed (Rs.82 lakhs).
- Tourism infrastructure is being developed near Pakhai Wildlife Sanctuary in Arunachal Pradesh (Rs. 5.00 crore)
- Gayaker Sinyi Lake at Itanagar is being developed at a cost of Rs.5.00 crore.
- Tourist infrastructure is being developed in Nathula-Memmencho-Kuppu tourist circuit in Sikkim (Rs.4.54 crore)
- MOT has sanctioned a project for development of Tizu Kukha as Adventure Destination in Nagaland (Rs.4.99 crore)
- Projects for Jammu & Kashmir.

MOT has sanctioned a project for development of tourism infrastructure in Leh (Rs.4.95 crore), Bungus Valley (Rs.2.31 crore), Kargil (Rs.4.84 crore), Poonch (Rs.4.50 crore), various villages around Sonmarg (Rs.1.08 crore), development of Gurez and Telail Valley (Rs.3.66 crore), Patnitop (Rs.2.83 crore), Dandi Pora (3.45 crore), Anantnag (Rs.2.1 crore), Shri Amarnath Yatra Marg (Rs.7.00 crore), Bhaderwah (Rs. 4.12 crore), Kishtwar (Rs. 2.81 crore), Wullar Lake (Rs.2.06 crore) and Rajouri (Rs.4.34 crore). Tourist Information Centre, Public amenities; approach roads, shelters, signages, etc. will be developed in these projects so that tourists who are visiting Jammu & Kashmir should have trouble free experience the beauty and bounty of the region.

5

Angling Eco-tourism

Angling Eco-tourism: Issues, Guidelines and Experience from Kamchatka

Recreational fishing is an important component of the tourism industry and an important component of regional economies around the world. When angling tourists reach threatened freshwater ecosystems, however, there is a risk of degrading the very fishery and landscapes that attracted them, thwarting long-term economic development prospects and reducing biodiversity. Following the emergence of catch-andrelease recreational fishing, we believe that angling can be legitimately considered a form of Eco-tourism that contributes positively to conservation, science, and local or regional economic development. With successful angling Eco-tourism projects, anglers and local populations can become viable constituencies for conservation. We describe the angler-sponsored research programme of the Kamchatka Steelhead Project as one case study where many aspects of a successful Eco-tourism project were present. We then propose guidelines for future angling Eco-tourism projects and address opportunities and obstacles to the continued development of angling Eco-tourism.

In the United States, over 34 million people participated in recreational angling and 29.4 million recreational fishing licenses were issued in 2001 (American Sportfishing Association, 2004; USFWS, 2002). The revenues from fishing licenses support fish and wildlife management agencies at all levels of government, and the expenditures from recreational fishing contribute to local and regional economies, especially in regions where fisheries have been preserved in pristine or near-pristine conditions. Recreational fishing in Alaska is a $1 billion per year industry, more than

$500million of which comes in direct in-state expenditures, including money spent on guides, supplies, accommodations and provisions. More than 11,000 Alaskans are employed to support the recreational fishing industry, many of them in regions that are otherwise job-poor (American Sportfishing Association, 2003). The value of these expenditures is multiplied as funds ripple through regional economies.

Reviews of recreational fishing tourism tend to focus on the economic impact of anglers travelling from one location to another in search of quality angling experiences (Ditton et al., 2002). Other analyses, however, have argued that a fish caught by a recreational angler may be worth 40 times more to the economy than the same fish caught as part of a commercial harvest (Hayden, 2000). The 1994 value to British Columbia, Canada (consumer, worker and business surplus, plus government revenue) of its 431,000 commercially-caught chinook in that year has been calculated at CDN$8.2 million, while the value from 239,000 recreationally-caught fish has been calculated at CDN$96.5 million (Gislason, 2001). Well-regulated recreational fishing is an economically viable use of a natural resource that can be both lucrative and sustainable for local communities and ecosystems.

Despite its attractiveness as a vehicle for economic development and sustainability, recreational fishing ventures in vulnerable ecosystems like those of Alaska pose potentially serious ecological risks. Shortsighted choices made by tourism promoters and regulatory agencies in terms of lodging and transportation options, energy and resource use, visitor quotas, and fishing techniques can degrade fisheries and stress the ecological resources of water bodies. Practiced recklessly, recreational fishing can lead to overfishing just as commercial fishing can. In the United States, for example, the recreational fishing sector is responsible for 23% of landings of 'species of concern' (Coleman et al., 2004).

Promoting a sustainable model for angling Eco-tourism is in the interest of natural resource managers, environmentalists, tourism promotion agencies, and local communities. In parts of the world, recreational fishing may be the primary tourism attraction and, if pursued as Eco-tourism, could form a vital component of sustainable development. To date, the literature has not examined the acceptable forms of angling Eco-tourism and only one regional Eco-tourism certification body has issued guidelines (Nature's Best, Sweden). It would be wise to address and discuss the issues in a comprehensive way rather than wait for Eco-tourism certification bodies or entrepreneurs to take the lead.

Angling as Eco-tourism

Perhaps the two fundamental attractions of Eco-tourism are that it can contribute positively both to conservation efforts and to local economies (Honey, 1999). While angling tourism holds these potentials, the literature has not clarified the status of angling tourism in regards to Eco-tourism. The concept of Eco-tourism encompasses three primary dimensions: a focus on nature, sustainable management, and environmental education (Blamey, 2001). These aspects position Eco-tourism primarily as a subset of nature tourism and entirely as a subset of sustainable tourism (Weaver, 2001).

Traditionally, the limit to viewing angling as a form of Eco-tourism has focused on the character of its environmental impacts without engaging with the question of whether or not those impacts are sustainable over the long term. Fishing is typically viewed as a consumptive activity that provides products – though the status of catch and release fishing is uncertain – and the implicit argument is that non-consumptive activities, which provide experiences, have lower impacts and therefore should uniquely qualify as Eco-tourism (Weaver, 2001).

There are problems with using the consumptive/non-consumptive dichotomy to define Eco-tourism, however, since all tourism involves consumption on some level. Virtually all forms of tourism burn fossil fuels in transportation, produce cumulative impacts from visitor footprints, and use resources to produce souvenirs (Weaver, 2001). It would be more appropriate to place tourism activities along a continuum that examines the particular impacts of each activity in detail and acknowledges that most tourism activities provide both products and experiences (Vaske et al., 1982). It is likely that most capture fishing would fall closer to the consumptive side of this continuum, while catch and release fishing would lie nearer to the middle.

Other, similar criteria have also been proposed as essential points for Eco-tourism. Duffus and Dearden (1990) draw a line by examining the mindset of the participant and excluding activities where the goal is to remove an organism from the natural world. Fennell (2000) has argued for a 'moral principle' to be included in definitions of Eco-tourism that would identify activities 'founded upon respect for plants and animals'. These two subjective metrics, however, are problematic criteria for defining Eco-tourism due to their emphasis on process and intent rather than performance. If defined solely by process, Eco-tourism may look good on paper and yet still irreparably harm the environment, as has been seen in the attempts to certify Eco-tourism ventures (Honey & Rome, 2001) or in case studies of failed Eco-tourism ventures. Performance on the ground must be the defining criteria of Eco-tourism.

The major definitions of Eco-tourism, including those of Ceballos-Lascura'in, The Eco-tourism Society, the Eco-tourism Association of Australia, the National Eco-tourism Strategy of Australia, and Tickell (all quoted in Blamey, 2001), support this view by placing emphasis on sustainability and minimal impact rather than non-consumption per se. For example, The Eco-tourism Society's definition is 'responsible travel to natural areas which conserves the environment and improves the well-being of local people' (1991). The National Eco-tourism Strategy of Australia mentions that Eco-tourism is 'managed to be ecologically sustainable', which involves an 'appropriate return to the local community and long-term conservation of the resource' (Allcock et al., 1994). Honey (1999) argues that, while generally nonconsumptive, Eco-tourism can include consumptive activities such as hunting if they are 'sustainable industries based on renewable resources'. Recreational fishing can be a sustainable industry when pursued responsibly. Without ignoring the poor status of overfished species, there exist many fish populations around the world that are healthy and can support smallscale extraction in ways that will not diminish future population health. For the purposes of angling Eco-tourism, the emergence and widespread acceptance of catch-and-release recreational fishing has created an unprecedented opportunity. Valuable sport fisheries in both saltwater and freshwater have recently been converted primarily to catch-and-release. By regulation, the most accessible and popular wild steelhead fisheries in British Columbia are managed on a catch-and-release basis (Hooton, 2002a).

Other advances in angler ethics also contribute to the potential sustainability of recreational fishing. The National Marine Fisheries

Service Code of Angling Ethics, developed with the participation of both angling groups and conservationists, specifies limiting catch to the desired species and size and using techniques that minimise harm to fish when releasing them (NMFS, 1999).

These approaches include many techniques. Fly hooks, for example, typically catch in the periphery of a fish's jaws or mouth and produce less damage than the deeper hookings of lures and, in particular, bait. Post-release mortality rates in steelhead fisheries in British Columbia, Canada, range from 10% for bait fishing and 3% for lures to 1% for fly-fishing (Hooton, 2002b). Reduced exposure to air (under 30 seconds for), handling with wet hands, and reduced 'playing' with a fish are also thought to decrease mortality rates in catch and release fishing (Catch and Release Foundation, 2001; Hooton, 2002b). Avoiding the use of non-native species as live bait and unwashed fishing gear in multiple waters can lower the risk of disease and invasive species being introduced into a river.

More generally, several practices can reduce angler 'efficiency' (catch per unit effort), including the avoidance of bait, fishing from shore rather than boats, flyfishing rather than spincasting, and using barbless hooks. For example, the probability of capture in flyfishing may be as low as one-fifth that of bait fishing. By reducing the number of fish caught per angler, a river's carrying capacity can support a larger number of fishermen, thereby providing a greater economic opportunity for the region. With healthy populations and moderate levels of fishing, the inevitable impacts on fish populations may be minimal and sustainable for the natural ecosystems in which a recreational fishing Eco-tourism operation occurs.

Beyond environmental sustainability, however, Eco-tourism's concept of sustainable management includes economic and social considerations. Minimising negative impacts is an identifying aspect of sustainable tourism, while Eco-tourism is additionally expected to contribute positively to conservation and local economies.

With this in mind, recreational fishing Eco-tourism presents particular opportunities to enhance conservation activities and local communities through new and alternative revenue streams. Fishing permits, a concept with which anglers are familiar, provide a straightforward method to raise funds for conservation or economic development, while park fees are an alternative method. The intensely local experience of fishing in a given water body has the potential to convince tourists to make direct donations for local conservation efforts if such channels are readily available. These donations can be facilitated and encouraged by travel operations.

Similar to many other forms of Eco-tourism, recreational fishing trips are often guided. Properly trained, these guides and other staff can be hired from local communities. Products and services for the fishing operation can be procured locally to maximise local economic impact. Where the infrastructure or capacity to provide tourism services and products locally does not exist, tourism operators can assist in developing these capabilities.

In Costa Rica, tourists practicing catch and release angling for billfish spent $17.8 million in the 1993–1994 season (Ditton & Grimes, 1995). British Columbia's Skeena River steelhead fishery, also managed on a catch and relase basis, is worth at least $1.9 million per year. The Togiak National Wildlife Refuge in Alaska provides more than 50 jobs and contributes more than $1.5 million to the local economy. Properly managed and practiced, recreational fishing Eco-tourism has a great potential to contribute positively to conservation and local development efforts while engaging in a sustainable activity. Implementing Eco-tourism on the ground, however, may be a complex task.

Case Study: Kamchatka Steelhead Project

Kamchatka is a 1250 km peninsula in the far east of the Russian Federation, bordered to the east by the Pacific Ocean and to the west by the Sea of Okhotsk. Economic development on this remote peninsula has been sparse due to historical isolation of the region under the Soviet Union, and large areas of the peninsula have been left relatively wild. Poaching is widespread, however, in part due to high unemployment rates, and constitutes a major threat to the health of certain salmon runs. Oil and gas development, which would pose a serious threat to salmon habitat, is being considered as an economic development strategy. There are few plans for the sustainable use of regional renewable resources, and Eco-tourism has been called the 'best opportunity for an environmentally sustainable industry employing a broad range of local people' (Newell, 2004). In the early to mid-1990s, however, tourism infrastructure was either scarce or non-existent.

From 1994–2003, a partnership between the Wild Salmon Centre (Portland, Oregon, USA), and the Ichthyology Department of Moscow State University (Moscow, Russia) operated an angler-sponsored scientific research programme on the Kamchatka peninsula. The Flathead Lake Biological Station of the University of Montana (Missoula, Montana, USA) also joined this effort in later years.

The angler-sponsored programme was designed to fund scientific expeditions and was one of the pioneers in bringing paying foreigners to the peninsula. Before its transfer in 2002 to an independent non-profit, the angler-sponsor programme was part of the Kamchatka Steelhead Project (KSP), a 20-year research effort dedicated to the study and conservation of Kamchatka's Oncorhynchus (parasalmo) mykiss – both the anadromous steelhead (syomga) and resident rainbow trout (mikizha) life histories. The steelhead and other salmonids of Kamchatka are unique for their large sizes, healthy populations, and wide range of life histories. Some individual river systems in Kamchatka host as many as six species of Pacific salmon, plus grayling, varieties of trout, and three species of char. In total, the rivers of Kamchatka are believed to serve as the spawning grounds for as much as one-quarter of Pacific salmon stocks. Numerous human communities rely upon these healthy salmon stocks, as do half of the global population of Steller's sea eagles, the world's largest population of brown bears, and 1800 Steller's sea lions.

Participants in the programme included scientists from the United States and Russia and conservation-minded anglers from the United States and elsewhere. Anglers supported the conservation mission both by funding the scientific research and by directly assisting in the collection of biological samples through catch and release fly-fishing. This is a method shown to have low post-release mortality in steelhead. After an angler caught a fish, the angler and researchers collected data on length, girth, weight, sex, scales (to determine life history), and tissue samples for genetic and protein analysis. Individual fish were tagged to track migrations and determine population structure.

The logistics of bringing visitors to Kamchatka were, and remain, complex, but can provide many opportunities for economic benefits to accrue at the regional and local levels, if properly planned. Anglers flew on Magadan Air, a regionally-owned airline for whom the programme was a major client. Anglers typically spent one night during the trip in a hotel in Petropavlosk-Kamchatskiy, the capital of Kamchatka. Due to the remoteness of the region, Russian helicopters were used extensively for transport to and from fishing lodges. The camps and lodges were small in scale and were Russian-owned. Local outfitters ran the trips in Kamchatka and cooks were hired locally, while guides came from Russia and the United States.

As local guides' language and service skills did not meet client expectations, the programme began to train guides from a pool of current students and graduates of the English language faculty of a local university. These efforts built critical local capacity for tourism. However, guide training did not emphasise natural history and guides typically placed little emphasis on education while in the field. From 1994–2003, more than 600 angler-sponsors participated in expeditions supporting the Kamchatka Steelhead Project. At the programme's peak in 2002, an estimated $650,000 in one year was contributed to the economy of the Kamchatka Peninsula through expenditures on local outfitters, helicopter transportation, and field expenses (Klimenko, 2004). Trip costs were high, making this a relatively elite activity, but such expenses may be unavoidable in areas of the world where travel and logistical costs are significant. High accessibility costs are also undoubtedly a key factor in the health of the studied steelhead populations.

The programme's major scientific advances include the discovery of five distinct life histories of O. mykiss in Western Kamchatka and the observation of anadromous O. mykiss parents producing resident rainbow trout offspring, and vice versa. Scientific papers were published from this project in the Journal of Ichthyology and other leading Russian and international journals. In addition, the presence of anglers and scientists on remote salmon-rich rivers during the spawning season caused reductions in illegal poaching for caviar, the primary threat to these salmon populations.

Environmental impacts of the programme included the heavy reliance on air travel, a necessity given the landscape but also an energy-intensive mode of travel. Lodge construction involved the installation of helicopter pads and other landscape modifications. Power at the lodges was produced with diesel generators, the fuel for which also had to be flown in. The project conducted feasibility studies into renewable sources of energy, including wind, solar and micro-hydro, but was not able to implement any of these proposals due to high costs.

Overall, however, environmental impacts would be considered low, primarily due to the small size of the angling and research operations and the efforts made to spread trips out over the fishing season and over the length of the river. On the healthy rivers where the trips occurred, mortality due to catch and release fly-fishing was not a significant factor. In the rare cases of direct steelhead mortality, the fish were taken for full laboratory analyses as part of the expedition's mortality take quota, issued by the Federal Ministry of Natural Resources. Cultural impacts were also low or non-existent, though in this case a key factor was the isolation of tourists in wilderness areas. Kamchatka Steelhead Project's angler-sponsored research programme offers one case study of a partnership between conservation groups, research teams, anglers, and local organisations that may serve as a valuable model for future angling Eco-tourism operations. Such operations would need to more fully implement educational and interpretive aspects to be considered Eco-tourism, however. While the Kamchatka project model may not be appropriate in all contexts, it demonstrates angling with a strong conservation science orientation, firm standards for environmental protection, partnerships between diverse groups, and progress towards sustainable development and local community involvement. The project produced tangible benefits to conservation through discouragement of poaching activities, increased knowledge about salmon and steelhead biology, donations to a conservation non-profit, support for local economic development through outfitter payments, and increased local and worldwide visibility for the threats facing a globally-important ecosystem. Potential future donors to Kamchatka conservation efforts were also identified.

With this case study as an innovative example, angling Eco-tourism has to potential to make a viable contribution to both regional economic development and social and environmental sustainability.

Guidelines for Angling Eco-tourism

To assist in the development of new Eco-tourism ventures and to evaluate operations marketed as Eco-tourism, many certification and eco-labelling programmes have been developed over the past decades, including over 250 voluntary initiatives around the world.

In referring to codes of conduct, a similar concept, Issaverdis (2001) commented that these initiatives can 'play a part in the overall continuum of developing industry professionalism and can be a useful means of introducing standards to sectors of the tourism industry'.

All such efforts must be based on firm standards and guidelines, but to date, angling Eco-tourism standards do not exist in the literature and the only Eco-tourism body to issue angling Eco-tourism certification criteria – in Swedish – is Nature's Best (The Swedish Eco-tourism Association and The Swedish Travel and Tourism Council, 2002a). Given the vast numbers of angling tourists, standards are a pressing concern.

Any guidelines should flow naturally from the definitions of Eco-tourism. Greater direction, however, can be found in expanded descriptions such as Honey's (1999) eight characteristics of Eco-tourism: (1) involves travel to natural sites; (2) minimises impact; (3) builds environmental awareness; (4) provides direct financial benefits for conservation; (5) provides financial benefits and empowerment for local communities; (6) respects local culture; (7) is sensitive to the host country's political environment and social climate; and (8) supports human rights and international labour agreements. A comparable example is the six overarching criteria of the successful Nature's Best Eco-tourism certification programme in Sweden: (1) respect the limitations of the destination – minimise negative impact in nature and culture; (2) support the local economy; (3) make all the company's operations environmentally sustainable; (4) contribute actively to conservation; (5) promote the joy of discovery, knowledge and respect; and (6) quality and safety all the way through (The Swedish Eco-tourism Association and The Swedish Travel and Tourism Council, 2002a).

Out of the above and other examples, we distilled the following six primary areas that guidelines should address in describing angling Eco-tourism.

Nature Experience

While many recreational fishing tourism operations will focus on catching large fish and/or many fish, an Eco-tourism operation needs to take a broader perspective and view the fish within the complex ecosystem needed for their survival. By building clients' appreciation for the beauty and complexity of these ecosystems through direct fishing experiences, Eco-tourism can enlist their support for place-based conservation efforts. Client expectations, impressions, and lessons are shaped from the moment they choose an Eco-tourism programme, and therefore Eco-tourism operations need to have clear objectives from their first interaction with potential clients (Gruin & Rogers, 2004).

Location

Tourism operations are centered around direct experiences and appreciation of fresh or salt water ecosystems and their native fish.

Marketing

Trips are advertised and sold to clients explicitly as angling Eco-tourism trips or as angling Eco-tourism components in broader tourism packages.

Education and Interpretation

Education is a central aspect of many Eco-tourism definitions due to its power to build an 'intellectual, emotional and even spiritual connection between people and places' (Weiler & Ham, 2001). In all interactions, operators should accurately describe the ecosystem in which anglers will be fishing as well as the cultures of surrounding areas.

Education can occur through direct interactions between clients and guides, as well as through reading materials, maps, and poster boards. Fish are important components of many aquatic ecosystems and anglers should be informed of the many processes that contribute to a healthy ecosystem – salmon for example support terrestrial ecosystems by carrying marine nutrients upstream during their spawning migrations (Cederholm et al., 1999).

In order to build future stewards, clients should be informed of the major threats to ecosystems and cultures, the conservation efforts being conducted in the area, and what they can do to help these efforts. As fishing guides will likely be a client's primary contact in an angling Eco-tourism operation, guide training is a critical aspect of a high-quality experience.

Training pertinent to the broader goals of Eco-tourism will be especially important in the angling Eco-tourism sector, since guides will likely come from a recreational fishing background where the traditional focus is typically more tightly restricted to catching numerous large fish.

Knowledge Sharing

Tourism operators share their knowledge of local ecosystems and cultures, and the knowledge of other competent bodies, with customers before and during operations in order to build awareness, respect, and a sense of stewardship.

Guide Training

Guides are trained in the natural history of the area, local cultures, and sustainable tour operating techniques.

Environmentally-sustainable Operations

It is important to understand whether a particular water body is appropriate for angling Eco-tourism and to know the level of angling that the ecosystem can support sustainably. The case study demonstrated how consultation with independent biologists and non-governmental conservation groups can help in finding answers to these questions. Government biologists can also provide assistance.

We suggest setting overall fish mortality limits for the tourism sector in order to avoid 'tragedy of the commons' situations where cumulative impacts from individuals add together to far exceed an ecosystem's carrying capacity. For ease of application, limits should be set by species and water basin – or other appropriate stock definitions – and businesses should coordinate with other tour operators in the area to remain within those limits. Fish mortality is the sum of all killed fish as well as expected mortalities from released fish given relevant mortality rates.

Tour operators and regulatory agencies also need to recognise the cumulative impacts of visitors and limit overall numbers to what the ecosystem can withstand without adverse effects (Honey, 1999). In recreational fisheries more intensively used than those in the case study, an effective regulatory, compliance, and enforcement regime may be necessary to ensure that angling and other activities are sustainably managed. A limited entry fishery may be necessary, whether imposed by the government through the issuance of permits or self-enforced among tour operators in the region. These tactics limit impact on the fishery and, when enforced through permits, generate revenue for management agencies.

Both the case study and the earlier discussion of recreational fishing as a sustainable activity provided examples of angling techniques that can be employed in angling Eco-tourism. As one of possibly a variety of techniques, catch and release flyfishing provides a proven method to ensure broad angling opportunities while limiting harm to hooked fish. More generally, several practices were discussed that can reduce angler efficiency, harm to released fish, and the spread of disease and invasive species. Locally applicable laws and guidelines should also be followed as a minimum but often not sufficient step towards sustainable operations (The Swedish Eco-tourism Association and The Swedish Travel and Tourism Council, 2002b) Implementing all of these techniques may require extensive angler education. More generally, angling Eco-tourism operations, as for all Eco-tourism operations, need to conduct their general operations in an environmentally sustainable manner with minimal negative impact (Blamey, 2001). The infrastructure required for recreational fishing operations typically includes lodges, transportation, and, at times, remote field camps. Minimising impacts may require the use of four-stroke rather than two-stroke engines on motorboats, energy efficiency and energy conservation in lodging, renewable energy generation, recycling plans, and the use of environmentally-friendly alternatives to conventional fuels and chemicals.

Planning Businesses and management agencies know the status of fish populations in their region of operation and the threats to these populations. Businesses operate within biological limits so that impacts from recreational fishing Eco-tourism will be minimal and sustainable given other pressures on the populations.

Angling Practices

All fish are caught and handled usingmethods that limit fish injury and mortality to minimal and sustainable levels. Anglers abide by applicable fisheries laws and regulations.

General Operations

All aspects of the Eco-tourism operation are conducted so as to minimise the consumption of natural resources and reduce the production of waste and pollution.

Respect for Local Cultures

For indigenous and local cultures around the world, fishing has played important subsistence, economic, and cultural roles. The annual migrations of salmon, for example, have structured societies from the Ainu in Japan to the Tlingit in Alaska (Roche

& McHutchison, 1998). Cultural aspects may provide a rich way to connect angler tourists to the traditions of an area or to learn about sustainable use. By the same token, tourism operations need to respect traditional customs surrounding fish and local community needs for fish resources. In Alaska, many native and non-native households continue to rely on locally available food for 'essential economic, nutritional, cultural and social benefits' (Kelso, 1982). The complexities involved in cultural matters will require careful cooperation between tour operators and local or indigenous communities. The most effective dialogues will likely begin early in the Eco-tourism planning process.

Interaction with Cultures

Operators and clients are respectful of local and indigenous traditions and needs regarding fish, land, and other resources.

Angling Eco-tourism in Kamchatka

Contribution to Conservation, Monitoring, and Research

The Eco-tourism concept includes the need to actively support conservation efforts (Blamey, 2001; Honey, 1999). This can occur through fees, business donations, and client donations, as well through participation in rehabilitation projects or scientific monitoring (Blamey, 2001).

As many recreational anglers are used to buying fishing permits, fees may be a particularly applicable method for governments or resource management agencies to raise funds for conservation. The case study showed, however, that the tour operator is probably not the appropriate actor to levy these fees. A more productive example for tour operator contributions may be a formula whereby businesses donate a percentage of yearly profits to conservation programmes (Alaska Wildland Adventures, 2004). This strategy requires strong partnerships with local conservation groups. The case study showed how this can occur when such groups are included in planning from the outset. In most parts of the world, a large opportunity also exists for angling Eco-tourism to participate directly in fisheries monitoring and research. Even in the United States, where a large agency structure supports fisheries data collection, information on recreational fisheries and fish populations are lacking (Donofrio, 2004). Throughout Far Eastern Russia, where the case study was located, scientific work is only just beginning to examine salmon distribution and population trends in many river basins (Augerot, in press). By enlisting angling Eco-tourism operations as partners in ecosystem monitoring, conservation efforts can gain access to more of the information they need to accomplish their goals.

Given the decentralised nature of tour operators, it seems unlikely that an appropriate data collection protocol will be developed or data aggregated in meaningful ways without cooperation between tour operators and scientists in the academic, non-governmental, or governmental sector. Preferably, all angling Eco-tourism operators in an area would participate in the same program using common standards, metrics, and data reporting formats. Data collection will likely include keeping accurate and thorough records of the size, weight, sex, and species of the fish caught and reporting data to the appropriate groups. These catch statistics are also important for evaluating an operation's environmental impacts (The Swedish Eco-tourism Association and The Swedish Travel and Tourism Council, 2002b).

Conservation

Tour operators support local conservation efforts through donations and cooperation and as well as by informing anglers about conservation organisations.

Monitoring and Research

Tour operators and guides work in cooperation with academic researchers, conservation groups, and/or government scientists to monitor and research fish populations and other environmental indicators. Accurate catch statistics are maintained.

Contribution to Local Economies

Eco-tourism can contribute to local economies in many ways, including foreign exchange earnings, employment, infrastructure development, longterm economic stability, and economic diversification (Blamey, 2001).

Preferential purchasing of local goods and services along with opportunities for residents to directly market crafts and other products to visitors can also play a part of these efforts. In the case study, Eco-tourism provided an alternative source of employment for communities that were turning to destructive practices such as poaching. Eco-tourism can thus provide a strong economic incentive for resource protection (Blamey, 2001). By demonstrating the economic value of a sustainably used resource, Eco-tourism can lead local communities to value healthy ecosystems and waters rich with fish (The Swedish Eco-tourism Association and The Swedish Travel and Tourism Council, 2002b).

Ideally, Eco-tourism must also contribute to the transfer of economic and political control to the local scale, a difficult and time-consuming process (Honey, 1999). In the case study, small steps were made in this direction by training guides locally. Local and/or indigenous involvement in Eco-tourism operations and planning is an important component of building capacity and sustainable development.

Local Residents

Significant economic benefits from angling Eco-tourism operations accrue to local residents in a manner that builds local support for resource protection.

Opportunities and Challenges for Angling Eco-tourism

As both recreational fishing and tourism expand in economically and ecologically important fisheries worldwide, the need to define angling Eco-tourism grows more pressing. It is necessary to set a high standard that recognises the need to conserve ecosystems and sets limits on the overall impact of anglers. In addition to promoting conservation and benefiting local economies, that high standard will add value for environmentally-conscious tourism operators and recreational fishing guides by enabling them to selectively market their services to discriminating customers and charge premium prices on the basis of a fishery's environmental attributes.

Despite these promising opportunities, there are challenges looming in the near future. Should the term 'angling Eco-tourism' or 'recreational fishing Eco-tourism' enter into common usage, it is likely that many tour operators and recreational fishing guides will use it in promotional material. Many of them will be sincere and diligent in their desire to minimise environmental impacts and promote conservation, but some will not.

As the vernacular of environmentalism has grown more prevalent, the number of travellers on ecotours has increased, but the conservation missions, ecological integrity of nature sites, and environmental education components have all been diminished (Honey, 1999). Travel industry 'greenwashing' of conventional tourism has devalued the market worth of Eco-tourism organisations and sustainably managed tour companies, crowding some out of the market.

In certain pristine and hitherto-remote regions, Eco-tourism has even served as a Trojan horse – attracting sustainable levels of tourism at first, before conventional mass tourism operations respond to growing demand (Butler, 1990).

Predictably, the environmental and social infrastructure of a region can be quickly stressed and degraded by increased numbers of visitors. Kamchatka is not currently subject to these demands, but some recreational fisheries of Alaska and British Columbia already suffer from overfishing and habitat degradation. Examples of degradation include erosion on riverbanks, noise pollution from motorboats, and improper disposal of human waste.

At the same time, regions wishing to use angling Eco-tourism as a form of economic development need to understand the limitations on the market for world-class angling tourism on the scale enjoyed by areas like Alaska. A clear attraction needs to be present, such as the steelhead in Kamchatka or the giant king salmon of the Kenai River in Alaska. When logistics are more complex or when tourists must travel larger distances for fishing, the cost of transportation will limit the potential tourism market to wealthier individuals. Certain regions may want to focus on local angling Eco-tourism markets, rather than trying to compete at the international scale. Regardless of the scale, angling Eco-tourism should almost always be considered in the context of a broader Eco-tourism development strategy that includes a diversity of Eco-tourism forms such as wildlife watching, photographic expeditions, adventure trips, agritourism, and ethnotourism.

For angling Eco-tourism to avoid the pitfalls encountered by other Eco-tourism ventures, conservation groups, fisheries regulatory agencies, local communities, and tourism operators must cooperate early and operate in good faith. They cannot expect the problems and possible contradictions of angling Eco-tourism to be solved from the outside. While certification bodies provide general Eco-tourism guidelines, the specifics of angling Eco-tourism remain largely ignored. For angling Eco-tourism to mature from a vague, looselyapplied concept to a thoughtfully implemented practice, carefully formulated standards and guidelines will be needed. As angling tourism expands, it brings with it not only great opportunities, but threats to sensitive and ecologically valuable fisheries worldwide. In the case study we present, anglers played an active role in advancing the scientific understanding of the salmonid fisheries of Kamchatka. Not only did the lowimpact angling fund the activity of fisheries conservation groups, but it directly contributed to data-gathering and environmental monitoring of the fishery. This study is only one of many possible examples, however, and more work is needed to examine fully the various challenges and opportunities presented by angling Eco-tourism.

To provide better clarity to the angling Eco-tourism concept, we propose guidelines for this activity designed specifically to minimise environmental impacts, generate support for local economic development, and contribute directly to conservation. Our specific principles are applicable in a range of ecosystems and emphasise the need for cooperation between stakeholders.

While angling Eco-tourism is an exciting and highly promising venture, it faces threats and challenges discussed above, particularly the danger of 'greenwashing' and the use of the Eco-tourism label to promote conventional, unsustainable angling tourism. For angling Eco-tourism to succeed, there is a pressing need to set high standards and coordinate the actions of all stakeholders. All parties will play integral roles in making angling Eco-tourism a valid and vital tool for science, conservation and sustainable development.

Angling in India

The Indian Himalayas are an ideal for sport fishing. Anglers from all over the world come to the Indian rivers to try and hook the Himalayan Rainbow trout or the mighty Mahaseer. Good fishing is possible in the north of the country on the Ganga, Kali rivers for mahseer and on the Tirthan, Tons and Sainj rivers for trout. In the east of the country, rivers like the Kameng, Teesta, Brahmaputra etc. provide excellent angling opportunities.

India with its dozens of rivers and thousands of streams, offers vast opportunities for fishing and angling. Whether you're a first time angler or an expert angler,-India's waters, both fresh and salt, can be a pleasant surprise for you. The country has an estimated 50,000 km of waters-rivers, streams, and lakes included-and an additional 3,000 km of coastline. There's definitely a lot of scope for some satisfying angling in India. Major rivers like the Ganga and its tributaries, the Yamuna, the Brahmaputra, the

Mahanadi, the Krishna and the Kaveri are home to a wide spectrum of fish, including mahseer, rohu, katli, and trout. The coastal waters caressing the shorelines of India harbour marine fish like-mackerel, marlin and sea bass.

In India, most major cities lie along the rivers, as a result finding a fishing zone is generally not a problem. In addition to this, most states have well-organised Departments of Fisheries, where special breeding areas assure that there's always a gene pool of local and exotic fish. Fish sanctuaries and breeding grounds in Jammu and Kashmir, Himachal Pradesh, Uttar Pradesh and other states through which major rivers flow, conserve a vast stock of fish which are specially bred for re-stocking rivers.

Licenses and Permits

Fishing licenses are mandatory for all anglers. Go to the concerned official before you throw your line into the water, or else you will be penalised for not having the fishing license. In most cases, fishing licenses are not issued during the monsoon (when most fish species breed); in addition, most licenses are issued for only a specified stretch of water. Furthermore, there are conditions that all fish caught must be released into the water, and anglers are restricted to catch a specified number of fish per day you can get the license from the Fisheries Department of the state where you have come for angling.

Foreigners, who are head towards the Lakshadweep or Andaman & Nicobar Islands for fishing & angling, will need a permit from the Ministry of Home Affairs in New Delhi-or an authorised official in the state. The same applies to certain areas of Himachal Pradesh, Jammu and Kashmir and other border states.

Things to Bring

The basic fishing equipment required includes rods, lines, hooks, reel, flies, spinners, spoons and bait-in the form of worms, paste or other lure. Light, waterproof clothing-brown or green in colour-is essential, as are waterproof shoes or light sandals which can easily be slipped off to drain out sand or water. Sunscreen, a light hat and dark glasses are necessary, and during the winter make sure you're well clad with sufficient woollens and a macintosh. Some travel agencies and tour operators in India provides everything from equipment and experienced guides to boarding, lodging and transportation to the anglers.

Some Best Zones for Anglers

The main river expanse suitable for angling are in the lower Himalayas, the Satpuras, and the Aravalis, all of which have rivers teeming with a broad range of fishes. India's rivers acquire about 31 species of freshwater fish which are of interest to anglers; these include trout (brown and rainbow trout, both introduced species); murrel, catfish and cyprinids.

Agritourism

Agritourism, as it is defined most broadly, involves any agriculturally-based operation or activity that brings visitors to a farm or ranch. Agritourism has different definitions in different parts of the world, and sometimes refers specifically to farm stays, as in Italy. Elsewhere, agritourism includes a wide variety of activities, including buying produce direct from a farm stand, navigating a corn maze, picking fruit, feeding animals, or staying at a B&B on a farm. Agritourism is a form of niche tourism that is considered a growth industry in many parts of the world, including Australia, Canada, the United States, and the Philippines. Agritourism overlaps with geotourism, Eco-tourism, and culinary tourism. Other terms associated with agritourism are "agritainment", "value added products," "farm direct marketing", and "sustainable agriculture".

Agritourism in the United States

Agritourism is widespread in America. Agritourists can choose from a wide range of activities that include picking fruits and vegetables, riding horses, tasting honey, learning about wine and cheesemaking, or shopping in farm gift shops and farm stands for local and regional produce or hand-crafted gifts.

According the USDA, Cooperative State, Education and Extension Service, "Tourism is becoming increasingly important to the U.S. economy. A conservative estimate from the Federal Reserve Board in Kansas, based on 2000 data, shows that basic travel and tourism industries accounted for 3.6 percent of all U.S. employment. Even more telling, data from the Travel Industry Association of America indicate that 1 out of every 18 people in the U.S. has a job directly resulting from travel expenditures."

Through the Small Farm Centre at the University of California, "Agricultural tourism or agritourism, is one alternative for improving the incomes and potential economic viability of small farms and rural communities. Some forms of agritourism enterprises are well developed in California, including fairs and festivals. Other possibilities still offer potential for development." The UC Small Farm Centre has developed a California Agritourism Database that "provides visitors and potential entrepreneurs with information about existing agritourism locations throughout the state."

In Western North Carolina, the organization HandMade in America is using agritourism to develop their local economy and craft trades, and to educate visitors about agriculture practices. On the web site, *Hand Made in America,* they look at agritourism as a "... niche market [that] not only assists communities with solutions to help diversify their economic base, but it also helps our regional urban centres and increasingly suburban populations to understand the important role that farming and rural life plays in our history, by highlighting the need for it in our contemporary society. Agri-tourism projects reinforce the need to support local growers and sources and allow the visitor to experience what it is to be part of the land..."

The publication *Promoting Tourism in Rural America* explains the need for planning and marketing your rural community and weighing the pros and cons of tourism. According to the publication, local citizen participation is helpful and should be included in starting any kind of a tourism program. Citizen participation in planning tourism can contribute to buliding a successful program that enhances the community.

Additional websites that promote and publicize agritourism in the United States include Rural Bounty, founded by agritourism consultant Jane Eckert, Sleep in the Hay, a nationwide directory of farm stays, and Farm Stay USA, a blog that profiles farm stays and tracks agritourism news.

Reasons for Popularity

People have become more interested in how their food is produced. They want to meet farmers and processers and talk with them about what goes into food production. For many people who visit farms, especially children, the visit marks the first time they see the source of their food, be it a dairy cow, an ear of corn growing in the field, or an apple they can pick right off the tree.

Agritourism was featured in the satirical NBC television comedy series *The Office* in the episode entitled "Money" from season . The character Dwight Schrute lives on a beet farm, and in this episode reveals that he has opened a B&B in his farmhouse. The characters Jim and Pam proceed to visit the farm, where they choose the "irrigation" themed room. They choose to participate in various farm activities, including plowing the fields, making wine from beets, and watching a table making demonstration. In the episode, Dwight explains that Trip Advisor is the lifeblood of the agritourism industry. The episode portrayed agritourism in a somewhat unappealing light, as Dwight's beet farm and rural lifestyle are often objects of ridicule on the show. Still, the episode brought the concept of agritourism to the show's many viewers.

Dude Ranches

Dude (or guest) ranches offer tourists the chance to work on cattle ranches, and sometimes participate in cattle drives. The fact sheet, *Promoting the Farm and Ranch Recreation Business,* gives farmers and ranchers information on marketing and developing strategies to win tourism dollars. Dude ranches are common in the United States and Australian Outback.

6

Travel and Destination Promotion

Destination marketing facilitates the achievement of tourism policy, which should be coordinated with the regional development strategic plan. Marketing of destinations should also guide the tourism impacts optimisation and the maximisation of benefits for the region. In order to appreciate the complexity of destination marketing this paper explains the destination concept and attempts to synthesise several models for strategic marketing and management of destinations.

Destination as an Amalgam of Tourism Services and Experiences

Destinations are amalgams of tourism products, offering an integrated experience to consumers.

Traditionally, destinations are regarded as well-defined geographical areas, such as a country, an island or a town. However, it is increasingly recognised that a destination can also a perceptual concept, which can be interpreted subjectively by consumers, depending on their travel itinerary, cultural background, purpose of visit, educational level and past experience. For example, London can be a destination for a German business traveller, whilst Europe may be the destination for a leisure Japanese tourist who packs six European countries in a two week tour. Some travellers will consider a cruise ship to be their destination, while others on the same cruise may perceive the

ports visited during the trip as their destination. Often destinations are artificially divided by geographical and political barriers, which fail to take into consideration consumer preferences or tourism industry functions. An example of that is the Alps shared by France, Austria, Switzerland, Italy by often perceived and consumed as part of the same product by skiers. For the purpose of this paper destinations are considered to be a defined geographical region which is understood by

its visitors as a unique entity, with a political and legislative framework for tourism marketing and planning. This definition enables Destination Management Organisations (DMOs) to be accountable for the planning and marketing of the region and to have the power and resources to undertake action towards achieving its strategic objectives.

Destinations offer an amalgam of tourism products and services, which are consumed under the brand name of the destination. Leiper (1995) explains that destinations are places towards which people travel and where they choose to stay for a while in order to experience certain features or characteristics-a perceived attraction of some sort. Cooper et al (1998) define destinations as the focus of facilities and services designed to meet the needs of the tourists. Therefore, a destination can be regarded as a combination (or even as a brand) of all products, services and ultimately experiences provided locally. It also enables us to assess the impact of tourism regionally, as well as manage demand and supply in order to maximise benefits for all stakeholders.

Six As Framework for the analysis of tourism destinations;

- Attractions (natural, man-made, artificial, purpose built, heritage, special events)
- Accessibility (entire transportation system comprising of routes, terminals and vehicles)
- Amenities (accommodation and catering facilities, retailing, other tourist services)
- Available packages (pre-arranged packages by intermediaries and principals)
- Activities (all activities available at the destination and what consumers will do during their visit)
- Ancillary services (services used by tourists such as banks, telecommunications, post, newsagents, hospitals, etc)

Although there is plenty of literature on destination planning and development of facilities, there are few textbooks examining destination marketing and even fewer illustrate destinations as an experience-provider for tourists and locals.

This is also reflected in the academic literature published in journals and other scientific publications.

The inadequacy of destination marketing literature probably illustrates the interest of researchers in the impacts of tourism on destinations. Hence, the management and marketing of destinations is often left to industry people and consultants and it is not frequently discussed in the literature or in academic debates. The competitive nature of destination marketing also prevents involved parties from publishing their strategies and marketing plans. In addition, there is an apparent difference between the marketing and planning tourism literature.

Traditionally marketing concentrates on increasing visitation and treats tourism like any other commodity. This approach fails to recognise the unique needs and limitations of each destination as well as their particular geographical, environmental and socio-cultural characteristics. In contrast, planning literature concentrates more on the impacts of tourism and on limiting tourism development, often ignoring the market dynamics and the requirements of entrepreneurs at the destination and the place of origin explains that companies and governments in tourism have applied only part of the marketing mix to tourism, i.e., promotion, with little attention being paid to the other components of marketing. However, if tourism is to survive by generating satisfaction among interacting tourists and hosts, it must adopt societal marketing strategies. This involves carefully monitoring tourist satisfaction levels and using these as part of the criteria for success, rather than increasing numbers of tourists; continually monitoring host reactions to tourists, for host-tourist interaction is an important component of the tourist experience; and being aware that infrastructure development of tourism resort areas has implications for the types of tourists that will be attracted.

The Strategic Purpose of Destinations and their Management and Marketing

Destinations are some of the most difficult entities to manage and market, due to the complexity of the relationships of local stakeholders (Sautter and Leisen,1999). Managing and marketing destinations is also challenging because of the variety of stakeholders involved in the development and production of tourism products. The destination experience is essentially comprised of regions, resources and amalgams of tourism facilities and services, which often do not belong to individuals. Instead they represent a collection of both professional and personal interests of all the people who live and work in the area. Managing often conflicting stakeholders' interests makes controlling and marketing destinations as a whole extremely challenging. Hence, strategies and actions should take into account the wishes of all stakeholders, namely indigenous people, businesses and investors, tourists, tour operators and intermediaries, and interest groups. Perhaps the most difficult problem is ensuring the rational use of zero-priced public goods, such as landscapes, mountains, and the sea for the benefit of all stakeholders and at the same time preserving the resources for future generations. Conflicts can easily develop, especially when some (perhaps greedy) stakeholders exploit resources for short-term benefits. A compromise encompassing all these interests is extremely difficult if not impossible, but is the key to long term success.

And yet tourists perceive the destination as a brand comprising of a collection of suppliers and services. Before visiting they develop an image about destinations as well as a set of expectations based on previous experience, word of mouth, press reports, advertising, and common beliefs. During their holiday, they "consume" destinations as a comprehensive experience, without often realising that each element of the product are produced and managed by individual players. Most service providers are small and medium-sized tourism enterprises which have a wide range of strengths and weaknesses whilst are also characterised by their independent nature. Tourists' overall experience is composed of numerous small encounters with a variety of tourism principals, such as taxi drivers, hoteliers, waiters, as well as with elements of the local attractions such as museums, theatres, beaches, theme parks etc. Their overall impression develops their image of a destination after their visitation. As a consequence there is much overlapping between strategic marketing of the destination as a whole and of each individual supplier at the region. Hence, the competitiveness of each player is often interrelated and almost indistinguishable from one another.

As consumers increasingly value environmental resources they are prepared to pay for them premium prices. Hence, local resources become a central asset for destinations and tourism suppliers and their sustainability a core function of tourism marketing. Middleton and Hawkins state that "a marketing perspective is essentially an overall management orientation reflecting corporate attitudes that, in the case of travel and tourism, must balance the interests of shareholders/owners with the long-run environmental interests of a destination and at the same time meet the demands and expectations of customers".

DMOs tend to be part of the local, regional or national government and have political and legislative power as well as the financial means to manage resources rationally and to ensure that all stakeholders can benefit in the long term. Destination management and marketing should act as tools and facilitators to achieve a complex range of strategic objectives, which will ultimately need to satisfy the needs and wants of stakeholders. The development and implementation of strategic objectives at destinations depends on relationships between stakeholders and thus the implementation of the key generic strategic objectives will be determined by the dynamics of the actors on this wheel.

Naturally each stakeholder aims to maximise the benefits emerging for themselves. Inevitably, the interests of some stakeholders may be conflicting with others and thus some of the four key strategic objectives may be jeopardised. This is often a result of some stakeholder trying to enhance its benefit at the expense of others.

For example a tour operator may try to reduce the prices paid to local suppliers in order to increase its profit margin and remain competitive in the marketplace. It is imperative, therefore, for DMOs to use legislative and management tools during planning and management of destinations in order to ensure that the benefits of tourism activity is shared fairly between all stakeholders and that sustainable practices safeguard the regeneration of resources utilised for the production of tourism. Failure to ensure and maintain a balance effectively jeopardises relationships between stakeholders, and threatens the achievement of the strategic objectives and the long term competitiveness and prosperity of destinations.

Strategic management and marketing objectives for destinations;

- Enhance the long term prosperity of local people
- Delight visitors by maximising their satisfaction
- Maximise profitability of local enterprises and maximise multiplier effects

- Optimise tourism impacts by ensuring a sustainable balance between economic benefits and socio-cultural and environmental costs

Hence, tourism marketing should not only be regarded as a tool for attracting more visitors to a region, as it has been the case for most destinations. Instead, tourism marketing should operate as a mechanism to facilitate regional development objectives and to rationalise the provision of tourism in order to ensure that the strategic objectives of destinations are achieved. Tourism marketing should also ensure equitable returns-on-resources-utilised for the production and delivery of tourism products, as well as the regeneration of these resources. It should also provide suitable gains to all stakeholders involved in the tourism system. Hence, marketing should be used as a strategic mechanism in coordination with planning and management rather than a sales tool.

Destinations may also involve de-marketing, i.e. the discouragement of certain market segments from visiting the destination during certain periods, through a range of prohibitive measures or by charging premium prices. Examples of these techniques include:

- visitor management techniques in theme parks which divert people from congested attractions to less busy ones by using a leading story/attraction;
- towns like Cambridge, which aims to attract only visitors who stay overnight and to discourage excursionists who contribute little to the local economy by controlling their parking processes; _ Mauritius which provides high quality resort accommodation and does not allow charter flights, therefore promoting high expenditure tourism; or
- Venice, which deters more visitors by charging premium prices for all services offered and recently initiated negative advertisement to reduce mass tourism.

In this way marketing is used as a mechanism to achieve strategic objectives of destination regions and thus, should be guided by the policies for regional development.

Main Markets and Destination Choice

Understanding destination types and characteristics is of paramount importance for its marketing. Each destination can only match certain types of demand and hence tourism marketers need to appreciate travel motivations in order to develop appropriate offerings and brand destinations for

the right target markets. In addition, destinations should be aware not only of the needs and wants of the active demand but also of the potential markets they can attract. It can then develop a product portfolio, which will enable the optimisation of benefits and adapt their marketing mix to their target markets. Consumer behaviour studies indicate that a wide range of criteria is used to select tourism products. These criteria are altered according to the purpose and features of the trip, elements of the external environment, the characteristics of the traveller and the particularities and attributes of destinations.

Classifying travel behavior and segmentation becomes increasingly more difficult as modern travellers combine pleasure with business, in order to take time and cost advantage. There are therefore endless variations between the two principle classifications of travel activities, i.e. business and leisure trips. However, leisure trips may include elements, characteristics and motivations of business travel and vice versa. Incentive travelling, extended conference stays and business meetings during leisure travel makes the distinction between the two categories increasingly blurred. Nevertheless the two principle categories are fairly identifiable and they are treated differently in this text for simplifying the concepts and marketing responses.

Business trips are fairly inflexible and it is often difficult for travellers to select their destinations.

Business travel, often referred to as MICE (Meetings-Incentives-Conferences-Exhibitions), is normally determined by business opportunities and involvement of the traveller with organisations at the destination. Perhaps more flexibility can be exercised by travellers attending optional meetings, which provide benefits but are not strictly essential to their business such as conferences, exhibitions, incentives, familiarization trips etc (Davidson 1994). Even though business tourism is much more

restricted in terms of choice, destinations providing a high degree of efficiency and safety, as well as elegance and leisure opportunities tend to be preferred for conferences and incentive travel. Business travel is seasonal, as people do not generally travel less during the holiday seasons, i.e. summer months and public holidays. Nevertheless, business tourism provide much higher revenue for enterprises as consumers are willing to pay more for their inflexible schedules and also destinations can increase their multiplier effects as some particular forms of business tourism use a much greater spectrum of local services than leisure tourism. Convenient transportation connections with major cities around the world, smooth arrangements at the destination and adequate provision of business related amenities are therefore very important. Urban destinations in developed countries with strong economic activity and vibrant markets tend to receive the majority of business traffic, as a result of the business meetings taking place locally. The location of meeting partners, host organisations, as well as company policy may determine the selection of destinations for business travel. In addition, corporate rates, membership of loyalty clubs (i.e. frequent flyer or frequent guest) as well as the availability of service providers are some additional criteria used to identify suitable destinations and service providers for the MICE market.

Leisure travellers, on the other hand, use a much more complex set of criteria in selecting their destination. They have a much higher price elasticity and therefore, price is a key element in the decision making process. In addition, leisure travellers are often time sensitive as families with children cannot travel during school time, creating the seasonality problem for the industry. However, different market segments have dissimilar seasonality patterns. For example, pensioners and elderly people tend to travel during the low season to benefit from discounts, whilst Scandinavian tourists tend to stay home during the summer months in order to enjoy the whether. School children and University students go on field research trips or excursions during the low season. Therefore, destinations have to identify the seasonality patterns of their various markets and attract compatible segments, which will enable them to maximise their total yield (both average expenditure and occupancy levels). It is also important to understand other factors that influence the decision of consumers to purchase. The social status and peer groups of consumers often influence what is acceptable and desirable as a destination. Travel intermediaries also play a significant role in determining the destination decision of consumers by using a wide range of promotional techniques and often channeling travellers to destinations and principals who offer higher remuneration for them.

This will also enable destinations to manage their resources according and attract the right market segments in order to optimize their impacts.

Nevertheless for both leisure and business markets, perhaps the most important criterion for selecting to visit or not to visit a destination is its image. Image is the set of expectations and perceptions a prospective traveller has of a destination. Past experience of the destination or the companies involved (i.e. airlines, hotels, tour operators); descriptions by friends and relatives; general information; and marketing campaigns develop these expectations and perception which may be true or imaginary representations. Interestingly, the sustainability of local resources becomes one of the most important elements of destination image, as a growing section of the market is not prepared to tolerate over-developed tourism destinations and diverts to more environmentally advanced regions. The degree of consumer satisfaction will depend on the assessment of the perceived overall experience of the destination versus anticipated expectations and perceptions. Developing the right image for destinations will therefore determine their ability to satisfy visitors as it will allow them to develop realistic and fulfil-able expectations.

Types of Destinations, Target Markets and Marketing Strategies Required

Developing a destination typology is a difficult task, as different visitors use destinations for different purposes. Nevertheless most destinations can be classified in several categories which represent their principle attractiveness. Understanding and appreciating the type of destination enables marketers to develop a suitable destination marketing mixes and deliver them to the appropriate target markets.

Urban destinations have been involved in tourism since the early years of the civilisation. People used to travel to cities and towns to meet politicians and business associates. Sports organisations, such as the Olympic Games in ancient Greece also generated tourism activity in main cities. People also travelled to cities on pilgrimage for religious purposes, as this is where all major cathedrals, mosques and temples were usually located. Urban destinations have also been attracting business travellers attending meetings, conferences and exhibitions. Most urban destinations are well equipped with conference and exhibition halls and transportation and accommodation infrastructure to facilitate the organisation of larger events. Urban destinations also attract leisure travellers, especially during periods of low business travelling activity, such as weekends and school holidays. Suppliers and facilities aim to reduce seasonality by developing the number of leisure visitors, despite the fact that they can only charge a fraction of the price they charge business travellers. On the other hand, leisure travellers can take advantage of some of the unique facilities and services of urban destinations to enjoy short-breaks or extended weekends.

London for example provides a wide range of heritage attractions as well as a wide range of entertainment opportunities such as theatre, concerts, bars, theme restaurants, discos etc.

Barcelona offers excellent conference facilities, combined with a culturally interesting and relaxed atmosphere. New York is highly regarded for shopping, sight seeing and theatre going. Urban destinations also attract education and health tourists, as they are generally equipped with good educational establishments and hospitals. Increasingly urban resorts take advantage of their industrial heritage and use obsolete industrial sites as educational experiences and leisure facilities. The Docklands in Liverpool and coal mines in Skipton are good examples of these facilities.

Seaside destinations and resorts traditionally serve tourists on holidays. Travellers from Northern regions and climates tend to spend a proportion of their annual holiday in the South where they can enjoy sunshine as well as sea sports. Seaside resorts nearby the place of residence were replaced by international destinations as a result of the emergence of mass tourism since the 1970s. For example, in the UK traditional resorts such Blackpool, Scarborough, Bournemouth and Brighton were replaced by the Spanish Costas through the development of package holidays. Typically European leisure travellers will take their annual holiday at Mediterranean seaside resorts, whilst Northern Americans visit Southern regions such as Florida,

California and the Caribbean. As the product in traditional seaside resorts matures, new long haul and exotic destinations, often in less developed countries attract sophisticated travellers who are looking for authentic and off-the-track experiences. The globalization experienced reduces distances and enables people to travel further afield. Examples include destinations such as Goa and Bali which take advantage of developments in transportation and attract travellers. Examples of seaside destinations and resorts can be identified globally.

Alpine destinations attract leisure travellers for winter sports, such as skiing, as well as holidaymakers who appreciate natural attractions in all seasons. They also attract activity holidaymakers such as naturalists, mountain cyclists, walkers etc. Although the majority of alpine sports are for recreational purposes a wide range of expeditions and challenges are organised for mountains such as the Everest or the Alps. Lakes may also offer facilities for sea sports such as surfing and skiing. Although the majority of alpine resorts are in near proximity to urban centres and thus can easily be accessed by private car, several are still unexplored and offer authentic experiences for travellers. Lakes and scenic landscapes make alpine resorts increasingly more popular for conference and incentive tourists and thus a certain business travelling activity can be observed in the last few years. The development of important business, political and economic meetings, such as the Davos Forum, attract a new market segment and expand the season for winter resorts. As a result a wide range of marketing and planning implications emerge to allow alpine areas to benefit from tourism and yet to ensure the sustainability of their resources.

Destinations in authentic (often Third World) countries are often off the beaten track. Tourists enjoy authentic experiences in places which have experienced limited tourism development.

Emerging destinations in Asia, South America and Africa attract a small number of adventurous tourists who are prepared to forego their comfort in order to interact with local communities and unspoiled surroundings. Although these regions may develop at a later stage to mass tourism destinations, they need to be planned properly in order to sustain their resources. They often lack the required infrastructure to deliver tourism services.

Finally certain destinations are branded unique-exotic-exclusive as they are regarded to offer a unique and precious experience. As a result, these destinations are promoted as "one-in-a-lifetime" experience and they are promoted premium prices. Examples include Bhutan, Mauritius, and Seychelles. In some destinations, there are several mechanisms controlling the number of visitors, often through managing their transportation and accommodating capacity or immigration procedures and visa allowances. These destinations focus on the non-charter and non-mass traveller reducing their visitation but maximising their income per visitor. They often epitomise the dream of the average traveller and thus are packaged and priced as prestigious products, for instance for weddings, honeymoons, anniversaries or a special occasion trip, or for incentive travel.

Marketing Research: Identifying Market Segments for Destination Products

Marketing research is used extensively by destination marketers to identify the types of customers that can be attracted (active demand), as well as the prospective visitors (suppressed demand) who do not visit for a variety of reasons (Athiyaman, 1997). Approaching the right target market and providing the most appropriate combination of local tourism products and services is the secret for successful destinations. Product design and formulation should therefore be based on research. As tourism bundles are formulated ad-hoc to satisfy specific consumer requests, a dynamic marketing research process will enable destinations to provide unique products by initiating local partnerships between all suppliers to address the needs of demand. Destination image is also developed through marketing research, which guides promotional activities towards branding and amending the brand values of the region. The effectiveness of promotional campaigns can be assessed so that the most cost-effective media is used to approach and persuade target markets to visit the destination.

Contribution of marketing research to destination marketing;

- Identification of the main attributes anticipated by each market segment
- Design and attributes required for tourism products and services
- Evaluation and development of destination image
- Segmentation of market and development of corresponding marketing mixes
- Opening new markets and reducing dependency on existing ones
- Evaluation of the elasticity of demand for each market segment
- Reduction of seasonality by matching market segments

- Examination of reasons deterring people (suppressed demand) from visiting destinations
- Assessment of compatibility with other target markets
- Examination of alternative distribution channels
- Assessment of tourism impacts to the destination and selecting the right segments
- Evaluation of marketing effectiveness and selection of media for promotion.

Marketing Destinations: Strategies and Practices

Developing a marketing strategy and mix for destinations is a complex process, mainly because there are many independent stakeholders and principals involved. Destinations cannot be managed or marketed as enterprises, due to the dynamics of interests and benefits sought by stakeholders. In addition, most destinations are amalgams of independent SMTEs, which already follow their own marketing strategies. Although DMOs have traditionally taken marketing responsibility for the destination product, they fail to control marketing activities and mixes of individual players and hence can only coordinate and guide, rather than undertake a comprehensive marketing strategy. Perhaps the most important challenge for destination marketing therefore is to bring all individual partners together to compete rather than to cooperate and to pool resources towards developing an integrated marketing mix and delivery system.

The international tourist industry is becoming an increasingly competitive marketplace where only the best-managed destinations are likely to prosper. Comprehensive strategic business plans therefore need to address all factors that have an impact on the product. Tourism strategies should not only concentrate on visitation, but also include the entire range of impacts such as overcrowding, environmental problems, visitor safety and security, seasonality problems, and sensitivity to local culture (Evans, et al 1995). This will enable destinations to develop comprehensive strategies to fulfil all strategic objectives.

The Position of Destinations and their Marketing

Perhaps one additional complication to tourism marketing is that in most cases destinations have already a rich history and legacy development which needs to be taken into consideration when developing tourism marketing strategies. Not only consumers develop certain images and views about places, but also previous development often provides several limits for marketing to address as well as stakeholders who need to be respected and consulted. Understanding therefore the stage and roots of tourism development is critical for development a strategy. One of the most widely used tools for undertaking this task is the destination life cycle. The main utility of the destination life cycle is to facilitate the understanding the evolution of tourist products and destinations and it to provide guidance for strategic decision taking. Cooper suggests that the life cycle concept illustrates that destinations experience a "birth to death" cycle and that the life cycle model has gained attention in tourism and hospitality as an explanatory tool.

Although in tourism life cycle analysis is often seen as a useful conceptualisation tool for destination area development, in hospitality management it is beginning to be used as a guide for strategic planning. However the main problems relate to identifying turning points, stages, length of stages and level of aggregation. Despite the many criticisms of the life cycle concept, it is quite critical for marketers to appreciate the stage of development of resort areas. A number of researchers have used the cycle as a framework for analysing changing destinations.

The different stages destinations are going through during their life cycle and illustrates how that effects their tourism impacts. This also illustrates that different stages of the life cycle require different marketing strategies and planning actions. This is largely due to the differences between demand and supply experienced at different levels. In the early stages demand exceeds supply whilst this relationship is reversed in the maturity and consolidation stages. As a result, marketing strategies should focus on building awareness and promoting the destination product on the early stages of the circle while they probably have to deal with image alteration and re-design and re-launch the product at the later stages. The entire marketing mix therefore will need to be differentiated to accommodate the needs of destinations at each stage of their life cycle. In addition, destinations experience different environmental and socio-cultural impacts during the different faces. As a result they need to use marketing to encourage sustainable practices for both consumers and industry as well as to communicate their environmental and socio-cultural policies.

Porter's Generic Strategies

Three main strategies proposed by Porter (1980) aimed to "outperform other firms in an industry", i.e.:

- Overall cost leadership, where organisations are required to minimise their costs, based on mass production and strict cost control of the main business functions;
- differentiation of products or services offered by "creating something that is perceived industrywide as being unique";
- focus on a "particular buyer group, segment of the product line or geographical market" and achieve either cost leadership or product differentiation.

This is well-developed generic model, which is widely used to all industries. It provides clear guidance for decision makers to position their products in order to maximise profitability and improve their competitiveness. However, this model fails to address the specific needs of tourism and in particular the scarcity of resources at the destination level. Therefore, similarly with commodities this model suggests unlimited resources are available to reproduce endless number of products. This is particularly the case for the cost leadership strategy where organisations are urged to increase their volume and to reduce their profit margin. Unfortunately environmental resources, both natural (e.g. coral reefs or mountain landscapes) and man-made (e.g. archaeological sites or architectural structures) have a limited capacity which they can accommodate. Resources in tourism are irreplaceable once destroyed and therefore a strategy should ensure that their use is limited to the degree that does not threat their sustainability in the long term. Once this is understood and appreciated, Porter's model enables tourism marketers to focus on differentiation strategies and to develop their mix accordingly. However, several destinations, which are on the consolidation phase of their life cycle, have exceeded the maximum capacity which would have enabled them to sustain their resources. Their ability to promote differentiated tourism products has also been jeopardised, as over-development has exploited and damaged their resources. This is experienced in some mass tourism destinations, such as Benidorm and Costa Brava in Spain, or Faliraki and Malia in Greece.

Once destinations have reached that stage there is limited choice. The majority try to attract more mass tourism so they can increase their profitability through volume. Increasingly however some regions aim to renovate their properties and facilities and re-launch their offerings. The Calvia example in Mallorca, which decided to demolish three hotels in order to improve public areas and to enhance the quality of its products set new best practices which may be followed by other regions.

Gilbert's Strategic Framework

Based on the above rational the second strategic framework introduced by Gilbert argues that destinations can classified on a continuum between a "status" and a "commodity" area. "Status areas" achieve intentional demand as a result of the unique product attributes perceived by the tourism market. These unique attributes may be genuine or imaginative and thus, a destination is regarded as irreplaceable, which increases consumers' loyalty and willingness to pay.

In the "commodity status" case, destinations are substitutable, very sensitive to price and economic changes, while consumers have a low awareness of any unique benefits or attributes. Thus, travellers base their decision to visit the area merely on price, while the demand for the destination is incidental and destinations are unable to attract high spenders. Despite the fact that the sustainability of resources is not discussed explicitly by the model, it is quite evident that "status areas" manage their resources as product attributes and therefore are appreciated by consumers who are willing to pay more.

Gilbert (1990) asserts that destinations should attempt to become "status areas", rather than a "commodity area" one, in order to improve their image, loyalty and economic benefits. It is suggested that destinations should differentiate their tourism products in order to achieve a unique "tourist product benefit". This will enable them to establish their position in the international market, and attract both high spenders and loyal tourists, who appreciate the uniqueness of their resources and offerings. Although the model clearly differentiates destinations to distinctive categories it fails to recognise that the majority of destinations lay between the two ends of the continuum.

It also fails to relate to the different stages of the life cycle and to the inevitability experienced in several regions where destinations are launched as status areas and gradually slip to commodity status (Buhalis,1999a). Nevertheless the model clearly contributes to tourism marketing by correlating product attributes with willingness to pay and also by illustrating clearly that destinations should decide on what direction they should plan and manage their resources and facilities.

Poon's Flexible Specialisation

A third strategic approach for tourism is proposed by Poon (1989 and 1993), based on the concept of "flexible specialisation" of the tourism business. Poon examines the tourism industry processes and proposes a strategy to enable tourism organisations to improve their competitiveness.

Commodity Area rigidly packaged". "The main sources of flexibility for service firms lie in the organisation, management, marketing, distribution and other forms of interaction and interrelationships among guests, hotels, suppliers, distributors. What is important however is not each of these stand-alone aspects but how they are coupled to create competitive advantages and hence, capabilities to move with the market". This is a timely model, which predicted the impact of information technology on the both decision making and consumer behaviour. Industry innovation is critical in this strategy and the utilisation of new technology provides the opportunity to customise products according to customers' specific requirements. Hence destinations can organise their assets and attributes in such a way which will enable them to specialise their tourism product according to particular demand needs.

Although Poon's model revolutionised tourism thinking it is still difficult to implement at the destination level. The majority of infrastructure and superstructure is based on fixed assets, which cannot be altered easily and therefore they have a limited degree of flexibility. This is more evident at destinations at the consolidation stages, which are unable to reinvent themselves and approach new markets.

Nevertheless, the model clearly contributes to the field by encouraging tourism organisations and destinations to challenge existing strategies and practices and to forcing them to approach new tourism with new tools introduced by technology. Concentrating on core functions and outsourcing all peripheral activities to networks of virtual co-operations should enable destinations and enterprises to innovate and to adapt to the needs of consumers constantly.

Aviation Promotion

Aviation Promotion Program

The Aviation Promotion Program helps stimulate aeronautical activity and promote aviation across the state by raising awareness in the business and public sectors about the programs and services provided and the economic benefits generated by Virginia airports. The program provides funding to airport sponsors for the promotion of commercial aviation services and general aviation activities. The Virginia Aviation Board has delegated the authority to review and approve funding requests for the Aviation Promotion Program to the Virginia Department of Aviation.

Project Eligibility

Promotion programs should feature public relations activities, advertising, educational activities, publications, and the development of business and financial plans. Programs for general aviation airports can cover a wide spectrum of projects based on the diverse needs of each community and an airport's target audience. Funding for a new project can only be requested after an existing grant agreement is closed.

Eligible projects for the Aviation Promotion Program include:

- airport flight guides
- newsletters
- annual reports
- promotional videos
- on-line services
- brochures and fliers
- print media, billboards, and sign boards
- air time on radio and television
- airport and aviation displays
- aviation educational activities
- acquisition of educational supplies
- business and financial plans that must include a description of the business, financial data, and supporting documents that verify up-to-date master and airport layout plans
- items or services that are contracted for the public's use and benefit at special events such as airport appreciation days, fly-ins, and air shows

- meetings specifically held for promotional activities, including administrative, legal, and incidental costs incurred in completing a project.

Ineligible projects include:

- a promotional item or activity that has the specific purpose of attracting business or passengers from another Virginia airport, including advertising or activities referencing the name, services, or economic advantages of one airport over a neighbouring Virginia airport
- the purchase, lease purchase, or long-term lease of office equipment, presentation equipment, audio-visual equipment, vehicles, uniforms, or similar items
- the physical enhancement, beautification, decoration, or improvement of airport facilities
- a promotional item, service, or event that is not available to the public
- the promotion of privately owned businesses as sole beneficiary of a promotional effort.

State Participation

For the Aviation Promotion Program, the VAB established a $25,000 annual ceiling per airport on state financial participation for air carrier airports and a $10,000 annual ceiling per airport for general aviation airports.

Careers in Tourism

Travel and Tourism one of the world's largest foreign exchange earner among industries, provides employment directly to millions of people worldwide and indirectly through many associated service industries.

A very wide industry, it includes Government tourism departments, Immigration and customs services, travel agencies, airlines, tour operators, hotels etc and many associated service industries such as airline catering or laundry services, Guides, Interpreters, Tourism promotion and sales etc. Travel and Tourism enterprises include major internationals with a workforce of thousands, to the small private travel agent with a handful of employees.

Work in the travel and tourism industry is essentially concerned with providing services for people who are away from home, on business or holiday. Travel can be leisure travel involving package tours, pilgrim travel, adventure travel etc or purely business. Work at every functional level in the industry involves dealing directly with people.

Travel agents assess the needs of tourists and businessmen and help them make the best possible travel arrangements from the many travel options available. Also, many major cruise lines, resorts, and specialty travel groups use travel agents to promote travel packages to the millions of people who travel every year.

Travel company personnel must be up-to-date on current rules and regulations and documentation required, in areas like cargo, ticketing and passports, visas etc. so as to correctly advise their clients, and to take care of the paperwork when necessary. Besides this, all tourism staff in marketing, counter sales, or guide services, should be knowledgeable about the places their clients visit, in terms of general background, how to get there connections by air, rail and road and the facilities available.

In India, Travel and tourism, as an industry, has been somewhat slower to take off than in many other places. However, with increasing worldwide interest in travel, and with the Government's encouragement of its activities, it is undergoing massive expansion and improvement.

This forecasts a bright future for all those who choose to make a career of travel and tourism. Young people with drive and a capacity for hard work can rise to top positions very quickly in travel and tourism or even head their own agencies. A job in the industry gives good returns as well as perks including opportunity to see many locales at low prices.

Eligibility: The eligibility criteria for admission to Travel and Tourism courses at the undergraduate level is, higher secondary examination pass. Job Prospectus: Job prospectus both in public and private sector's, are bright. However, the best prospectus for qualified tourism professionals are in the private sector with travel agencies, tour operators, airlines, hotels, transport and cargo companies etc.

Remuneration : Jobs in the travel and tourism industry offer good remuneration and perquisites, which include free travel for employees and their families. Salaries can vary somewhat within the industry and are higher in foreign airlines and agencies.

Travel and Tourism Competitiveness

The *Travel and Tourism Competitiveness Report* was first published in 2007 by the World Economic Forum. The 2007 report covered 124 major and emerging economies.

The 2008 report covered 130 countries, and the 2009 report expanded to 133 countries. The index is a measurement of the factors that make it attractive to develop business in the travel and tourism industry of individual countries, rather than a measure of a country attractiveness as a tourist destination.

The report ranks selected nations according to the Travel and Tourism Competitiveness Index (TTCI), which scores from 1 to 6 the performance of a given country in each specific subindex. The overall index is made of three main subindexes: (1) regulatory framework; (2) business environment and infrastructure; and (3) human, cultural, and natural resources.

The Report also includes a specific Country Profile for each of the nations evaluated, with each of the scores received to estimate its TTCI, and complementary information regarding key economic indicators from the World Bank, and country indicators from the World Travel and Tourism Council.

Variables

For the 2008 index, each of the three main subindexes is made of the scoring of the following 14 variables, called pillars in the TTC Report. Several changes were introduced in the 2008 TTCI in the definition of the variables as compared to the definitions of the 2007 TTCI.

First, the "environmental regulation" pillar was improved with help from the IUCN and the UNWTO, and for the 2008 index was re-named the "environmental sustainability" pillar to *"better reflect its components and to capture the increasingly recognized importance of sustainability in the sector's development."*

Second, the original pillar "natural and cultural resources" was divided into two separate subcomponents: "natural resources" and "cultural resources", thus, allowing to differentiate those countries which do not necessarily have the same strengths or weaknesses in these two different resources.

In general, the model was improved with better data and new concepts were introduced.

Travel and Tourism-related Policy and Business Decision Making

Tourism Infrastructure in India

Tourism plays a vital role in the economic development of a country. Tourism is the second largest foreign exchange earner in India. The tourism industry employs a large number of people, both skilled and unskilled. It promotes national integration and international brotherhood.

India has fascinated people from all over the world with her secularism and her culture. There are historical monuments, beaches, places of religious interests, hill resorts, etc. that attract tourists. Every region is identified with its handicraft, fairs, folk dances, music and its people. The Departments of Tourism promotes international and domestic tourism in the country. The Tourism Advisory Board recommends measures for promotion of tourist traffic in India. Indian tourism is adversely affected by terrorism, tours and pollution. Sincere efforts could help to further develop the Indian tourism industry.

Tourism is one of the fastest growing industries of the world. It plays vital role in the economic development of a country. India is one of the popular tourist destination in Asia. Bounded by the Himalayan ranges in the north and surrounded, on three sides by water (Arabian sea, Bay of Bengal and Indian Ocean), India offers a wide array of places to see and things to do. The enchanting backwaters, hill stations and landscapes make India a beautiful country. Historical monuments, forts etc. add to the grandeur of the country. They attract tourists from all over the world.

Tourism is the second largest foreign exchange earner in India. The tourism industry employs a large number of people, both skilled and unskilled. Hostels, travel agencies, transport including airlines benefit a lot from this industry. Tourism promotes national integration and international understanding. It generates foreign exchange, it promotes cultural activities. Tourism also promotes the traditional handicrafts sector. The tourist gets an insight into the rich and diverse cultural heritage of India.

India has a composite culture. There is a harmonious blend of art, religion and philosophy. Thought India has been subjected to a serious of invasions, she has retained her originality even after absorbing the best of external influences. Religions like Christianity,

Buddhism, Islam, Hinduism, Jainism, Sikhism and Zoroastrianism etc. has co-existed in India. India has fascinated people from all over the world with her secularism and her culture.

The diverse geographical locales of India delight the tourists. The monuments, museums, forts, sanctuaries, places of religious interest, palaces, etc. offer a treat to the eyes. Every region is identified with its handicrafts, fairs, folk dances, music and its people. Some of the places that attract a huge number of tourists are Agra, Jaipur, Jhansi, Hyderabad, Nalanda, Mysore, Delhi, Mahabaleshwar, Aurangabad etc. Hardwar, Ujjain, Shirdi, Varanasi, Allahabad, Puri, Ajmer, Amritsar, Vaishno Devi, Badrinath, Kedarnath, Rameshwaram etc. are places of religious importance. Srinagar, Kullu, Manali, Dehradun, Nainital, Darjeeling, Ooty etc. are famous hill resorts.

The Department of Tourism was formed to promote international and domestic tourism in the country. It provides infrastructure and carries out publicity campaigns. It provides information aimed at promotion of tourist sites in the world market. It formulates policies and programmes for the promotion of tourism in India. It has officers in India and abroad. The Indian Institute of Tourism and Travel Management, The National Council for Hotel management and Catering technology etc. provide professionally trained personnel to the industry.

The Tourism Advisory Board recommends measures for promotion of tourist traffic in India. It reviews the tourist trends and suggests appropriate measures. Some of the places, havelis and castles have been converted into heritage hotels. In these hotels, the tourists get the experience the exotic lifestyle of the bygone era. The exotic train 'palace on wheel's which travels through Rajasthan attracts a lot of foreign tourists. The Indian Tourism Development Corporation (ITDC) organizes entertainment programmes like folk dances and songs and provides shopping facilities. Today many private companies like Sita Travels, Club Mahindra etc. arrange domestic as well as foreign tours.

With the growth of urban professional middle class, the tourism in India is flourishing, Many states have taken necessary steps to promote tourism. Goa promotes water sports like sailing, scuba diving and rafting. Kashmir offers the pleasure of winter sports like skiing and mountaineering. Kerala has introduced the concept of houseboats in its lagoons. Himachal Pradesh has developed winter sports in the state. In 2005 The Indian Tourism Development Corporation (ITDC) stared a campaign called 'Incredible India' to encourage tourism in India. For a better growth, the department divided different places in different section like 'spiritual tourism,' 'spa tourism', 'Eco-tourism' and 'adventure tourism'. Things have now started looking bright for the Indian tourism industry.

However the Indian tourism industry has been hit by pollution. The effluents emitted by the Mathura Refinery has led to the decolonization of the Taj Mahal in Agra. The condition of many or our monuments is deteriorating due to the negligence of the concerned authorities. On the other hand, beaches have become the dumping grounds of garbage and waste left by tourists. This nuisance should be properly monitored.

Terrorism nowadays has become a global problem. Our country is also not an exception. The terrorism in Jammu and Kashmir, Maoists attacks in West Bengal and Bihar, Bodo agitations in north eastern hill areas greatly affect the tourism in our country. Kashmir is the paradise for domestic and international tourists. The terrorism in this valley not only affects the life of the common people but also the tourism, which is very important for the economy of the sate. Necessary steps should be taken by the state government as well as central government to prevent this menace.

The tourist infrastructure in India should be strengthened. Airports and railway stations should provide information to the tourists about the tourist destination. Government owned hotels should be properly managed. The Government should also take steps for the maintenance for the tourist destination. Steps should be taken to restore the ancient splendour of the monuments. Sincere efforts could help to further develop the Indian tourism industry.

Medical Tourism

Today India is emerging as a favoured place of medal treatment. Our country has witnessed a remarkable growth in the service of hospital and well-qualified doctors, which has not only attracted the patient population from neighbouring counties but also from the Middle East and the West.

As the concept of medical tourism continues to gain momentum in India, the Ministry of Health and Family Welfare, with the help of the Ministry of Tourism, is taking numerous initiatives in order to maintain international standards in medical facilities. With some of the best hospitals in the world, Delhi is competing with foreign countries. Even there are countries where critical patients may have to wait for months. But in Delhi, any kind of treatment is available in the shortest possible time.

The cost of treatment is substantially less than those in developed countries. Besides personalized nursing care, Delhi is superb place to rejuvenate. Our country also integrate traditional medical concepts Ayurveda, Unani and Homeopathy with complimentary therapies like Yoga, Acupuncture and Aroma therapies progress the process of healing.

Infrastructure: Key to Accessible Tourism in India

The travel and tourism industry in India is being exposed to the need and opportunity of Accessible Tourism. While this aspect was touched upon in the previous cover story, the important step forward, once the awareness is created, is for the industry to start formulating and implementing plans to tap this segment. However, the moot question which arises is, are we ready to provide services for this particular segment?

The needs of Accessible Tourism, broadly defined as a set of services and facilities for individuals with specific needs that may include the disabled, elderly people, pregnant women, parents with children or people with temporary disabilities, has been voiced by the American Society of Travel Agents (ASTA) India and various Non-Government Organisations (NGOs) like Samartayam (a civic body and National Centre for Accessible Environments), Access Ability (Universal Design and Disability Employment Specialist), Svayam (organisation for people with reduced mobility), National Association of the Blind, etc. These NGOs have been working with civic and government agencies and various other corporate houses to press home the needs of this segment and to create the required infrastructure.

In India, the first step towards Accessible Tourism will involve making public infrastructure accessible to people with reduced mobility.

Hospitality Sector

The Ministry of Tourism (MoT) has listed some amenities for the disabled as criteria in order to obtain four-star or five-star classification for hotels. These include, one room for physically challenged, easily accessible lifts, four-star and above hotels should have bathrooms for physically challenged, ramps with anti-slip floors and handrails at the entrance, wheelchair access with suitable table in at least one restaurant, facilities for visually impaired persons, public rest rooms to have low height urinal (24 inches maximum) and exclusive parking for PwDs near the entrance.

There are no budget hotels that have accessible rooms or supporting infrastructure. MoT will soon make provisions for the two-star and three-star hotels to be accessible as well. However, information is lacking and it is always word of mouth, which the disabled community has to depend on. Hotels with accessible features should provide this information on their websites.

Transport Sector

"Inaccessible railways, road transportation, airways and transit infrastructure is a deterrent not only for travellers with disabilities but also for the elderly, children and travellers with temporary disabilities like a fractured leg or arm, etc. "Indian carriers do not allow two wheelchair travellers to sit together, refuse to take responsibility for the disabled travellers, charge travellers for stretchers and ambulifts and lack in developments like seat numbers in Braille, etc. Such lack of infrastructure can discourage tourists for repeat visits to India.

The Railway Ministry has announced projects for provision of world-class facilities at metro railway stations. The new design concept will have all the Universal Design features in place that will make railway stations accessible to people with reduced mobility. Even local transport like accessible taxi services, trains are needed. However, efforts are being made, though on a small scale and on a private level like Tata Group working with Samarthyam to provide low floor buses in Delhi, Chandigarh, Indore, Ahmedabad and Mumbai

Tourist Sites

"Unfortunately all the tourist attraction sites, as well as historical monuments remain inaccessible to most people with reduced mobility. Historical monuments because of their status of protected monuments under the Archaeological Survey of India were never really considered for incorporating changes to make them accessible to all," stated Kavita Agarwal. Qutab Minar is one of the tourist sites in India which has ramps for tourists on wheelchairs.

"Universal Design is the need of the hour, especially in countries like India. With India on the brink of exponential growth in infrastructure development this is the right time to take up the issues related to barrier free and inclusive public infrastructure and transportation.

The organisations involved in the development of tourism at the Centre are Ministry of Tourism, Indian Institute of Tourism and Travel Management, National Council for Hotel Management and Catering Technology, India Tourism Development Corporation Limited, Indian Institute of Skiing and Mountaineering and National Institute of Water Sports.

The Ministry of Tourism is responsible for formulation and implementation of policies and programmes for the development of tourism within the country and for attracting foreign tourists to India by way of developing tourism infrastructure, publicity and promotion, dissemination of information, coordination and supervision of activities of various segments of industry such as hotels, travel agencies, tour operators, etc.

There are 20 field offices of the Ministry of Tourism in India and 13 in other countries to undertake both developmental and promotional activities. While the overseas offices are in constant contact with tourists, travel intermediaries and media to promote tourism in India, the field offices in India provide facilitation services to tourists and coordinate with the State Governments on tourism infrastructural development. The main objectives of the overseas tourist offices are to position India in the tourism generating markets as a preferred tourism destination, to promote various Indian tourism products vis-a-vis competition faced from various destinations and to increase India's share of the global tourism market. These objectives are met through an integrated marketing strategy and synergised promotional activities undertaken in association with the Travel Trade and State Governments.

India Tourism Development Corporation Development Limited

India Tourism Development Corporation (ITDC) came into existence in October 1966 with the objective of developing and expanding tourism infrastructure in the country and thereby promoting India as a tourist destination. Working on the philosophy of public sector, ITDC succeeded in achieving its objectives by promoting the largest hotel chain in India and providing all tourist services, i.e. accommodation, catering, transport, in-house travel agency, duty free shopping, entertainment, publicity, consultancy, etc., under a single window. It also offers consultancy services from concept to commissioning in the tourism field both for private as well as public sector.

In pursuance of the disinvestment policy of the Government, 18 hotels have been disinvested. Keeping in view the changed scenario, the Corporation has suitably been restructured so that it continues to fulfil its original mandate for tourism development in the country. Besides consolidating and expanding its existing business areas, ITDC has made diversification into new avenues/ innovative services like full-fledged money changer services and Western Union Money Transfer, Training Consultancy in hospitality sector, event management and consultancy and execution of tourism and engineering projects.

India Tourism Development Corporation (ITDC) came into existence in October 1966 with the objective of developing and expanding tourism infrastructure in the country and thereby promoting India as a tourist destination. Working on the philosophy of public sector, ITDC succeeded in achieving its objectives by promoting the largest hotel chain in India and providing all tourist services, i.e. Accommodation, Catering, Transport, in-house Travel Agency, Duty Free Shopping, Entertainment, Publicity, Consultancy, etc., under a single window. It also offers consultancy services from concept to commissioning in the tourism field both for private as well as public sector.

In pursuance of the disinvestment policy of the Government, 18 hotels have been disinvested. Keeping in view the changed scenario, the Corporation has suitably been restructured so that it continues to fulfil its original mandate for tourism development in the country. Besides consolidating and expanding its existing business areas, ITDC has made diversification into new avenues/ innovative services like full-fledged Money Changer Services and Western Union Money Transfer, Training Consultancy in hospitality sector, event management and consultancy and execution of tourism and engineering projects.

ITDC has been a pioneering tourism organisation which provides all the tourist services/facilities under one roof. ITDC's present network consists of 8 Ashok Group Hotels, 7 Joint Venture Hotels including one under construction, two Restaurants (including one Airport Restaurant), 13 Transport Units, 1 Tourist Service Station, 37 Duty Free Shops at International as well as Domestic Custom Airports, 1 Tax Free outlet, 1 Sound & Light Show and 4 Catering Outlets. Besides, ITDC is also managing a Hotel at Bharatpur and a Tourist Complex at Kosi and a SEL show at Sabarmati, Ahmedabad owned by the Department of Tourism.

The Ashok International Trade Division of ITDC offers world class duty free shopping facilities to international travellers at its 38 outlets, earning crucial foreign exchange for the country and showcasing Indian products to the world.

The Ashok Travels and Tours (ATT) handles work relating to Domestic/International ticketing, hotel booking and tour packages, car and coach rentals, money changing services, money transfer services, overseas insurance and organizing exhibitions.

The Ashok Reservation and Marketing Services (ARMS) Division of ITDC, which is mainly responsible for marketing of Ashok Group of Hotels, participated in national/international events like ITB Berlin to ensure direct interaction with Foreign Tour Operators to promote various services of ITDC.

The Ashok Institute of Hospitality & Tourism Management (AIH&TM) of ITDC has been associated with the pioneering efforts in human resource development for more than three decades. Awarded the ISO-9001-2000 Certification, the institute conducts 18 months Craft/Certificate courses in the field of Culinary Skill Development, besides providing training to management trainees/ apprentices and organising Executive Development programmes for the officials of ITDC. Under an MOU signed with the prestigious Kurukshetra University, the AIH&TM started 4-year Bachelor's Degree Course in International Hospitality Business Management from August 2004.

Hotel Management and Food Craft Institutes

The Ministry of Tourism has accorded high priority to the development of manpower to meet the growing needs of Hotels, Restaurants and other Hospitality-based Industries. For this purpose, 21 Institutes of Hotel Management and Catering Technology and 10 Food Craft Institutes (3 of these are now also State IHMS) have been set up in the country. In addition to the above, four more Institutes of Hotel Management are in the pipeline at Uttarakhand (Dehradun), Jharkhand (Jamshedpur), Chhattisgarh (Raipur) and Haryana (Kurukshetra). These Institutes conduct Degree courses in the field of Hotel Management, Catering Technology and Applied Nutrition and Craft Courses in Food and Beverage Services, Accommodation Operations, Dietetics and Hospital Food Service, Food Production and Patisserie, House Keeping, Front Office, etc. IHM's Mumbai, Bangalore and Pusa (New Delhi) have started 2 Years M.Sc Hospitality courses also. Food Craft Institutes conduct Craft Courses for duration ranging from six months to one year for operational staff. All these training Institutes are affiliated to the National Council for Hotel Management Catering Technology and Applied Nutrition (NCHMCT) at apex level which regulates academics for all these Institutes.

Capacity Building for Service Providers (CBSP)

In the year 2002, the Ministry launched a programme called CBSP to train the persons engaged in small hotels, dhabas, eating joints, restaurants, etc., and also handling tourists like Immigration staff, airport staff, security/Police personnel, guides, taxi operators, bus drivers, etc. The objective was to provide short term training to improve their etiquette, behaviour and attitude towards tourists.

The scope of this scheme has been further enlarged and the training programmes of 3/6 months duration have been added for skill development of existing as well as fresh service providers. Under this scheme, a new programme called 'Project Priyadarshini' was also launched in 2005 aimed at imparting training to women in taxi driving/operation, entrepreneurship like setting up souvenir kiosks, etc, to adopt tourism as their profession.

Hotel Accommodation

The hotel sector forms one of the most important segments of the tourism industry with high potential for employment generation and foreign exchange earnings. To give impetus to this sector, the government provides concessions under EXIM Policy and other incentives. The Industrial Policy has now placed hotels and tourism related activities as a priority industry. Foreign investment and collaborations are now facilitated under the new economic policy. Automatic approval is available for foreign direct investment upto 100 per cent in Hotel and Tourism sector.

Travel Trade

The Department of Tourism has a scheme of approving Travel Agents, Tour Operators, Adventure Tour Operators and Tourist Transport Operators. During 2005, keeping in view the spurt in Domestic Tourism, a new category for the recognition of Domestic Tour Operators has been introduced. The aims and objectives of this scheme are to encourage quality, standard and service in these categories so as to promote tourism in India. The Travel Trade Division also interacts with the travel trade associations like Travel Agents Association of India (TAAI), Indian Association of Tour Operators (IATO), Indian Tourist Transport Operators Associations,(ITTA), etc., and other agencies like India Convention Promotion Bureau, Pacific Asia Travel Association (PATA), etc.

The Travel Trade Division also deals with all matters pertaining to the regulation and training of tourist guides at Regional level and also co-ordinates with other Ministries such as Civil Aviation, Culture, Railways, Surface Transport, External Affairs and Home Affairs on various issues to improve the facilities for the tourists visiting various destinations in India.

Celebration of Various Tourism Events

A number of events and road shows have been organised during 2005-06 for spreading awareness about India Tourism in domestic and international tourism market to attract more tourists to India. The major events organised by the Ministry in collaboration with various State Tourism Departments are: Golf open tournament, Srinagar; Sindhu Darshan at Leh; Heritage Festival, New Delhi; All India Crafts Mela, Hyderabad; Heritage International Festival, Jaipur; India International Boat Show, Kochi; Paragliding Show and Tourism Conclave in Himachal Pradesh; Mega Folk Festival "Virasat" in Dehradun; Prithivi 05-Global Eco-Meet, Kochi; Domestic and International Photo Exhibition "A Confluence of Cultures" and Essay and Photographic competition on "What Tourism Means To Me" on World Tourism Day on 27 September (every year); India National Tourism Day on 17 March 2006; Designer's Night Bazar, Surajkund Crafts Mela, Haryana; 3 Global Interline Golf Championship, Photo Exhibition, Eco-Tourism Marketing Meet; Mussorie (Uttarakhand), WTTC, Himalayan Run and Trek and Photo Exhibition on Hindu, Buddhist and Islamic monuments of Kashmir. The Ministry of Tourism also participated in various travel and tourism events, trade fairs and exhibitions in India and abroad. The important fairs and exhibitions are Tourism Travel Fair in New Delhi, Mumbai, Bangaluru, Chennai and SATTE (South Asia Tourism and Travel Expo), New Delhi. India Tourism offices located in 20 cities in India also participated at local important fairs. The Ministry of Tourism participated in several overseas travel and tourism trade fairs, notably World Travel Market, London; ITB (International Tourism Bourse), Berlin; Arabian Travel Market (ATM), Dubai; EIBTM, Spain; IMEX, Frankfurt; Pata Travel Mart, Malaysia; FITUR, Spain; and World Travel Fair, Shanghai. India Tourism offices located in 13 overseas cities also participated in various travel and tourism fairs.

National Tourism Policy 2002

A National Tourism Policy-2002 was announced by the Government with, inter-alia attempts to position India as a global brand to take advantage of the burgeoning global travel and trade and the vast untapped potential of India as a destination.

Tourism in 10th Five Year Plan

In order to further accelerate the development of tourism in the country, the thrusts during the 10th Five Year Plan has been to:

Position Tourism as a Major Engine of Economic Growth

Harness the direct and multiplier effects of tourism for employment generation and economic development

Provide Impetus to Rural Tourism

Provide a major thrust to domestic tourism which will act as a spring board for growth and expansion of international tourism

Position India as a global brand to take advantage of the burgeoning global travel and trade and the vast untapped potential of India as a destination

Acknowledge the critical role of private sector with government working as an active facilitator and catalyst

Create and develop integrated tourism circuits based on India's unique civilisation, heritage and culture in partnership with states, private sector and other agencies

Ensure that the tourist to India gets physically invigorated, mentally rejuvenated, culturally enriched, spiritually elevated and "feels India within him".

By 2020, Tourism in India could Contribute Rs 8,50,000 Crores to the GDP

In other words, every man, woman and child could become richer by Rs 7,000. India has yet to realise its full potential from tourism. The Travel and Tourism industry holds tremendous potential for India's economy. It can provide impetus to other industries, create millions of new jobs and generate enough wealth to help pay off the international debt. That is why we have included Tourism amongst the Core Sectors of the Indian Economy.

Incredible India !

India is probably the only country that offers various categories of tourism. These include history tourism, adventure tourism, medical tourism (ayurveda and other forms of Indian medications), spiritual tourism, beach tourism (India has the longest coastline in the East) etc.

Explore India-choose the locales of your choice, and see what each state has to offer. Lose yourself in the wonder that is India. Meander through lands steeped in chivalry and pageantry that begin before recorded history. Explore modern cities that have grown organically from the roots of a multi-hued past. Make a pilgrimage to holy shrines that echo with tales of antiquity. Frolic on a vast array of golden beaches that dot an enviable coastline, washed by two seas and an ocean. Sport with adventure in style. Let the jungle lure you to a fascinating world at a diverse array of wildlife sanctuaries and national parks....... this is the wonder that is India.

India on the World Map

The Indian tourism industry has not had it so good since the early 1990s. Though the India economy had slowed, it was still growing faster than the rest of the world. In 2009, the country is seen rising 6.5 percent, compared to the world output, which is seen falling 0.4 percent. With Indian economy growing at around 7% per annum and rise in disposable incomes of Indians, an increasing number of people are going on holiday trips within the country and abroad resulting in the tourism industry growing wings.

It is fast turning into a volume game where an ever-burgeoning number of participants are pushing up revenues of industry players (hotels, tour operators, airlines, shipping lines, etc). Thus, the tourism sector is expected to perform very well in future and the industry offers an interesting investment opportunity for long-term investors.

The Indian tourism sector is seen generating $42.8 billion by 2017, a 42 percent surge from 2007, according to an industry research note by auditing and consulting firm Deloitte Touche. Despite the challenges being faced in terms of a slowing economy, sluggish demand and security concerns, the country was fighting back and tourism developments were taking place, it said." Although there will inevitably be some short-to medium-term set backs, the long-term outlook remains positive," it said." Despite the deepening world economic crisis, India's economy remains in decent shape and is still experiencing some of the strongest growth rates in the world," the Deloitte report said.

Despite the numerous problems, tourism industry was the second-largest foreign exchange earner for India. Realising the potential in India, international and domestic hotel chains were rushing to cash in on it.

According to the global authority for hotel real estate, Lodging Econometrics, there were 73,793 hotel rooms in the pipeline of which 11,207 were due to open in 2009 and 22,522 in 2010, it said.

International tourists account for a little over 5 million visitors, while domestic market is seen at more than 500 million. Limited infrastructure pose a constraint to the free flow of tourists, but the Indian government is addressing the issue through upgradation of existing airports and building new ones.

Medical tourism was poised for rapid development in the future and India is busy developing first-class facilities to attract this multi-billion dollar niche market. The government has already relaxed the criteria to receive a visa for medical tourism.

It is also considering other incentives such as offering air travel and accommodation for foreign tourists who visit India for the third time. It may also pick up the bill for tour operators promoting domestic and medical tourism and is mulling income tax exemption for hoteliers if they invest 50 percent of profits into infrastructure.

Tourist arrivals in the country slowed throughout 2008, after rising 13 percent year-on-year from 2005-2007, due to a slowdown in the main source markets for India, the U.S. and U.K., which account for more than 15 percent of all inbound tourists.

India : An Idea who's Time has Come

Conde Nast ranked her amongst the top 10 tourist destinations. JBIC ranked her as the fifth most attractive investment destination. The World Social Forum, AdAsia, World Bamboo Congress, Commonwealth Games, Laureus World Sports Academy Global Submit, F1 alongwith some of the biggest expos and conferences of the world chose her to play host.

Presenting India to you Readers. The subcontinent to whose splendour, diversity and world-class facilities the world has finally woken up to. Away from threats, untouched by SARS and politically stable India is the flavor of the season. Take a fresh look at her flourishing economy (double digit growth in third quarter of 2003-2004), geographically strategic location, faith fortified by major software firms to make it a global backup hub for software, the staggering figure of over 366 national/international level expos and about 100 congress already scheduled for leap year 2004 (of which over 50 in January alone), her forex reserves, her rising Sensex, rapidly growing consumer markets, presence of world's finest and choicest brands and the exceptional growth in interest from FIIs, to understand why India offers a feel good factor. Truly, India is one of the most exciting emerging markets in the world.

The Scene Till Now

Some major international events like 9/11, US-led war against terror and SARS hit the tourism industry over the past few years. Cutting down of routes by domestic airlines and increase in airfares last year also led to a fall in the movement of people in the country. The Mumbai terror attacks, targetting two premium hotels, also tarnished the country's reputation, drastically reducing hotel occupancy levels, and affecting year-end travel. The adverse travel advisories by many countries to their citizens too contributed to a significant slowdown in tourism in India.

There were other negatives too. Consider this-Expenses per night of stay for a tourist in India during the SE Asian currency crisis was $100 whereas it was around $35-40 in the SE Asian countries. This hurt Indian tourism. Though this discrepancy has come down, still there is some gap. Some of the reasons for this are high luxury and entertainment taxes and high landing charges applicable in Indian airports.

Costs are also high because tourism is a state subject. Each state separately spends on tourism and tourism related activities, whereas if these funds were spent in a cohesive manner by a nodal agency to showcase the entire country as one destination, the results would probably have been far more spectacular. Currently, the centre is only allocating finances for tourism projects. But the government is trying to convince states on the benefits of bringing tourism under the aegis of the Central government on to the concurrent subject on to the concurrent list.

Government Policy Initiatives

Keenly aware of the unfolding boom in the tourism industry, the government is lending a hand to the growth of the industry. In the Union Budget for 2003-04, government has extended infrastructure status to tourism, thus opening the doors to cheap, long-term funds to help finance tourism infrastructure.

Outlay for tourism for the Tenth Five Year Plan is Rs. 2900 Crore. For the financial year 2003-04 the outlay is Rs 325 crore. This is up sharply from Rs 150 crore allocated in the previous financial year. State governments such as Kerala lay a lot of stress on boosting tourism. The state has an outlay of Rs. 74.25 crore for the financial year 2003-04.

The Government of India has extended the benefits of Section of the Income Tax Act, 1961 to institutions financing hotels of three-star category and above. A top level executive of Travel Finance Corporation of India (TFCI) is all smiles as he says, "This has benefited TFCI as the company has a major part of its portfolio in the exempted category." And this smile is now strongly percolating down to all tourism industry players in the country.

The divestment of government's stake in government run hotels is another step in the right direction. Professionals are increasingly stepping in to take over this service-oriented industry. Global best practices, cost cuts and service with a smile are fast turning a norm.

Going Forward-Destination India

India is now chalking up one of its strongest growth charts in a long time. As the Indian economy continues to open up in an effort to integrate with the world economy, benefits of doing business with and in India are increasing. With the results, hundreds of thousands of jobs are moving to the Indian shores from the West. This brings in its wake transit travellers, business travellers, business meets and holiday seekers.

This is resulting in greater room occupancies and average room revenues (ARRs) in the country. ARRs have moved up from Rs. 3200-3400 last year to Rs 4000-4200 this year. Room occupancy rates have shot up from 75-80% in 2002 to over 90% now. Infact, in Bangalore it is now estimated at 100%.

International Tourism in India

Tourist Arrivals on Track for Target

Data released by India's Ministry of Tourism in November 2008 indicate that foreign vistitor arrivalscontinued to grow strongly in the first 10 months of the year, despite the slowing global economy. Intotal, 4.32 million visitors arrived in India between January and October, up by 9.4% y-o-y. This was also positive for foreign exchange earnings, which rose by a higher 17.1% y-o-y to total INR40,712 crore overthe period.

This growth rate represents a slight slowdown from double digit arrivals growth in the first two quartersof the year. However, given the global economic slowdown and the regional diversion effect of the Beijing Olympics in August, we view growth of 9.4% y-o-y as highly positive. Indeed, given that tourism arrivals within the region as a whole are beginning to slow, it is encouraging that India continues to post such strong sector growth. We view this relative resilience as the result of long-established links between India and its chief tourism markets, the US and the UK. In addition, visits by Indian nationals living abroad, which traditionally spike during the Western hemisphere summer season, have also offered support to arrivals figures. As such, we remain positive regarding the prospects for full-year growth, and maintain our forecast for arrivals of 5.2 million. Looking ahead, we expect tourist arrivals to continue tomoderate in 2009, as the global economic slowdown weighs on the global travel and tourism industry.

However, we expect India to continue to be one of the top global performers, with sector growth likely toremain one of the highest in the Asia-Pacific region.

India Focuses on Cruise Sector Potential

The government is seeking to encourage stronger growth in the cruise sector, in order to exploit the potential of India's long coastline. Tourism Secretary Shilabhadra Banerjee announced that the government is targeting stop-off arrivals of 10 million by 2010. Banerjee added that achieving this targetwould imply an inflow of US$9 billion in revenue, and the creation of 15 million new jobs. While this target appears somewhat optimistic, especially given the deteriorating global tourism environment, boosting India's cruise sector would offer valuable support to the industry. India has avaried and extensive coastline, which to date has not been exploited in terms of cruise potential. As such, the government has stated that it will seek to improve cruise infrastructure, encouraging a diversification from concentration on cargo ports to those more oriented towards tourism. As part of this plan, it will setup cruise terminals at Chennai, Mumbai, Goa and Kochi, and reform the tax on bunkers systems to provide more incentives for investment in the cruise industry.

International Tourism in India

Strategic Significance, Gaps and Vulnerabilities

India initiated economic reforms as an aftermath of a serious foreign exchange crisis. The number and the pace of reforms have been increasing ever since. The scope of external liberalization has increased many-fold in several fields, with difficult with drawl conditions under WTO agreements. Despite all these efforts, the Balance of Trade continues to be adverse, and so is the case with balance in the current account, if the private transfers were not supporting the same. Even then the Balance of Payment position can not be said to be satisfactory, if one takes into account the transfers in capital account and the external debt position, the latter having crossed U.S. $ 100 billion mark in the year 2002.

The importance of it for India can be realised from the fact that a 2.5% share in even one year can wipe off India's total external debt and an increase by 0.25% share can more than off set the adverse balance of trade, and ease foreign exchange pressure on the economy.

If India wishes to negotiate and open Tourism sector further to benefit from the international tourism business, it has to think strategically and gear up internally to develop appropriate physical, human resource, and other organisational infrastructure in an integrated manner, which can meet the varied needs of international tourists. Failing this, if the tourism sector is opened further for the external players, India may become only a minor tool in the value creation process in the international tourism business in India. It must prepare for playing the role of the main player, who not only helps in enhancing the value creation, but also captures and controls the value created. The major benefits otherwise would be captured by other international players.

To understand the strategic gaps and vulnerability, it is necessary to revisit three basic concepts, the concepts of (tourism) business, strategic management and value creation, value capture and value control in the (tourism) business.

Needless to add, tourists do not go to destination to gain theoretical or visual knowledge of it; which they can do even by being at their place, thanks to technological development in the present internet era. They come to experience it, personally, in the total setting. In this context the *arrangements of foods, stay (and travel) too can add to* attractiveness, if they are unique, tasty (comfortable) and hygienic (safe and affordable). It may be noted that *as the distance between the place of origin and the* destination (place of interest) increases, tourist tends to visit larger number of sites/spend larger number of day to maximise satisfaction from *the amount of money and time spent*. It is rare for an international tourist to come and see just one place, spending thousands of rupees (equivalent) and several days in travel. *He then starts seeking package* of places of interest. Packages are sought not only in terms of sites, but also services (stay, food and travel etc.), cities/ states and groups of people to enhance pleasure together and guard against lack of familiarity.

There are *other needs too, which are not easily realised* such as availability of necessary amount of money as and where required. The tourist needs to know the details of the site, its attractiveness *as well definitiveness and the ease of making arrangements* for travel, stay and food. Over and above this, the requirements of certainty, reliability and prompt information about *disturbance causing events also assume significance for him*. An additional demand arises on account of differences in languages. The above *does not purport to be a comprehensive and exhaustive, but* only an indicative list of all the needs of tourists emanating from different origins and conveys the variation in the nature and magnitude of requires *as the distance between place of origin and destination increases*. These need to be elaborated and prioritized through research studies.

The significance of the above *discussion lies in the fact that these* requirements of the tourists get determined by the definition of target in *terms of place of origin and the demographic variables of tourists*. The requirements of tourist from Kenya would be different from those of Sweden, the requirements of senior citizens as tourists would be different from the adolescents. *The preparation required to be made for attracting* tourists and catering to their needs at the destination may go haywire, if *the customer requirements are not properly defined before hand.*

The *uniqueness of tourism business lies in the fact that it is not a single* service, but involves a large variety of different, exclusive and specialized *services*, which can be provided by different group catering to hospitality, transport and travel, unique, attractive site etc. *There is thus, an additional task or business: that of integration of these services.* For example, the tourist would like to know about the places he may like visit, and as he goes to decide it, he wants whether accommodation and travel reservation within his budget are possible and if so, could he have them confirmed. Any loose link in the entire value chain of services needed by him, may jeopardize his plan and pleasure. *He is willing to pay the price for the role of integrator is ensuring certainty and reliability.* The *success of tourism business perhaps depends as much, if not more, on this integration aspect*, as the quality and variety of the specialized saves of transport, accommodation etc.

Value Creation, Value Capture and Value Control in Tourism

Business

The value chain of tourism business starts from the activity of identifying the customer, presenting them the attractiveness of destination in an interactive manner, helping him in travel, accommodation & other reservations, helping in money transfer etc, and actually taking to and entertaining him at the destination site, besides taking care at nodal, transit points. The total money spent by a tourist is the total value created in the tourism business. Income from impulse purchases like specialities, memoirs etc. and *all other money spent by him on account of his "pleasure travel" constitute the total value added* in the tourism business.

The sharing or capture of the total value created by different service providers depends not only upon the absolute quality of service provided by individual supplier, but their ability to control it. It is much the same way as in the case of computer hardware sales. Out of a total price of a PC say Rs. 40,000, half of it is captured by the supplier of processors and mother board etc. With every effort to assemble and sell a PC, the sale of processor is assured. Though a high amount of efforts are required to assemble and sell PCs, the major value is captured by processor supplier and it can strategically control the entire sales.

The same may turnout to be the case of Tourism also if due care is not taken to develop adequate safeguards measures when the sector is opened for the foreign players. Further discussion on the issue is deferred to a later section.

Strategic Management

The concept of strategic management can help in analysis of strategic gaps with reference to management of International Tourism in India. Strategic Management can be understood by looking at the types of managerial decisions. Ansoff has classified the organisational decisions into three broad categories; namely, the strategic, the administrative and the operating decisions. The strategic decisions (covered under strategy formulation) are concerned with the issue of setting the direction in which the organisation will move or the course that the organisation would follow in the future. These cover the decisions regarding the organisation's mission, objectives and the strategies (i.e., the product/ market scope).

The administrative decisions (commonly referred to as strategy implementation), on the other and relate to the task of gearing, up the existing setup i.e., physical, human and organisational infrastructure to meet the requirement of business/operations in the future. Typically they cover such issues as the resource allocation, changes in the organisational structure, systems, skills technology, organisation culture and key functional policies. Taken together they cover the entire scope of strategic management function. Finally, there are operating decisions concerning various transactions or the actual operations. Strategic management deals with decisions that fall in the strategic and administrative decision categories mentioned above. Strategic management may be defined as a stream of decisions and actions which lead to the development of effective strategy or strategies to help achieve corporate objectives.

Strategic management may thus be called as a process by which the top management determines the long term direction and performance of organisation, by ensuring that careful formulation, proper implementation and continuous evaluation of strategy takes place.

It is necessary here to explain the concept of corporate strategy. Corporate strategy can be defined as "a statement of organisation mission, objectives, strategy, policies and major plans and programmes of actions, described in a way that conveys what business we are in and why are we in this business".

This definition brings out the need for organisational clarity about the mission, objectives and strategies, to integrate or unify the organisational efforts. Corporate strategy may, thus, be understood as the outcome of strategic formulation process.

The Strategic Gaps

Gaps in the Concept of Business

As mentioned earlier, the strategic management forces the management to be clear on what business an organisation is in. Strategic management concerns with two significant discussions related to a future of an organisation. These are:

(i) What business the organisation would be in the future (in terms of produces market scope) and why?

(ii) How it proposes to gear up to meet the requirements of physical infrastructures, human resources (skills, style etc.) and organisational resources (structures, systems, shared values etc.) of the future business?

As elaborated in an earlier section, the value system of tourism industry tends to encompasses all the services required from the place of origin of the international tourist to the destination. The total gamut of services that need to be provided can be broadly classified into two categories.

A. Promotional and developmental (to induce, attract bring tourists from his place of origin to the state of destination).

B. To cater to his requirements once they reach the place, to help them gain memorable experience of the visit.

The *first major strategic gap that is stunning one, is observed in the concept of business itself.* At present, the country seems to be geared only for entertaining the international tourists on their arrival, focusing on activities related to "B" part mentioned above, *rather than focusing equally* on inducing and attracting international tourist to India.

A visit to tourist developments corporations will reveal the glaring nature of this gap. An international tourist can not know and get the services *relating to "A" part from the place of his origin*. The websites of different tourist corporation are not integrated even for information, leave alone providing other services, like booking/reservation of accommodation, air/rail ticketing etc. Each website seems to be quite independent of other and does not provide information in an integrated, building block manner.

Customer Segmentation Gaps

The international tourists are taken as a homogeneous group. The word "international" is thus used loosely rather than identifying and focusing on different geographic and demographic segments to develop appropriate infrastructure to uniquely meet the requirements of different tourists segments. This is exemplified by the publicity material that is available in English Hindi or other vernacular language which can not meet the requirements of a nature German, Swiss, French, Italian, Spanish Swede, Dutch or other European tourists. *One may be surprised to learn that the* hotels, reservation and such other agencies may not even know from where is the potential market, USA, Europe, Japan, Kenya or Singapore. A knowledge of the fact that the biggest chunk in the international tourism is constituted by European tourists, may considerably help in sharpening and focusing strategy. Efforts are made to design Buddha Circuit, Taj Circuit etc. But these may not be items of common/ equal level of interest to international tourist from Japan and Europe. Same is the case of lack of understanding about their demographic patterns. For example, there seems to be no cognition of the fact that there are different segments by age group and that the requirements of each age group is different.

Lack of Clarity on Objectives

The individual services providers like hotels, airlines etc. cater to tourist alright, but they can not be sure of attracting them because all by themselves they can not determine it. The tourism development corporations were expected to do the job. *But a typical list of objectives would indicate that* they had various activities listed to entertain the tourist ones they come to *country*. There is no mention that they wish to earn foreign exchange and bring more tourists from different parts of the globe. They thus reduce themselves to play the role of individual service provider, concerned primary with increase in their capacity utilisation through variety of customers, rather than gearing up to bring the international tourists here.

Gap in Integration Value Chain Activities

The essence of strategic management is not only futuristic but also ensuring integration; ensuring that the requirement of infrastructures and operations for international tourism in India are properly taken care of. Presently there seem to be lot of gaps in the inter-linkages between various services. *The* hospitality industry (hotels etc.) treat tourism more as an as add on *activity.* The local site seeing is some what better connected in physical terms, but *there is little standardisation and assurance of quality of service.* The international money transfer facility is not provided by any domestic agency. *The list of certified hotels and guest houses is not available to the* tourists except though foreign travel agencies There is little or no interconnectivity *across various service providers and across the states.* The international tourist has to decide various arrangements before commencement of journey. But at present an international tourist *may not* even know about tourist facilities available at different sites, directly from *any domestic, Indian travel agent and other players.* He has to reach the country before he decides finer details. There is no integrated system to system to let international tourist get successive levels of information. There is no single agency to take care of missing links and ensure integration of various services as a cohesive whole, rather than presenting services in a fragmented manner.

Objectives of A State Tourism Development Corporation

- To promote, take over, develop, start, purchase, construct, take on lease, maintain, manage and operate hotels, restaurants, motels, travellers' lodges, guest houses and other places for the purpose of boarding, lodging and stay of the tourists; canteens, cafeteria, places of tourist interest like wild life sanctuaries, beauty and recreational places like parks, avenues and galleries, handicrafts emporia, establishments, undertaking enterprises and such other activities of any description with a view to develop, facilitate and promote tourism in the stat.
- To enter into any arrangement for taking over any or all of the assets and liabilities of any department of the state government or of the Government of India connected

with the development of tourism and in particular as a going concern all or any of the Tourists' Homes/State government Guest Houses/Travellers' bungalows and catering establishments already established and maintained by the state Government or by the Government of India in various places and to run the same with the object of promoting tourism.

- To establish and manage transport units, travel and transport counters, import, purchase, lease and run or otherwise operate buses, coaches, trucks, launches, ropeways, aircraft, helicopters, inland, waterways and other modes of transport and to act as travel agents I for airlines, railways, shipping companies etc.
- To provide, arrange or conduct entertainment for tourists by way of cultural shows, dances, music concerts, cabarets, ballets, film shows, sports and games, son-et-lumiere spectacles and others.
- To provide or arrange shopping facilities for tourists, establish or manage shops including duty free shops, emporia and other places for selling travel requisites and other articles of tourist interest.
- To carryon the business of restaurant keepers, wine and spirit merchants, licensed victualers, theatrical agents, box office keepers, concert room proprietors, hotel keepers, dramatic and musical publishers and printers and any other business, which can be carried on in connection with any of those objects as may seem calculated to render profitable any of the company's property and rights for the time being.
- To establish art galleries for the exhibition of paintings, engravings, sculptures, jewellery and other works of art and to buy, sell and deal in works of art of all kinds.
- To acquire land and construct, develop and maintain wayside amenities and picnic spots.
- To organise or conduct all inclusive tours by roads, rail, sea, air or otherwise and to enter into agreements for this purpose.

The task of ensuring appropriate integration is not so difficult in the present internet era, But major players who can effectively play the role of *integrator* such as State Bank of India, Bank of

Baroda, etc. who have large network of branches both in India and abroad and also have close interaction with railways, airways, hotels etc. for other businesses, *are feeling shy of entering the tourism business* and playing critical integrative role and really make tourism a money spinning and foreign exchange earner.

Strategic Vulnerability

The fact that tourism world wide is a U.S.$ 4 trillion business, opens up great opportunity for India to benefit from it in terms of earning foreign exchange and mitigate adverse balance of trade account. *An increase of* 0.25% share in the international tourism business can overcome the pressure of earning foreign exchange that has to be arranged through high interest bearing bonds and deposits, which add to self perpetuating *crisis*.

The potential business may be lost if India does not gear up to bridge the strategic gaps mentioned above. Worse still these potential may be exploited to the hill by the foreign players by bridging the gaps. Despite huge international tourism business in India, the country may not benefit in terms of getting foreign exchange as the same may be appropriated by *them*. The booking of international travel may be done by foreign carriers and exchange and commission associated with transfer of money may be appropriated by the international players like American Express, Thomas Cook etc, using Indian labour only. Even the booking of hotels may be done in foreign country and the foreign exchange may not flow to India. *A big* chunk of total value created in the tourism business in the form of travel, accommodated money transfer, even shopping may be captured by the strong armed multinational player with world wide network and Indian service providers reduced to play only second fiddle.

Some recent *studies show that the country has not gained benefits as expected by opening of Indian economy* in terms of reducing international trade gap, technological capability building and globalization or enhanced global competitiveness and ability to earn foreign exchange on its own. The same may happen in the tourism sector if it opened without necessary ground work.

Action Strategies

International tourism is an *extremely tempting proposition in terms of* potential of business especially foreign exchange earnings, for opening of tourism sector in the next round of negotiations.

It may, however, turnout *to be a mirage* if the sector is opened without adequate preparation to gear up the strategic gaps. India currently is not geared to reap the advantage of first movers. Hence must avoid straight jacket opening. *It has to fine tune* this gearing up with speed of opening tourism sector as per the provisions *of negotiations at WTO. It has to carefully examine when and how much* to open through (almost irreversible) specific commitments and what should be limitations put into effect to achieve this fine tuning.

The preparations for exploitation of international tourism business *require* as much attention of the government and industry as of the academicians. The governments need to play the first level integrator role in terms of setting priorities and expectations from the international tourism business. It has to play the role of promoters, persuading different providers (to bridge the gaps), who have not come forward to play the role like the banks. The industry has to *develop mechanisms to ensure strong linkages among various service providers to make it an integrated whole,* rather than behaving like a large number disjointed service providers. The academicians have to *provide strong analytical support through research* studies for identification of missing links in providing various services, *pointing conceptual confusion in mission, objectives and strategies.* In a nutshell the international tourism business has to be considered in its entirety by the three major contributors.

Issues for Future Research

The paper highlights the need for several types of in-depth studies required to gear up for benefiting from the growing international tourism business. Firstly, there is a need for *study of international tourists needs (especially those related to the promotional and developmental aspects* explained in section 3 of the paper) coming from different geographical areas. There is also a need for *studying the appropriateness of existing infrastructure in* light of the needs identified to understand the degree to which the present *infrastructure is adequate or inadequate.* Only the in-depth studies can show whether there is need to focus more on utilisation of infrastructure already created rather than creating new ones. The country has paid a huge price in the race for creating assets in the nineties in various sectors of industry leading to excessive infrastructure created in the industry sector as a whole. The mistake does not need to be repeated once again in this sector. There is also a need for validating the *strategic gaps identified in the concept of business*. This will help in identifying to what extent the thrust of tourism strategy in India has been a lopsided one; focusing mainly on entertaining the international tourists who have come to India vs. bringing them to India and its different states. *Studies are also required to ascertain* the nature and level of efforts and investment required for bringing the *international tourists to India*. Further, *studies are also required to clarify* the strategic focus of tourism industry; how much domestic and how much international tourism and why?

Studies are also required to clarify the assumption of considering all the *international tourists as a homogeneous group*. Are there demographic segments that can help in designing the infrastructure in a better manner to meet specific and varied requirements of different segments?

There is yet another set of studies required to *identify the missing links in* the tourism business at the country, state and city level that need to be *taken care of*? There is also a need for ascertaining *whether tourism in* general, and international tourism in particular, is being consider as an integrated business or an assortment of hospitality, entertainment and *travel businesses by various players in the field*. If so, what is the consequence of it in terms of loss of tourism business in general, and international tourism business in India, in particular.

Last but not the least, there is a need for studies to understand *how much of* the value created in the international tourism in India is being captured and retained (especially the foreign currency part) in India and how much of it is captured and repatriated out of India by the international players. This is important as if due care is not taken then India may not benefit in terms of foreign exchange earning from this lucrative sector, what is a key consideration in negotiation at WTO for opening this sector.

7

Natural Disasters and Tourism

Tourist Safety and Security in the Coastal Zones of the Greater Caribbean

The Importance of the Tourism Industry to the Greater Caribbean

Tourism has proven to be a pillar of economic development for many regions around the world. In 2003, tourism was the largest business sector in the world economy, employing 200 million people, generating 3.6 trillion in economic activity and accounting for 1 in every 12 or 8% of jobs worldwide.

Across the economies of the Greater Caribbean too, the importance of tourism for generating income, creating and sustaining jobs, encouraging foreign investment and facilitating trade opportunities cannot be denied.

In 2007, the Caribbean travel and tourism economy is expected to account for 5.1 per cent of world demand; to contribute 16.5 per cent to the region's GDP; and will experience a 19.9 percent real growth in capital investment of total investment. In fact, today, tourism stands as the primary source of foreign exchange revenue in half of the countries in Central America. The statistics therefore clearly demonstrate the value of tourism to the Greater Caribbean region.

The Vulnerable Nature of the Tourism Industry to Different Disaster Triggers

The vulnerability of tourism to risk, crisis and disaster has long been evident (Sharpley, 2005). In fact, the historical record is full of cases in which the tourism industry has been affected by a range of disasters each with different disaster triggers, whether they be:

1. Natural;
2. Biological;
3. Man-made; or
4. Technological.

Each of these types of disasters have affected tourism over the years and we have several notable examples that we can call to mind:

Natural

a. The Indian Ocean tsunami of 2004 which has without doubt shown how international tourists were, with tragic consequences, caught up in the unfolding of a natural disaster (Sharpley, 2005). Thousands of western tourists were the victims of the tsunami. One estimate puts the overall death toll as surpassing 280,000 and the number of tourist causalities at more than 3,500.

Such was the scale of devastation, that the World Tourism Organisation's Francesco Frangialli has been known to refer to that event as 'the greatest catastrophe ever recorded in the history of world tourism' because it caused the biggest loss of life in terms of the number of tourists as well as those working in the tourism industry; and

b. The impact of Hurricane Katrina on New Orleans in 2005 which left more than 80% of New Orleans underwater and blew away that state's biggest source of revenue-tourism which in 2004 drew more than 10 million visitors and created 80,000 tourism-related jobs;

Biological

a. Foot and mouth disease in England in 2001 which affected travel flows in the United Kingdom, Europe and Asia;
b. The Severe Acute Respiratory Syndrome (SARS) epidemic of 2003 which severely affected Southeast Asia, Europe and China; and
c. The Bird Flu epidemic in 2003, 2004 and 2005 which affected Asia and Europe;

Man-made

a. Persistent crime against tourists such as we experience here in our Caribbean islands, and on a much larger scale, terrorist acts such as September 11 in 2001 which crippled the global economy and eroded traveller confidence; and

b. The Bali bombings in October 2002 which for some territories such as Indonesia resulted in a substantial decrease in international arrivals, a retardation in new holiday bookings and a cut in international airline services;

Technological

a. Airplane crashes such as TWA flight 800 in July 1996, a scheduled international passenger flight from John F. Kennedy International Airport New York, to Charles de Gaulle International Airport, Paris which due to a technical malfunction crashed and killed all 230 people who were on board.

Events like these threatened the safety of tourists, host communities and tourism employees. Moreover, there has been a downturn in the tourism product of individual destinations as a result in each case, for reasons that are only too obvious.

The Geographic and Climatic Setting of the Greater Caribbean Increases the Risk of the Occurrence of Natural Disasters

As these examples have shown, no region on the globe is safe or immune from the risk of the occurrence of a disaster. In our own region, we are likely to be visited by the precursors of disaster every year in the form of tropical storms and hurricanes. This is because as each and every one of us knows, the Caribbean lies in the North Atlantic Ocean, one of the six main tropical areas of the Earth where hurricanes may develop from June to December every year.

Interestingly, at the regional level, several other facts about the location of the territories of the Greater Caribbean make their vulnerability to certain natural hazards inevitable. For example, several of the islands of the Eastern Caribbean are volcanic in origin and the volcanoes in the region are considered to be either active or dormant. The only known submarine volcano in the region-Kick 'em Jenny-which is located 9 km north of mainland Grenada, also puts the island of Grenada and the rest of the Eastern Caribbean open to the threat of a tsunami should a major under-water volcanic eruption occur. Studies have suggested that a tsunami generated by a violent eruption at Kick'em Jenny would realistically reach heights over 7 metres on the north shore of

Grenada within 5 minutes of the eruption. What is more, the Tectonic Setting of the Caribbean is such that many Greater Caribbean countries lie close to tectonic plate boundaries and thus face the threat of earthquakes. In fact, the level of seismicity in most of the Caribbean is considered to be moderate to severe. Thus, all the countries of the Greater Caribbean are to some extent vulnerable to the impact of geological and hydro-meterological hazards.

The Special Case of Coastal Tourism

Add to this scenario, the fact that over the past three decades the predominant style of tourism in the region has been based almost exclusively on the attraction of the climate and of beaches. International visitors simply like visiting the beach and as receiving destinations in the Greater Caribbean, we have made an economic commitment to satisfying international demand by providing a coastal tourism product (UNECLAC, 2003). However, the coastal zone is seen to be in the direct and immediate area of risk for the following reasons (Mahon, 2007):

- Hurricanes and tropical storms make landfall with all their force in this area and wind force is likely to be most destructive on the coast;
- Shear wind force acting on coastal waters throws up sea water on coastal land producing storm surge and conditions ripe for severe coastal erosion that threatens the stability of coastal buildings and other structures;
- The coastal zone is the most low lying area in Caribbean SIDS and as a result is prone to coastal flooding due to runoff from mountains; and
- Tsunami impact is greatest closest to the shore as the coastal zone is the first zone of impact.

Yet, despite information on the numerous risks associated with building on the edge of the water, tourism plant continues to be built in the hazard-prone area of the Caribbean coast. For example, in the island territory of Barbados, there about 420 places of accommodation divided between hotels, villas and condominiums and about 90 percent are located on the coastline (Daily Nation, 2006); while World Bank (2000) estimates that generally the typical tourism development in the Caribbean is located on the coast and is sited within 800 metres from the high water mark.

The Impact of Natural Disasters on the Coastal Tourism Product

In the realm of natural disasters, the focus of the region and tourism industry has traditionally been on the hurricane hazard – and for good reason. The impact of tropical storms and hurricanes has been significant.

For example, the impact of Hurricane Georges on the Caribbean tourism sector in 1998 has been well documented. In Antigua, six hotels were closed; while in Barbuda, there were two hotels with extensive damage. 15% of the 5,800 rooms in the Dominican Republic were damaged. In St. Kitts, 500-600 rooms were closed for one month; while in Nevis one hotel was closed for two months with eight of ten guest houses at the hotel being destroyed (Collymore, 2006).

More recently, in the case of Hurricane Ivan in 2004, 50% of Grenada's physical tourism assets was destroyed. Such a sharp contraction in Grenada's overall hotel room stock translated into a sharp decline in almost every other area of tourist activity on the island. Preliminary data covering the period January to April 2005 placed stay-over visitor arrivals (which account for 88% of total visitor expenditure) at 31,331 compared to 49,550 for the same period in 2004, a decline of 37%. All major source markets except Germany experienced declines – USA (29%); UK (65%); Caribbean (32%); Canada (42%); with an attendant decline in visitor expenditure for the four month period by 41%, from approximately EC$ 177 million to EC$ 104 million. The total impact of Hurricane Ivan on the sector was plugged at EC$ 264.3 million (OECS, 2004).

In 2005, Wilma which was the strongest Atlantic storm ever recorded wrecked Cancun and other beach resorts, washed away whole beaches, killed 7 people and caused $2.6 billion in damages (Reuters, 2007). Wilma made several landfalls with the most destructive effects felt in the Yucatan Peninsula of Mexico, Cuba and the US state of Florida. The popular Mexican resort towns of Playa del Carmen, Cozumel and Cancun all suffered significant damage. Tourists in the resort city of Cancun and its adjacent islands were told to return to their places of origin or head inland while those unable to, were relocated to designated hurricane shelters throughout the city. During the storm, waves five to eight meters (high enough to reach the third floor of many hotels) slammed against the coastline.

The passage of Hurricane Dean in August of this year which became the first major hurricane and first category 5 hurricane of the 2007 Atlantic hurricane season, saw thousands of tourists leave the 'Mayan Riviera' and head for makeshift shelters on Mexico's Yucatan peninsula. In Quintana Roo's Costa Maya region, where Dean made landfall as a category 5 storm, a state of emergency was declared and involved the evacuation of some 80,000 tourists.

In September, the situation for the region was no better. Hurricane Felix slammed into Nicaragua's Miskito coast as a Category 5 storm while Hurricane Henriette made a direct hit on the Cabos resorts of Mexico's Baja California peninsula. Amazingly, twin Atlantic and Pacific hurricanes had made landfall on the same day. This was unprecedented as no such thing has happened in the recorded history that dates back to 1949. If we remember that Hurricane Dean had struck Mexico further up the Caribbean coast, then also unprecedented was the fact that two Category 5 hurricanes had made landfall in the same year (Associated Press, 2007).

Hurricane Henriette was powerful enough to snap young palm trees in two and rip branches off others. Tourists were urged to stay indoors after a middle-aged female tourist was killed while walking on the beach. You see as this storm approached Mexico's Pacific beach and golf resort of Los Cabos, it sent 13 feet (4-meter) waves crashing onto the shore.

Most recently, in fact in earlier this month, the impact of Hurricane Noel on the Bahamas has made headlines as costing the popular island destination millions (Nassau Guardian, 2007).

So this is what has happened in the last decades; it is what we are facing now; and it is what we can expect to face in the future. However, our purpose is here today is to make sure that when we face it, we are prepared and that every caution is taken to secure the safety and security of visitors in the event of a natural disaster.

Issues Related to Tourist Safety and Security in the Event of a Natural Disaster

Good Tourism Planning Practice Ought to Recognise That

There are different types of tourists that visit the region and we must know how best to respond to their needs in the face of a disaster. For example, tourists on organised tours will have different needs when compared to independent travellers simply because accommodation arrangements and tourist activities tend to be different. In addition, destinations that promote family vacations versus honeymooners will have slightly different issues to consider as children have different needs to adults. As do the physically challenged and what is needed to keep them safe in times of disaster. For tourists that visit by yacht, evacuation of these vessels ought to be a priority as rough waves can break vessels from their anchors. We have to think too not only about coastal hotels but also about coastal and marine based tour operators; about their situation and about their needs;

The seasonal nature of Caribbean tourism dictates that in the peak season tourists tend to be spatially concentrated on the narrow coastal zone (UNEP, 1999);

The location of most important tourism developments visited by international tourists lie in the path or location of natural phenomena with a high potential for disaster (UNECLAC, 2003);

Due to the small size of Caribbean islands and the narrow physical nature of the coastal zone, tourists will not have many options for evacuation upon receipt of warning of impending disaster (UNECLAC, 2003); and

While resilience of physical structures is essential in an earthquake, or hurricane events where occupants take refuge within the structure, appropriate evacuation design implemented in the physical layout of structures is a priority in cases of tsunamis, volcanic eruptions and storm surge when occupants seek to flee to higher or safer ground (Garcia et al, 2006).

Of foremost concern too is the high occupancy density of hotels, as is the need, unlike other businesses, to cater for both employee and visitor safety (Johnston et al. 2007). This makes a strong case for the consideration of safety concerns as a central part of the appraisal process of any coastal tourism project.

Learning from Past Experience

There can be no doubt that tourism is a valuable industry that is worth protecting. In trying to achieve this goal of protecting our tourism product, our tourists, and our tourism employees, we have to determine from past experience what are the optimal approaches to managing a crisis arising out of the passage of a familiar natural event such as a hurricane or earthquake as well as unfamiliar events such as tsunamis.

Lessons from the Great Hanshin Earthquake of 1995 (APEC,2005)

In the Great Hanshin Earthquake in Kobe, Japan in January 1995, which was measured at a magnitude of 7.3, 249,180 buildings collapsed, 6,436 people lost their lives and 43,792 were injured. However, in the midst of this destruction, for the tourism industry, precautions such as earthquake proof architecture, fire proof equipment and the value of frequent fire and evacuation drills had paid off. In addition, although in many cases, guests had to stay in hotel lobbies for 2 to 3 days, they were given frequent situation reports in order to prevent panic and employee morale was kept high. Four key points have come out of that disaster:

1. The basic rule of prioritizing human life prevailed – each employee must act for guest safety soon after an emergency event. This was evident by the fact that most guests were evacuated from their rooms on hour after the event;
2. The importance of having a unified information flow that prevents the spread of rumors that may lead to panic and confusion;
3. Moving down decision making power to the front lines in emergencies; and
4. Maintaining a good relationship with the local community so that there is rapid cooperation during disasters.

Lessons from the Tsunami of 2004

The Indian Ocean tsunami of 2004 demonstrated how the tourism industry despite its technological advances and sophisticated building methods turned out to be the most vulnerable sector located on the coast (Garcia et al., 2006). For example, it was observed that due to the demand for scenery rather than safety, the tourist trade was the least environmentally sustainable form of human settlement on the coast of Thailand and the least integrated into the natural ecology.

A glaring example of this was the fact that although resorts and hotels were built along the lowest-lying areas of the coast for the convenience of beach access, such areas proved to be the most prone to wave action and flooding.

The Indian Ocean tsunami experience has taught us several lessons:

- That keeping a decent registry on clientele is critical. Hoteliers ought to know who is there and what language that person speaks;
- That management and security functions such as communications centres, back-up power generators, safety deposit boxes, reservation desks, and offices should be relocated to the upper floors so that they can still function during and after the disaster;
- That in the event of a sudden onset disaster, where there is a verbal warning, death rates are significantly lower. The dissemination of warning messages is critical in the event of a disaster. Tourists may not have mobile phones; few will have or be close to a radio. Have we determined who are equipped with warning devices such whistles, bull horns, sirens etc? We remember 10 year old Tilly Smith who saved a hundred fellow tourists from the tsunami because of a geography lesson about the giant waves. Tilly sounded an alarm and urged her family and others to get off Maikhao beach in Thailand;
- That in disaster events, where there is no warning, we need to be prepared to operate in a bottom up manner. This usually means that it is the staff closest to the tourist that is in a position to make life and death decisions. Therefore, the role of knowledgeable, well paid, enthusiastic staff that are both ready, able and willing to make an effective response cannot be underestimated.
- That shelter and/or evacuation options must be available and tourists must know how to access them. The importance of tourist sensitisation even while on vacation to the likely event of disaster and what to do if this occurs should not be underestimated. Tourists are usually not aware of the geography of their surroundings. Yet, tourists need to know where critical support services such as shelters, evacuation routes, hospitals, fire stations, police stations, and airports are;
- That the tourism industry must be prepared to assist itself in times of emergency. Hotels and upscale restaurants in that region were dependent on imported goods, services,

and power, isolating it from local communities, which produce their own food, transport, and energy resources. Hotels administrations however, ought to make a list of critical items and keep these readily in supply. Since the amount of damage due to a disaster can never be known beforehand and it may not be possible to leave the hotel facility to obtain supplies, do we have emergency supplies of food and water safely stored at all times? In addition, items necessary for search and rescue operations such as shovels, hammers, saws, axes must also be kept. Alternatively, are we encouraging visitors to invest in travel insurance to cover events that necessitate evacuation and repatriation?; and

- That good community relations and integration is essential in times of disaster. Stranded and injured visitors often had to get first aid, food, water, shelter and transport from local fishermen and shopkeepers rather than from tourism operators.

The experience around the world has confirmed that regardless of the type (public or private) and size (large or small), organisations that fail to take action prior to a disaster are more likely to respond with ad hoc measures. The tourism industry is too important to the region's development for such an approach.

The Role of the Regional Network for Tourist Safety and Security in Promoting Initiatives Related to Visitor Protection

The territories of the Greater Caribbean remain committed to the creation and implementation of this network that fosters a safe and secure environment for visitors and host populations alike. Their latest initiative to achieve this goal comes in the form of the Regional Network for Tourist Safety and Security which is envisioned as providing an overall, comprehensive framework for addressing various threats to visitor safety and security. The focus of the Network thus far has been on crime, crime management, and occupational health and safety concerns in the tourism industry. However, more remains to be done in executing a truly holistic approach to the issue of tourist safety and security in our region.

The Sustainable Tourism Directorate sees this High Level Conference as an opportunity to partner with the Natural Disasters Directorate to address some of the pressing concerns of tourism stakeholders in our Member countries in the realm of dealing with natural disasters. The Natural Disasters Directorate has considerable expertise on which to draw, having already produced material on early warning systems (2003); executed a project aimed at updating the building codes of the Greater Caribbean for Winds and Earthquakes (2003); produced a Caribbean audio soap opera for hurricane disaster preparedness (2005); and held workshops on the exchange of successful experiences of the disaster management offices/agencies of countries of the Association of Caribbean States (2005). Likewise, in January of this year, the CDERA in conjunction with its regional partners has undertaken the Regional Disaster Risk Management for Sustainable Tourism in the Caribbean Project which promises to contribute to the reduction of the vulnerability of the tourism sector in the Caribbean to natural hazards. No doubt, we look forward to assimilating the policy considerations that come out of the Caribbean Regional Sustainable Tourism Development Program which is an initiative of the CTO.

It is generally believed that human institutions and their decisions have a real influence on whether a community, and we make particular reference to the tourism community, suffers substantial damage due to an extreme event. Each of the organisations represented in this workshop today has a special and significant role to play in this regard. Therefore, this workshop should prove to be useful not only to gather the views of the disaster risk management community and other regional partners on matters of common interest but also to identify areas of organizational synergy and establish a harmonised direction for the future.

The RNTSS has an important role to play in identifying and promoting best practices, such as the Barbados Model of Tourism Emergency Management Committee and the Tourism Emergency Operation Centre, which can be integrated into the National Task Forces, Committees on Tourist Safety.

We would like to see, for example, a system where a pool of information collated from Immigration Authorities showing which tourists are in the country, where they are from, where they are accommodated, information from tour operators and accommodation establishments, showing the language of the tourists, any special needs (medical related), emergency contact information, etc.

This added to updates on evacuation of these tourists who was relocated to where, who are accommodated on flights off the island and on which ones.

Collation of this information will be facilitated by a network of hoteliers, hotel associations, immigration authorities, airlines, police (Interpol), CARICOM Regional Security Mechanisms, the national sub-teams for disaster management in the tourism sector. The objective is to provide comprehensive record and tracking of the tourists visiting the region at any given time.

This information is already available and needs to be reorganized for this special purpose. Some of the considerations which will impact on instituting this system relates to:

- Systems for guest recording in hotel and other accommodation establishments
- The quality of record-keeping by tour operators and other ancillary service providers
- The willingness of the tourism sector to maintain up-to-date records and to share this information
- Confidentiality of the information in terms of the institution in which it would be housed, who will have access regionally and internationally
- The use of technology to capture, store and manipulate the information.

8

World Eco-tourism Summit

This report contains the summaries of the debates held and conclusions reached at the World Eco-tourism Summit and its preparatory process, as well as the Quebec Declaration on Eco-tourism. The World Eco-tourism Summit, was held in Quebec City, Canada from 19 to 22 May, 2002. This was the principal event to mark 2002 as the International Year of Eco-tourism.

The Summit was an initiative of the World Tourism Organisation (WTO) and the United Nations Environment Programme (UNEP). It was hosted by Tourisme Quebec and the Canadian Tourism Commission. These four organisations were the partners responsible for the Summit. The purpose of the Summit was to bring together governments, international agencies, NGOs, tourism enterprises, representatives of local and indigenous communities, academic institutions and individuals with an interest in Eco-tourism, and enable them to learn from each other and identify some agreed principles and priorities for the future development and management of Eco-tourism.

Main Themes

UNEP and WTO, in consultation with other organizations and Eco-tourism stakeholders, had defined and adopted the following main discussion themes for the International Year of Eco-tourism and for the Summit.

Theme A-Eco-tourism Policy and Planning: The Sustainability Challenge

Sustainable Eco-tourism plans, policies and programs at international, national and local levels; integration of Eco-tourism policies into sustainable development plans and frameworks; land use planning; use of natural parks and protected areas; balance between development and conservation objectives in policies; development agency programs on Eco-tourism and their role in funding related pipeline investments; plans for human resource development in Eco-tourism.

Theme B-Regulation of Eco-tourism: Institutional Responsibilities and Frameworks

Legislation, norms and other regulations for Eco-tourism activities; voluntary schemes and self regulation; certification, accreditation and ecolabels; international and inter-governmental guidelines, principles and codes; roles of different stakeholders in ensuring compliance with regulations or voluntary schemes.

Theme C-Product Development, Marketing and Promotion of Eco-tourism: Fostering Sustainable Products and Consumers

Building sustainable Eco-tourism products; multistakeholder cooperation for product development especially in protected areas and biosphere reserves; market research, marketing techniques and promotional methods; information to tourists; ethical behaviour; environmental education for consumers; public-private sector relationships for marketing and promotion; cooperative marketing for small Eco-tourism operations.

Theme D-Monitoring Costs and Benefits of Eco-tourism: Ensuring Equitable Distribution Among all Stakeholders

Measuring economic, ecological and social costs and benefits of Eco-tourism; contribution to conservation; assessing potential and actual environmental and socio-cultural impacts of Eco-tourism; taking precautionary measures at local, national, regional and international levels; integrating monitoring and evaluation procedures; research needs and adaptive management systems.

Cross-cutting Themes

Throughout the discussions on the four themes the focus was on two main cross-cutting issues:

- The sustainability of Eco-tourism from the environmental, economic and socio-cultural points of view;
- Involvement and empowerment of local communities and indigenous people in the Eco-tourism development process, in management and monitoring of Eco-tourism activities, and in the sharing of benefits resulting from it.

The Preparatory Process for the Summit

During the latter half of 2001 and the first four months of 2002, 18 preparatory conferences were held. These conferences took place in all the regions of the world, either under the aegis of WTO or of UNEP (in association with The International Eco-tourism Society). A list of the conferences can be found later, in the reports of the regional panels. The preparatory conferences provided an opportunity for all kinds of stakeholders in Eco-tourism to come together to present their experiences and discuss matters of local, regional or international concern. In total over 3,000 delegates attended the conferences and over 300 papers were presented at them.

The preparatory conferences addressed each of the four main themes of the Summit. The combined results of the conferences were summarised in four papers, one for each of the themes, which together formed a discussion paper circulated at the start of the Summit.

During April 2002, a web conference was held. This enabled any individual or body, at no cost, to participate in the debate about the four Summit themes. There were 948 registered participants in this conference.

Participants and Presentations

A total of 1,169 delegates attended the World Eco-tourism Summit, from 132 different countries. The range of delegates included:

- International agencies engaged in supporting conservation, tourism and sustainable development.
- National ministries of tourism, culture and the environment. In total 30 ministers of state attended the Summit.
- Non-governmental organisations working at an international or local level, representing conservation, indigenous communities, travellers and other interests.
- Private sector enterprises engaged directly or indirectly in Eco-tourism.
- Academics, consultants and other experts in the field of Eco-tourism.

Registered delegates were invited to submit statements relating to the Summit themes. A total of 180 statement proposals were received. From these, 120 were selected for presentation during the event, considering time limitations of the three-day programme. The selection was based on the relevance and originality of the contribution and on the need to achieve a representative balance of presentations from different types of organisation and parts of the world. In addition to the registered statements, participants had the opportunity to intervene freely throughout the debate sessions.

All statements, whether presented or not, which were received by the deadline were included in a CD-Rom, which was distributed to each delegate. This CD also included the reports from the preparatory conferences.

Structure of the Summit

Following introductory presentations from the partners, the Summit consisted of the following elements:

- A plenary session at which four panels reported on the preparatory conferences held, respectively, in Africa, Asia, the Americas and Europe.
- Four parallel working group sessions, covering the four main themes of the Summit.
- A ministerial forum, and two special forums covering the business perspective and development cooperation in Eco-tourism.
- A plenary session to receive and debate reports from the four thematic working groups.
- A final plenary session to receive and debate the draft Quebec Declaration on Eco-tourism.

Summit Outputs

This report, including the annexes, sets out the issues, key points, recommendations and conclusions arising from the Summit.

The main output from the Summit is the Quebec Declaration on Eco-tourism. This has been taken forward to the World Summit on Sustainable Development at Johannesburg, 2002, and has been widely circulated. The full text is included in this report.

The complete text of this report, also the content of the above mentioned CD-Rom, including all statements received and the final reports of the preparatory conferences are available at the following websites:

Reports From the Regional Panels

The opportunities presented by Eco-tourism and the need for its careful management are apparent in all regions of the world. Evidence from the preparatory conferences suggested that the fundamental principles and issues relating to the development of Eco-tourism are similar in all areas. However, it was also apparent that differences in resources, ecosystems, markets and socioeconomic structures, mean that priorities and practicalities vary from region to region.

These similarities and differences were brought out during the reports of the regional panels at the Summit. During each panel session, short presentations were made by selected spokespersons on the preparatory conferences held in that region. In the main, these conferences had focused on the region in which the conference was held, but in a few cases the conferences covered types of destination (e.g. islands, deserts, Arctic lands) irrespective of continent.

Following the presentations on the preparatory conferences, the sessions were opened up to interventions from the floor and a discussion. At the end of each session, the key points that had arisen were identified by the rapporteurs.

Session on Preparatory Meetings Held in Africa

Four reports were presented to the Summit on the preparatory meetings held in the following locations:

- Maputo, Mozambique, March 2001-for all African states with an emphasis on planning and management
- Nairobi, Kenya, March 2002-for East Africa
- Mahé, Seychelles, December 2001-for Small Island Developing States (SIDS) and other Small Islands
- Algiers, Algeria, January 2002-for Desert Areas

The presentations in this panel demonstrated that Eco-tourism is one of the main forms of tourism in which Africa has a comparative advantage.

Africa features extensive protected areas hosting a variety of ecosystems and traditional cultures that are major attractions for nature-oriented tourism. In many African countries, vast national and wildlife parks count for many forms of Eco-tourism activities. Eco-tourism seems the best way to prevent controversial effects and negative impacts on prevailing ecosystems, local communities and traditional cultures and to be a viable source of economic benefits for African countries, if developed and managed in a sustainable manner. The specific circumstances and needs for different areas were separately identified.

Africa's International Comparative Advantage: National Parks and Protected Areas

Eco-tourism is a great opportunity for African countries and its parks, reserves and protected areas are an international level resource. Thus, many African countries can base their tourism development on exploiting their natural assets on the condition that the rules of sustainable development-the basis of Eco-tourism-are respected. Conservation of natural resources can become mainstream to socioeconomic development in Africa. National parks and reserves in Africa should be considered as a basis for regional development, involving communities living within and adjacent to them. Given their strong international recognition, parks and reserves can be turned to sort of brands, providing advantage in tourism marketing and promotion.

Small Islands and Coastal Zones

Particular attention must be focused on tourism development in small islands as development, even Eco-tourism development, can be at the origin of environmental and social problems-even before large number of tourist arrivals. This is the case of coastal zones in small islands where ecosystems, notably lagoons, are particularly vulnerable. Appropriate liquid and solid waste treatment systems must be put in place whenever any Eco-tourism activity is created.

Moreover, ecolabels are particularly important for small insular countries as shown in the example of the Seychelles. Ecolabels can be very useful for achieving landscaping and beautification objectives, such as by encouraging better use of gardens, and for stimulating environmental management, such as energy conservation, waste treatment plants and recycling systems.

Due to the natural and economic specificities of tourism in small islands it is not realistic to focus on Eco-tourism in the stricter sense. Rather, the broader concept of "sustainable tourism" is often a more effective policy position, though Eco-tourism plays an important role in further setting the standards for the protection of the natural and cultural environment.

The fragility of island ecosystems must be the cornerstone of any Eco-tourism plan and any action must respect the island's local, natural and cultural environments.

Desert Areas

Desert areas represent comparative and even absolute advantages for Africa, which has the largest desert in the world. Deserts are also some of the largest conservation areas in the world. The seminar in Algiers concluded that there are great opportunities for Eco-tourism in desert areas-particularly for Africa because of its location near the large tourist generating markets of Europe. Desert areas represent complex Eco-tourism attractions, showcasing natural, geological, and archaeological features, nomad and other specific cultures and traditions. A special attention should be paid in Eco-tourism development and management in desert areas to the fragility of ecosystems, the extreme meteorological conditions, the presence of unique archaeological and geological remains, the scarcity of water resources and the difficulties of access.

Importance of Trans-boundary Cooperation

Many natural zones cross the political borders of several countries and this must be taken into account when developing Eco-tourism. Indeed, it is impossible to envisage diverging or even opposed development policies in zones shared by several States where there is natural, human and social unity. In this case, trans-boundary cooperation is fundamental for all types of Eco-tourism development, which implies common policies between countries in the same region. This cooperation is particularly necessary in areas where wildlife crosses administrative and political borders. The development and management of trans-boundary natural resources and parks has to become a central issue in Africa, recognizing the need to maintain ecological integrity and free movement of wildlife in certain territories that are divided by country frontiers.

The Need to Find Commercial and Financial Solutions

The commercial viability of Eco-tourism initiatives is a recurring theme in the debates such as in the case studies presented in the preparatory seminars, specifically in Maputo. Participants emphasised the importance of strengthening small and medium enterprises and particularly micro enterprises to enable them to successfully engage with the tourism industry in Africa. The importance of identifying and demonstrating to funding sources the value of conservation and of Eco-tourism to national economies in Africa has to be recognised.

The Need to Reinforce Capacity Building

There is a lack of awareness of tourism among African local communities. Local communities need to appreciate the benefits and the demerits of tourism. It is important for governments to ensure that communities are trained to administer joint ventures, as without capacity building it is difficult to sustain an equitable approach to management. Capacity building is essential if local communities are to be real stakeholders in the development of Eco-tourism in Africa.

African Necessity to Focus on Benefits for Local People

Speakers and participants identified the need to generate local community benefits from Africa's natural heritage tourism as the critical issue. Eco-tourism as a concept has most to offer in the African development context, linking to the rural economy to avoid leakages and maximise local economic benefit from tourism. In Africa, national parks, wildlife reserves and other protected areas have to play a significant role in encouraging local economic development by sourcing food and other locally produced resources.

Session on Preparatory Meetings Held in Asia and the Pacific

Five reports were presented to the Summit on the preparatory meetings held in the following locations:

- New Delhi, India, September 2001-International NGO Workshop Tourism Towards 2002
- Gangtok, India, January 2002-Conference for South Asia
- Maldives, February 2002-Asia-Pacific Ministerial Conference on Sustainable Development of Eco-tourism
- Chiang Mai, Thailand, March 2002-Conference for Southeast Asia
- Fiji, April 2002-Conference on Sustainable Development of Eco-tourism in the South Pacific Islands.

The papers and debates from the Session on Asia and the Pacific highlighted a number of issues and perspectives, as follows.

Need for Baseline Studies

The importance of baseline studies was highlighted, in order to provide a better knowledge on ground conditions, and changes over time. It was recommended that innovative approaches be examined, instead of reliance on government, particularly in under-resourced areas. Suggestions included involving volunteer organisations (e.g., those that provide programmes in which conservation and community development work is combined with educational, cultural exchange and tourist activities), or involving educational institutions (e.g., through PhD students).

Commoditisation in Tourism

Particular mention was made of commoditisation in tourism in the region, in large part due to poverty. Commoditisation refers to the degradation of the intrinsic value of cultural items, beliefs, goods, and practices, and may even refer to treating a human being as a good for sale. This trivialisation of culture is demonstrated by the sale of culturally related trinkets, and even by people selling themselves (sexually) to visitors. Organisations developing or managing Eco-tourism are urged to focus on the improvement of basic human conditions.

Managing Impacts

A range of approaches were mentioned for managing impacts, from pricing and fees, to diversification of product offers (to alleviate crowding). However, a serious impact with no solutions offered, was that of global warming in the region.

The need to Integrate a Range of Perspectives, with Communications Being Key

In some Asia-Pacific destinations, ministries try to push their own agendas on other departments and vice versa (e.g., Tourism and Forestry). This achieves very little except resistance. There needs to be awareness and capacity building in government departments, to understand that Eco-tourism can be a force to assist both mandates.

It was observed by some participants that some NGOs always feel government actions are wrong, and governments tend to pay less attention to constant criticism. Other participants felt that

NGOs have some valid perspectives whether in critique of governments or not, and that NGO comments deserve appropriate attention. It was also felt that some NGOs or governments actually undermine private business. The issue that emerged was: how to integrate the range of perspectives, and how to cooperate to mutually beneficial ends.

Improved communications are required. In particular, it was recommended that:

- governments should establish an open dialogue with local communities, private companies and NGOs;
- governments should develop transparent communication, consultation and decision making processes; and
- public-private partnerships should be seen as a key facilitating mechanism, particularly for informing and educating the travelling public about the consequences of their travels as well as their potential for beneficial action.

Challenges of Implementing Community Participation

The challenge of how to implement sustainability through empowerment and participation was discussed, since local participation has an important role in preserving biodiversity.

- Bottom-up participatory processes were recommended (e.g., as in Fiji, where the Fiji Eco-tourism Association was formed, so that government and others could more easily communicate with an umbrella industry organisation).
- Top-down participatory mechanisms were also recommended, as well as a mechanism for multi-sectoral involvement. It was suggested that communities should be consulted on a range of topics, from product development to elements of marketing.

It was acknowledged that time is required for awareness and capacity building, so that communities are able to participate effectively and make decisions.

Community control of local resources was said to be a key need in the Asia-Pacific region. It was suggested that communities should be involved in all levels of activity, including management.

Participatory management was said to be a key tool in ensuring participation in planning, decision-making and management. An example was given of Sri Lanka, where both poachers and policemen communicate together, and although it has taken five years (as well as time, patience, energy, and the efforts of the Eco-Development Committee), both parties now have confidence in the process, and poachers are using their locally-developed skills in a more sustainable way.

It was agreed that Eco-tourism is best developed to enhance and complement current community lifestyles and economic activities, rather than basing community economies solely or predominantly on Eco-tourism, or introducing a completely new activity. It was also frequently stated and agreed that communities should have control over Eco-tourism, including whether they wanted to have it at all, and if so how much, where, when and of what type.

Human Resource Development is Required

It was recommended that there should be a bigger emphasis on training for local people. In the Asia-Pacific region there is a very great need to incorporate local indigenous peoples into any training programs. It was also felt that communities in general need to have awareness training or information related to Eco-tourism, and also to be made aware that they may have a choice about tourism or other activities.

A challenge related to this topic was how to develop mechanisms to ensure that revenues from Eco-tourism activities are invested in training (e.g., on-the-job training, management training, or sending workers to attend conferences).

Regulation and Monitoring is Required

Regulations can either have a positive role in facilitating movements of tourists and foreign exchange in SE Asia, or can be restrictive. It was suggested that very often poor planning has had adverse consequences and needs to be improved. Also, the lack of enforcement of current regulations is a problem.

Session on Preparatory Meetings Held in The Americas

Six reports were presented to the Summit on the preparatory meetings held in the following locations:

- Cuiaba, Brazil, August 2001, for all American states
- Belize City, Belize, November 2001, for Mesoamerica
- Lima, Peru, February 2002, for the Andean region
- Oaxaca, Mexico, March 2002-Oaxaca Declaration on Indigenous Tourism

- Buenos Aires, Argentina, April 2002-First National Conference on Eco-tourism
- Web Conference on the Sustainable Development of Eco-tourism, April 2002.

The Americas are probably one of the regions in the world where Eco-tourism is developing fastest. There is also an increasing concern about the involvement of indigenous peoples and local communities both in the planning and development of Eco-tourism.

The preparatory conference reports showed clearly three main concerns about the development of Eco-tourism: the involvement of local communities; the need for certification schemes easily accessible to everybody regardless of their economic capacity; and much needed training at all levels. In general, there is consensus about the fact that Eco-tourism can and is contributing actively to nature conservation in the region, and also to a better quality of life for local people. It has also been recognised that it is very important to learn from past mistakes as well as successes.

Planning

One of the issues raised around planning was the specific problem of trans-boundary areas where there is a need for international regulations. Another important point was that very often not all available scientific information is used for planning.

A further concern was that it is important to have a diverse range of activities besides Eco-tourism such as agriculture, livestock, forest non-timber products, and others, thus avoiding over-dependence on Eco-tourism. Shifting from traditional sustainable use of resources (when these uses are sustainable, which is not always the case) to Eco-tourism is a high-risk strategy for local communities. Besides, in areas where Eco-tourism products mix with other kinds of tourism, it is agreed that there is a need to increase the sustainability of all tourism products.

Regulation and Certification

A suitable approach regarding regulation is to follow a process leading from optional guidelines to obligatory regulations. Codes of conduct need to be established as well as procedures and all stakeholders should adopt these. The importance of ethics among operators, the community and consumers was also identified as one of the key issues. Another important point raised was that regulation of Eco-tourism needs stakeholders sharing a similar concept of Eco-tourism. It was agreed that there is a need for more transparency in certification processes and that these should relate both to environmental aspects as well as quality and participation of local communities. International certification systems are believed to be too expensive and it was suggested that local initiatives should be recognised by international systems. It was suggested that certification should occur at different levels that are more suited to specific regional and local conditions and allow community-based companies to take part in the process. There were proposals to establish incentives for certified companies. Finally it was recognised that in some areas there is a risk of a proliferation of eco-labels.

Participation of Indigenous and Local People

One of the main concerns was the lack of public participation in the process of planning for Eco-tourism in many places. It was stressed that local communities need to be the main actors and that they must take part not only in the planning process but also in the management of Eco-tourism products, which generally means also taking risks. A particularly sensitive issue was the concern among indigenous people about the fact that in some of their lands Eco-tourism development is being imposed by governments and private companies, without proper consultation and participation.

Capacity Building and Training

Capacity building and training were identified as key points in the proper development of Eco-tourism in the region. This included the need for capacity building of local communities, training and technical support. An important point raised was that training needs to be realistic, not creating too high expectations for local communities. Policy makers were also identified as important targets for training and it was shown that they need to learn about Eco-tourism in the field. Very often policies are in the hands of people with very little practical experience in the subject. Another target much in need of education about Eco-tourism is the media in general, who very often cover Eco-tourism but without reflecting properly its real essence.

Marketing

A fairly common problem in the Americas is that marketing generally focuses in landscape, wildlife and cultural issues and does not put enough emphasis in social, environmental and sustainability aspects, which should be part of responsible marketing communications and very often can be of interest to potential visitors.

In recent years there has been a great development of communications within the region and the Internet has become an important tool for marketing, even for small companies and communities, as well as in remote areas where Cybercafes can be accessible. The Internet can fulfil its potential only if capacity-building and access to modern technology is provided in order to empower Eco-tourism stakeholders for the adequate use of this media.

Session on Preparatory Meetings Held in Europe

Four reports were presented to the Summit on the preparatory meetings held in the following locations:

- St. Johann / Pongau and Werfenweng, Salzburg, Austria 12-15 September 2001-for mountain areas, with an emphasis on European Eco-tourism
- Almaty, Kazakhstan, 17-18 October 2001-for the transitional economies of the CIS countries, Mongolia and China
- Thessaloniki, Greece, 2-4 November 2001-for European, Middle East and Mediterranean countries
- Hemavan, Sweden, April 2002-for the Arctic countries, including North America and Asia as well as Europe

In addition, a paper was presented by the Minister of Tourism of Turkey.

Although the term 'Eco-tourism' is less frequently used in Europe than in other continents, the presentations showed that the principles and concepts associated with it are equally important here as elsewhere. Europe has many wilderness areas, yet in much of the continent attractive rural landscapes and biodiversity are dependent on traditional land management practices. There is increasing recognition within Europe of the important and mutually supporting relationship between tourism, agriculture, viable rural communities and the conservation of nature.

The preparatory conference reports demonstrated the contrasts to be found within Europe, in terms of landscapes, climate, culture and management priorities. The specific circumstances and needs of different areas were separately identified.

Mountains

Mountains are important locations for Eco-tourism. The report from the conference in Austria recognised the important linkages between the objectives of the International Year of Mountains and the International Year of Eco-tourism, both declared for 2002 by the UN. Mountainous areas often display a particular cultural richness, economic fragility, a decline in traditional populations and activities, and sensitive biodiversity. Mountain communities can use Eco-tourism to address these issues. There is a close relationship between the needs and opportunities of Eco-tourism and sustainable activity tourism in mountains.

The Mediterranean

This area receives some of the largest volumes of tourist arrivals in the world, concentrated on the coastal belt. Yet, this is an area of rich biodiversity and also has immense cultural resources. The report from the conference in Greece identified the opportunity for Eco-tourism in the coastal hinterland and more remote inland areas, as a way of improving the image of Mediterranean destinations, diversifying the offer, reducing seasonality and bringing economic benefits to areas suffering depopulation. Careful planning will be essential.

The CIS Countries

These countries have extensive natural areas including forests, wetlands, plains and mountains. Potential for Eco-tourism is considerable. However, as economies and societies in transition they have particular needs, especially in terms of the general services and infrastructure for tourism. Important issues include clarifying national objectives for Eco-tourism, stimulating and catering for the domestic market, filling knowledge gaps, easing visa restrictions and promoting cross-border cooperation.

The Arctic

This is a sensitive area with its own particular needs. The traditional values and practices of the indigenous peoples of the Arctic, in protecting and using natural resources, should be recognised, as should their rights over land and water. The report from the conference held in Sweden identified the need for certification programmes for Eco-tourism which take account of the particular circumstances of the Arctic. Appropriate codes of conduct for visitors and operators need to be applied. A restructuring of the cruise ship licensing system was called for, with local people having control over the use of their areas for Eco-tourism.

In addition to these priorities relating to specific areas or ecosystems, a number of general themes of particular importance in the European context can be identified from the presentations and the subsequent discussion.

Taking an Integrated Approach to Destination Planning

There is strong recognition in Europe of the need for a holistic approach to the planning and development of destinations for sustainable tourism, both in terms of providing a quality experience for visitors and addressing all the impacts of tourism. Eco-tourism should be seen within this context. There should be concern about physical infrastructure, destination marketing and information services, linkages with other economic sectors, and relationships with other forms of tourism.

The important role of local authorities in supporting the development and management of sustainable tourism, including Eco-tourism, is well understood in Europe. This is helped by well-established local democratic structures, effective land use planning and development control processes. At the same time, the need to foster a participative approach at a local level, for example through engaging village communities, is recognised.

Addressing Transport and other Access Issues

The use of transport to, and within, the destination was a key concern of the preparatory conference in Austria. Where possible, Eco-tourism should be based on forms of mobility which have low environmental impact. Discussion at the Summit widened the debate on access, with a call for more attention to be paid to facilitating access to rural and natural areas, including mountains, for example through networks of hiking trails.

Being Concerned about Demand and Equity Amongst Users

Demand management was felt to be an important issue in the European context. Points made about this during the discussion included:

- avoiding discrimination and increasing access to Eco-tourism experiences for people with disabilities and disadvantages;

- promoting opportunities to domestic visitors, ensuring that they are not put off by high prices (e.g. in the CIS countries); and
- influencing larger tour operators as well as more specialist operators (e.g. in the Mediterranean).

Showing Responsibility in Promoting Eco-tourism in Less Developed Countries

Europe is a source region for much global Eco-tourism. The responsibility of European governments and operators in encouraging more sustainable forms of Eco-tourism, and in providing technical advice and support in this field, is recognised.

Reports From the Thematic Working Groups

The second full day of the Summit was devoted to four separate working groups on the four Summit themes.

Each working group meeting started with the presentation of a report from an expert, appointed by WTO and UNEP, which summarised the results of the preparatory conferences and served as discussion paper for the Summit concerning the theme in question. These reports are reproduced in Annex 1.

A total of 71 presentations were made to the four working groups. These were restricted in time, to enable a range of topics to be covered and to give as many people as possible a chance to speak. Two presentations from the host country, Canada, were made during the first session of each group. The presentations were grouped into four sessions throughout the day, and after each one at least half an hour was allowed for interventions from the floor and for debate. In the closing session, the WTO/UNEP experts summed up the main points to be taken forward to the final day of the Summit, and these were further discussed and expanded by delegates during a final hour of debate.

On the third and final day, a report from each working group was made to a full plenary session of the Summit. This was followed by a discussion period which enabled all delegates to have a chance to make further points about each theme, and to comment on the conclusions of the working groups.

The four reports which follow set out the issues discussed and the key points and recommendations arising from the working groups, while also taking account of the points raised in the final plenary session. These reports build on the summary reports of the preparatory conferences, adding to, illustrating and emphasising points made in them.

A short resume of the key points arising from the preparatory conferences is given, before the points arising from the Summit are presented. Reference should be made to Annex 1 for the full coverage.

Many of the points made were repeated in more than one workshop.

This is inevitable as most of the principles of Eco-tourism relate to all of the themes and each of the topics are interdependent. For example, Eco-tourism planning needs to take account of product development and regulation issues, and vice versa.

Working Group-A

Eco-tourism Policy and Planning: The Sustainability Challenge

Eco-tourism is a complex activity, often seeking to meet a range of objectives, involving a variety of stakeholders and taking place in environmentally and economically fragile locations. It therefore needs careful planning. This working group was concerned with the frameworks, structures and processes of Eco-tourism planning and policy-making to maximise sustainability and local benefit. There were eighteen presentations to the working group, which covered:

- National Eco-tourism planning, policy-making and strategy development-Botswana, Chile, Cote d'Ivoire, Haiti, Rwanda, France, Brazil, Senegal, Tanzania, the Mayan World.
- Eco-tourism planning systems in federal and provincial parks-Canada
- A case study of ecosystem changes in tourist destinations-Nepal
- Guidelines to minimise negative impacts of Eco-tourism in vulnerable ecosystems (the Convention on Biological Diversity) or small islands (Seychelles)
- Integrated planning and management in rural areas-Greece, Chile Policies developed by origin countries for minimising tourism impacts in destinations-The Netherlands.

Issues Discussed

The main issues discussed were:

- The best structures and tools for effective Eco-tourism planning, which relate to all objectives
- Planning for environmental conservation
- Planning for economic development
- Gaining social and cultural benefits
- Multi-stakeholder participation.

The Relationship Between Eco-tourism and Sustainable Tourism

It was suggested that planning and policy development for sustainable tourism was the appropriate context for Eco-tourism planning, since Eco-tourism embraces the principles of sustainable tourism concerning the economic, social and environmental impacts of tourism. On the other hand, it was also suggested that there was merit in highlighting the particular characteristics of Eco-tourism, bringing positive benefits for conservation and communities and not simply avoiding negative impacts. It was recognised that Eco-tourism products may vary considerably, but that all should adhere to basic Eco-tourism principles.

Lack of Appropriate Infrastructure and Services in Destinations

In many destinations with Eco-tourism potential, it is felt that there is a lack of infrastructure (e.g., accommodation) and services (e.g., well-trained guides).

Foreign Ownership or Low Levels of Local Jobs Minimise Local Benefits

The issue of foreign ownership draining many of the benefits at the local level was raised. This is particularly the case with respect to infrastructure. In addition, the level and quality of jobs in which local people are employed is too often inadequate (e.g., in Senegal).

Eco-tourism Brand

The themes of the Summit are in many cases strongly interrelated. Within the Planning and Policy Development sessions, there were discussions about the desire to prevent the use of the word Eco-tourism by those who do not adhere to its principles, through some type of trademark or branding protection, although the difficulties in this were also acknowledged. This whole topic was the focus of considerable discussion in Session B, and reference to that section provides further insight.

Uncontrolled Penetration of Eco-tourism Activities into New Areas

The penetration of Eco-tourism (or other forms of tourism) to remote areas can create management and monitoring problems. For example, in Egypt treks go to very remote areas of the country, which are mostly desert. The difficulty of monitoring tourism operations in remote areas enables the stealing of artefacts, fossils, etc.

Key Points and Recommendations

A number of key points and recommendations arising from the working group were specifically related to conservation, economic development, social benefits and stakeholder participation. However, there were many points that cut across these issues and these are presented first.

Key Crosscutting Recommendations

Main recommendations from the preparatory conferences:

- Integrate Eco-tourism policies and planning across national boundaries
- Ensure national governments provide necessary leadership and guidance
- Create a planning framework for protected areas
- Formulate Eco-tourism plans jointly between public agencies, NGOs and other stakeholders, with a long term vision and clear goals
- Develop tools to assist in planning and management of Eco-tourism (e.g. appropriate land use planning and visitor management techniques)
- Provide adequate and appropriate funding for projects, protected areas and partnerships
- Involve governments, development agencies, NGOs, private businesses and others in building local capacity, to encourage participation and employment of local people
- Ensure careful consultation and participation of all stakeholders in planning and policy development processes.

Using Transboundary Management Approaches

The need for trans-national policies was emphasised, related to many aspects of tourism, such as easier movement of peoples between regions, and cooperation with respect to shared ecosystem management.

Humans should be recognised and acknowledged as being a part of the ecosystem (as opposed to only using ecosystems). Transboundary movement possibilities should be built into plans and policies.

There was a recommendation that a world fund be established to enable appropriate Eco-tourism development particularly at the trans-national level, with the focus intended to be on enhancing cooperative activities between jurisdictions. However, no specific proposal was made on the nature and source of the fund.

It was proposed that global regions (e.g., the Caribbean) should come together for a range of planning and policy development functions (e.g., to highlight issues which have regional relevance)

Taking a Collaborative Approach to Planning and Policy Development

There should be an overall national vision of how Eco-tourism can serve biodiversity, as well as how biodiversity can serve Eco-tourism. One of the biggest problems is lack of a sectoral planning perspective (e.g., the frequent divorce in dialogue between tourism agencies and environmental agencies). All agencies need to work together. It is recommended that lessons and failures be taken from such planning processes as Integrated Coastal Zone Management Studies, for integrating Eco-tourism planning. Integrated planning should be actively pursued, including collaboration with stakeholders.

Government must take a holistic perspective when developing sustainability strategies, which is both spatial and sectoral (e.g., as in Greece). Eco-tourism planning should be conducted within the context of sustainable tourism planning, which in turn should relate to the wider context of planning for sustainable development. Eco-tourism planning, actions and policies should be developed with the knowledge that they are likely to be applicable to other forms of tourism, and in all likelihood will be a force for positive change throughout tourism, considering the trends towards mainstreaming Eco-tourism values and principles. For example, in Tanzania, there are major policy reforms stimulated by the International Year of Eco-tourism, which are focusing on poverty reduction through a range of sectoral perspectives such as developing economic opportunities and empowering communities through community participation.

Sectoral integration should be a foundation of all planning and policy development (not only in Eco-tourism). For example, Chile's National Action Plan is based on an integrated approach, and has been done with the private sector, in a bottom-up manner. Another example is found in the Seychelles, where there are not only various topical themes within their National Environmental Management Plan (including tourism and aesthetics), but there are significant cross-cutting themes (education, awareness and advocacy; partnerships, public consultation and civil society participation; training and capacity-building; management; science, research and technology; monitoring and assessment; vulnerability and global climate change).

It was recommended that whatever the mechanisms, all decision-making be transparent, and also accountable.

Developing Appropriate Tools for Planning and Management

It was recommended that appropriate scale in Eco-tourism development be a part of planning considerations. For example, some destinations build in development controls ahead of time (e.g., Botswana has, as part of its planning framework, deliberately stipulated small-sizes for their ecolodges and camps, or temporary facility structures to enable them to be moved in the future).

There was a comment that in many areas, policies and regulations may exist, but are not implemented. While appropriate planning and policy development is one requirement, rigorous implementation is fundamental.

Planning Systematically for Protected Areas

It was emphasised in debates that a protected area system must form a key part of planning and policy making for Eco-tourism, and that protected area managers be involved in planning initiatives (not only senior government officials).

A severe problem for protecting biodiversity and protected areas was felt to be the fragmentation of ecosystems. It was recommended that the issue of adequate size of protected areas be addressed in development and planning. It was suggested that a useful educational and management tool is the creation of maps to illustrate locations, threats, or other spatial variables, so indicating where it is most necessary to conserve biodiversity.

Committing Adequate Financial and other Resources

Some countries lack the ability to mobilize the resources necessary to address significant Eco-tourism planning and policy development needs. Multilateral aid is required in the form of various types of assistance. One recommendation was that there be support for centres of development and dissemination of knowledge and cooperation; another was that there be a fund for trans-national Eco-tourism development.

The public may be encouraged to contribute funds. It was suggested that visitors and others should be able to donate funds to projects, and should receive some recognitions and benefits which reinforce the value of their donation. For example, the Coral Reef Action Network offers donors a range of educational reminders: stickers to heighten awareness, CD with a tool kit for customers, wall calendar, passport, poster, boaters' chart, quiz and similar items. These educate and keep donors involved with the project. In addition, they give donors guarantees that all their contributions will go to the chosen project.

It was suggested that some funding for education, in schools and elsewhere, be set aside from Eco-tourism revenues.

Capacity Building

Training and capacity building is required for those professionals who are involved in planning and policy development. It is recommended that the WTO and other international institutions support or fund programs which train public officials who will be planning and developing policies, in order to build capacity within ministries and similar institutions (e.g., this could be through national level training institutions). This suggestion of appropriate training was also made for the personnel of park and protected area authorities.

At a more local level, it was suggested that the WTO and other institutions should continue to expand training programs, such as for local authorities, indigenous people and other stakeholders. Another suggestion was that a range of types of support be examined to develop capabilities locally, such as guiding skills. It was recommended that tour operators also be involved in education and training. Education and awareness-building is recommended as a significant tool for all players, from lodge owners and tour operators to local communities and young people. Suggestions included such innovative ideas as developing education caravans for community awareness building, or creating coursework for schools to better understand the concept of impact.

The views and perspectives of youth are a key influence on positive future directions. It is recommended that sustainable tourism education of young people be built into educational programs and ministry curricula in all countries.

It was recommended that the Internet be better used for information exchange. International agencies should collaborate to compile a database of information, which is web accessible, continually updated, and includes information on best practice for sustainable tourism and for Eco-tourism. It was suggested that qualified websites with useful information should be able to link to this site.

Building Multi-stakeholder Participation into Policy and Planning Processes

Mechanisms should be developed to include a range of stakeholders in planning and policy development. It is always easier for governments to deal with umbrella organisations than with operators directly, thus developing industry organisations may assist. For example, Parks Canada and the Tourism Industry Association of Canada have developed an accord concerning heritage-based tourism, which is currently focussed on agreement about principles, which acknowledge shared stewardship in managing and protecting national heritage places.

Indigenous peoples' representatives (e.g., Shushwap Nation, in Canada) emphasised the need to build targeted participative mechanisms into planning and policy development. Since indigenous peoples tend not only to be the poorest members of society, but also to have land based economies and cultures (involving hunting, fishing and gathering), it is critical to involve them early in any processes.

Other suggestions for including stakeholder participation came from Tourism Quebec, who suggests that integrated management requires that there be government centres close and accessible to citizens (decentralised communications points).

It was also emphasised that past experience should be brought into the planning and policy development processes (e.g., South Africa) so that there is greater integration of Eco-tourism activities into the way of life of communities. It was recommended that the Global Code of Ethics developed by the WTO should be adopted by all stakeholders, to promote a balanced perspective in different forms of tourism development, including Eco-tourism.

It was also agreed that Eco-tourism should not be developed if consultation revealed that local communities did not want to have it.

Recommendations for Environmental Conservation

Main recommendations from the preparatory conferences:

- Conserve energy, water, and other resources, reduce waste and favour materials that are not imported.
- Plan more sustainable transport options.
- Promote awareness of conservation and biodiversity amongst local people and visitors.
- Use appropriate tools to identify limits to use and to manage impacts.
- Seek to influence demand as well as managing visitors who do come.
- Use economic tools, information and interpretation in visitor management.

Educating Communities about Biodiversity and Conservation

It was felt that many local communities did not understand the value of biodiversity very well, and that education was needed. Visitors should also be educated about the value of biodiversity and that natural resources belong to local peoples and should not be removed by visitors (souveniring, biopiracy, or removal of fossils, etc.).

Managing Impacts

Primarily, it is essential to ensure that Eco-tourism does not have negative impacts, and that operations adopt minimum impact practices and guidelines (e.g., in the St Laurent or Yukon areas of Canada). Other options are planning in the destination to exclude certain activities (e.g., in the Seychelles, where there are certain banned activities). In some locations, government regulations are required (e.g., to ensure that cruise ships adhere to minimum environmental standards where ships do not take voluntary action). It is recommended that management decision-making be built into plans, together with other techniques (such as forecasting, environmental and social impact assessments or monitoring), to address potential problems or impacts as a preventative measure.

Managing Visitors

Overall, it was recommended that an integrated approach is applied for the management of many variables, including supply and demand. Supply considerations, such as resources or culture, should be of primary concern, but management should also take full account of markets and demand.

Recommendations for Economic Development

Main recommendations from the preparatory conferences:

- Provide training, micro-credit and other assistance to small, medium and micro-enterprises.
- Provide incentives for enterprises to pursue sustainability
- Provide infrastructure, such as access and telecommunications, to assist communities in Eco-tourism development.
- Emphasise the role of governments as facilitators rather than operators.
- Place an emphasis on increasing retained economic value per visitor rather than expanding visitor volumes.

Providing Government and other Support for Community Level Eco-tourism

It was confirmed that the state should be a partner, not a developer of Eco-tourism operations.

In recognition that there is a spectrum of market interests, and a spectrum of tourism opportunities, there may be scope to link nature to cultural tourism and even to mass tourism (e.g., in Greece) particularly in areas where there are fewer pristine environments, in order to heighten the attraction of the destinations, and to generate community benefits. Communities need a source of funds which can be linked to development. There may be opportunities to create community institutions and link them to forms of income generation; or to create Community Conservation Funds for donors, so Eco-tourism is viewed as a business by communities. International assistance should be targeted more towards Eco-tourism projects. Assistance can be given in the form of finance, technology, training, information, mentorship, or in other ways. Loans might be given to countries, for example for training. Assistance could be targeted and conditional upon performance (e.g., demonstrating environmental protection). It is recommended that international agencies coordinate sources and conditions of assistance, and provide centralised and up to date information (e.g., on a website) for easy access by needy destinations. Other forms of assistance may include staffing and human resources, and volunteer labour. This can provide a sense of ownership of the project by participants (e.g., in Senegal there are agreements between Parks and volunteers).

Recognising Mutual Benefits

Often, there are contributions which local communities bring to Eco-tourism or other developments, which are not viewed in terms of having conventional value (e.g., in Uganda, these might be spiritual, medicinal, or other information or cultural activities). It was felt that while Eco-tourism development can bring value to local communities, at the same time local communities can contribute valuable knowledge and information, practices, traditions, etc. to agencies, entrepreneurs, visitors, or others. In some cases, local people provide such information or knowledge without any recompense or benefit. It was recommended that such local contributions and sharing should be valued through financial or similar means. In this way there is likely to be more understanding that contributions are mutual, rather than the view that benefit flows are uni-directional to communities. Exchanges of information can be of equal value to communities and to planners and policy makers. For example, imported technologies must be appropriate to the communities. However, indigenous technologies must also be acknowledged (such as India's Care and Share program), since traditional ecological and other knowledge and technologies will also have great value. For example, the Austrian Parliament has just called for a respect for the knowledge of indigenous peoples as a basis for sustainable development, and for indigenous land rights as a basis for human rights.

Recommendations for Social and Cultural Benefits

Main recommendations from the preparatory conferences:

- Use historic buildings and other heritage resources, thereby contributing to their protection.

- Involve communities in social and cultural programmes, to ensure local control, ownership and authenticity.
- Mount community awareness campaigns.
- Ensure that tour operators and other external companies are aware of their responsibilities towards communities.

Involving Communities and Ensuring Local Ownership

A number of areas have problems due to overpopulation (e.g., European coastal areas) while other areas (e.g., mountains) may suffer from depopulation. It was suggested that Eco-tourism may provide some benefits to both areas, by alleviating pressures on the coast, while attracting visitors (and development) to rural areas. For example, in Greece the planning process aims to link natural areas with cultural tourism and to link these to mass tourism destinations. It is recommended that governments consider providing communities with land or resources which can enable them to act as partners in Eco-tourism operations. Botswana has allocated wildlife management areas to local communities for consumptive or non-consumptive use in tourism, so they can share in Eco-tourism benefits. An additional benefit is that this has led to decreased poaching. Communities should have input to planning processes through, for example, local narratives and guides, wherein they provide information to visitors, plus develop their own self-esteem. Communities should be involved and empowered, such that there is no Eco-tourism development where there is no desire for involvement in tourism. Opportunities should be sought to build on current economic and community activities rather than developing some totally new product.

Recommendations for Multi-stakeholder Participation

Main recommendations from the preparatory conferences:

- Build support for joint ventures into planning and policy initiatives
- Facilitate community-level joint ventures, such as co-management of protected areas
- Encourage strategic alliances between private businesses and local communities.

Encouraging Joint Ventures

Origin-destination joint ventures were suggested. One innovative example is in the Netherlands, where there is increasing awareness by tourists or tour operators that they may be the source of problems when they visit other destinations. An outgoing tourism policy has been developed, and moves to link outgoing tourism with NGOs in receiving destinations.

It was emphasised by Tanzania that there needs to be strong involvement by the private sector in partnerships, not just governments or NGOs. The Tanzanian delegation to the Summit included a great many industry representatives as well as government representatives. Overall, throughout the discussions on policy and planning, the points made at the preparatory conferences were reinforced, with the topics summarised above being the main focus of discussion. In addition, it was also said that the International Year of Eco-tourism has already stimulated some of the actions and directions identified above.

Working Group-B

The Regulation of Eco-tourism: Institutional Responsibilities and Frameworks

The impacts of Eco-tourism on society and the environment can be positive and negative. The theme addressed by this working group was about providing the right regulatory frameworks and systems to ensure that products that are developed and marketed as Eco-tourism are beneficial and not harmful to environments and communities. Nineteen presentations were made to the working group, covering:

- Examples of regulation and control of Eco-tourism-Quebec, Mexico, Japan and Seychelles.
- Certification systems-The experiences of existing and planned new certification schemes in Australia, Peru, and Costa Rica as well as the examples from the USA and Europe.
- International guidelines for Eco-tourism-Austria, Germany and Europarc.
- The need for quality control and for the identification of indicators-emphasised in two Canadian presentations.
- Specific methodologies and practical examples, from Uruguay, Indonesia, India and Korea.
- Eco-tourism and ethics, presented by the representative of The Vatican.

Issues Discussed

The following were the main issues discussed by the working group.

Institutional Frameworks

Legal frameworks and regulations are not always established for Eco-tourism only and very often are common to other kinds of tourism. The need to have specific legal frameworks and policies for Eco-tourism was stressed by different speakers, although in some cases it has proved difficult to have the same framework in different regions of a single country.

In some cases the work of individual countries is not enough to guarantee that Eco-tourism is properly developed. There were proposals in the Korean presentation to promote action for Eco-tourism development at the international level.

The need to develop Eco-tourism strategies at the national level through a consultation process was well demonstrated in the Seychelles.

Regulation of Eco-tourism

The role of the private sector in the establishment of regulations and in the certification process was discussed and different viewpoints were expressed. While some people felt that the private sector should take part in defining regulations, others considered that governments and NGOs should establish regulations in order to guarantee the preservation of natural and cultural resources.

Certification and Labelling

These were issues that brought a number of questions and discussions. One of the points was whether certification should be just a voluntary process, or whether it should be an instrument to complement the regulation of Eco-tourism ventures. Another important point raised by different people concerned the components of certification schemes. Other aspects, beyond environmental issues, need to be taken into account and included.

The scale of certification met with a great deal of interest. How can certification schemes work at the local level and at the same time have international recognition? In relation to this, how to cover the cost of certification at the local level was a big concern in many areas and proposals were made to overcome this problem so that it can be made accessible to all sizes of business as well as to local communities. In Peru, for example, some communities receive technical and financial support from academic bodies, while in Australia, the cost of certification is proportional to the size of the business.

A final point discussed is the problem of the appearance of pseudo-eco-labels: too many labels are confusing and there was agreement that something should be done in this respect. A possible solution is the example of VISIT, a joint European initiative for the promotion of ecolabels and sustainable tourism development. VISIT has cooperated with 10 leading ecolabels in Europe and developed common basic standards for their criteria and verification procedures. These standards allow the identification of those ecolabels which guarantee a high environmental quality of their certified hotels, campsites, beaches or marinas. In 2004, VISIT will be established as a European accreditation body for ecolabels in tourism.

Sustainability Indicators and Monitoring

The need to monitor sustainability of Eco-tourism products was discussed and a number of approaches were presented. The difficulty of identifying indicators for social and cultural aspects was pointed out. Surveys to determine visitor satisfaction could be used to evaluate the quality of the visitor experience. At the same time, local people should be made aware of what was being done to the environment and how this would affect them.

A good example was the "European Charter for Sustainable Tourism in Protected Areas" which has proved to be a valuable tool for ensuring that tourism in protected areas is managed according to the principles of sustainable development.

Capacity Building, Training and Education

This was considered a key issue for the sustainable development of Eco-tourism. Without adequate training and education of all stakeholders, from government to the private sector and consumers, in matters relating to regulation, certification and monitoring, it is impossible to progress towards sustainability in Eco-tourism. All players need to understand why some sort of regulation is necessary in many situations, why certification can help both the business and the environment, and finally why monitoring is essential to demonstrate that progress is being made towards sustainability.

Other Issues

The impact of transport in relation to Eco-tourism was a key point in some of the discussions and suggestions were made on how to take it into account in Eco-tourism products and in certification schemes.

Key Points and Recommendations

Institutional Frameworks

Main recommendations from the preparatory conferences:

- Ensure coordination between government ministries in the planning and regulation of Eco-tourism.
- Develop a framework of cooperation between public, private and non-governmental organisations.
- Ensure institutions understand the different dimensions of sustainable tourism and Eco-tourism.

Key Points Arising from the Summit

There is a need to reach agreements between protected area management bodies, tourism departments or ministries as well as the tourism industry in general. A good example of this is the progress being made by the Canadian certification program. Good coordination among protected area managers and tourism departments is extremely important. The development of legislative frameworks at the regional level should be supported, because they can positively influence sustainability issues, including the promotion of Eco-tourism and similar types of tourism harmonized with the environment. The recent establishment of quality and specifically Eco-tourism product rules in Québec, Canada, is a promising example in this field.

Incentives should be set up, such as lower taxes or public land concessions at lower rates, for Eco-tourism operators that promote environmentally-sensitive land use (e.g., the ones working on Crown land in British Columbia, Canada). At the same time, in Ontario, Canada, regulatory requirements ensure that resource stewardship agreements are established between the State and tour operators working within an area covered by the agreement, to preserve natural areas of high tourism value. This approach reserves the most pristine areas for Eco-tourism operations. The idea, in both examples, is to stimulate proper Eco-tourism in sensitive and valuable natural areas with a high potential.

Regulation of Eco-tourism

Main recommendations from the preparatory conferences:

- Move gradually from optional guidelines and simple codes of conduct towards obligatory regulations.
- Establish suitable legal frameworks underpinned by effective tools for regulating Eco-tourism.
- Develop guidelines and best practice information at all levels.
- Ensure protected areas are consulted and involved in regulatory procedures.

Key Points Arising from the Summit

Tourism operators, local government, and conservation departments should establish regulations. They should guarantee the protection of sensitive natural resources and cultural integrity. Legislation and regulations should be specific for Eco-tourism A good example was the case study of Tourisme Quebec where a very specific legal framework is being established, clearly separating adventure tourism activities and Eco-tourism with an objective of avoiding a severe impact upon natural assets.

In some areas regulations need to be compulsory since in many countries voluntary regulations do not work and very often the public asks for minimum obligatory regulations, as it was presented in the example from Mexico. Certain laws and regulations within protected areas should be extended beyond their frontiers. Legally binding instruments for the implementation of sustainable Eco-tourism and avoidance of non-sustainable forms of tourism for sensitive areas should be established. Strict regulations for Eco-tourism at an international level should be avoided, while guidelines are acceptable. The potential negative impact of visitors should be taken into account from the beginning of the planning process. This can be realised through some measures such as reservation systems, routing in sensitive points, zoning within the site according to carrying capacity. The Bodogol Education Centre, in Indonesia, has successfully put in place some of these preventive measures.

Certification

Main recommendations from the preparatory conferences:

- Provide guidelines on certification schemes for Eco-tourism.

- Avoid penalise very small scale enterprises and facilitate their access to certification schemes.
- Involve all stakeholders in developing and implementing certification processes.
- Ensure certification processes are transparent, understandable and updated.

Key Points Arising from the Summit

Certification processes need to be global in concept, following international guidelines and recommendations, but local in application. An example of this is the need for ecolodge guidelines, which can always be adopted at the local level and can then be followed by some sort of international ecolodge certification.

Auditing teams must be independent and ideally should have representatives from different countries and proper training. They should also have different cultural backgrounds.

Certification should take into account social, economic and cultural aspects, besides the environmental ones. Most of the existing concepts for eco-labels, brands and certification systems have to be enlarged by social and cultural aspects to reach the aims of sustainable Eco-tourism. NGOs should take part in the process of identifying certification schemes. In many cases NGOs have developed voluntary certification schemes which have afterwards been regulated and spread by governments.

International certification schemes must be multistakeholder. They should be promoted by international organizations including governments, academia, conservation NGOs, the private sector and with proper consultation with local and indigenous people. It was suggested that organizations such as WTO and UNEP could play a role in establishing an international framework for tourism certification systems and all existing certification schemes should be considered in this process.

Certification and accreditation should be industry driven and paid for by the operators, as they can use it as a marketing tool and possibly marketing advantage over competitors, therefore it can be beneficial and profitable. The case of Australia is particularly interesting with well-established Eco-tourism and ecoguides certification programs.

In the case of very small businesses in developing countries, there should be technical and financial support through grant or loans or micro-credit systems to assist in making the necessary changes and to cover the costs of certification, either from strong NGOs, local government, academic bodies, larger profitable businesses or development agencies. There was agreement that environmental certification very often leads to economic benefits since energy, water and other resources are saved.

Easily accessible funding formulae to cover the cost of international certification schemes should be explored, so that small businesses can have access to them. Other funding and capacity building mechanisms should be identified and promoted for this purpose.

Eco-tourism certifiers must be guided by social criteria geared to facilitating the integration of small businesses at preferential rates and through technical contributions or the promotion of collective certification alternatives.

Financially sound NGOs should shoulder the role of a certification body at a cost more affordable for local entrepreneurs.

Certification should provide powerful incentives and guidelines for responsible business practices.

A multistakeholder Sustainable Tourism Stewardship Council, such as the one being considered by Rainforest Alliance in coordination with a range of international organizations, could help local certification programs exchange information in a forum that allows for accreditation of certifiers, marketing and credibility.

The obligatory introduction of certification systems for Eco-tourism facilities and operations should be considered at least at regional and national levels, to guarantee that the quality provided is consistent with the principles of sustainability. This is the case of the national ecocertification scheme which will become compulsory in the near future in the Seychelles.

Capacity Building, Training and Education

Key Points Arising from the Summit

In the certification process, there is a need to train and educate all stakeholders, including the industry, operators and customers or consumers. This latter case is particularly important since the interest of consumers in true Eco-tourism will reward good products and punish examples of "greenwashing". A good example of consumer education is the brochure "Your Travel Choice Makes a Difference" from The International Eco-tourism Society. Certification programs should be promoted and explained to the public by both the tourism and the environmental authorities.

Education, transfer of know how, exchange and respect for local people must drive the development of Eco-tourism in all destinations. In the long term, customers will reward or punish Eco-tourism products according to their sustainability.

Demand from consumers and tour operators is a prerequisite for a certification system to work. Tourists must be informed of certification schemes and therefore, the promotion by government (by both the environment and tourist departments) is essential.

Monitoring and Indicators

Main recommendations from the preparatory conferences:

- Include the economic, social and environmental impact of tourism in monitoring.
- Define targets to be achieved in a certain period of time.
- Establish continuous data collection, involving businesses and tourists.
- Ensure monitoring is a prerequisite of providing assistance to projects.

Key Points Arising from the Summit

The issue of monitoring and indicators was central to the discussions of Working Group D, but the following specific points were raised within this working group.

The definition of sustainability indicators should not be left only to the private sector and should be the result of consensus among all stakeholders including local people, NGOs, government and protected area managers.

Sustainability indicators should be integrated with local planning.

Indicators must be identified at the local level and should take into account environmental, social and cultural factors.

New methods of evaluation of progress towards sustainability in Eco-tourism need to be identified, that are accessible to the local population both from the technical and economic point of view.

Index

□□□